IMPACT
BLACKS IN OKLAHOMA HISTORY

Rochelle Stephney-Roberson

ACTIVITIES EDITION

© 2011 by Rochelle Stephney-Roberson
This book and its contents are copyrighted by the author.
Publishing rights acquired by Books of Impact

All rights reserved. No part of this book may be reproduced in any
form or by any electronic or mechanical means, including
information storage and retrieval systems, without permission in writing from the publisher,
except by a reviewer who may quote brief passages in a review.

First Edition

Cataloging-in-publication Data

Stephney-Roberson, Rochelle, 1963-
Impact : blacks in Oklahoma history /
Rochelle Stephney-Roberson
188 p. : ill. ; 28 cm.
ISBN-13: 978-0-9817105-6-3 (alk. paper)
ISBN-10: 0-9817105-6-5 (alk. paper)
1. African Americans--Oklahoma--History. 2. Oklahoma--History.
3. Oklahoma--History. I. Title.
E185.93.O4 2011
976.600496073 dc 22

Printed in the United States of America

www.thingswithimpact.com

CONTENTS

Oklahoma Territory	1
Oklahoma's All-Black Towns	5
Boley	6
Brooksville, Clearview and Grayson	8
Langston	10
Lima	14
Redbird	15
Rentiesville and Summit	16
Taft and Tatums	19
Tullahassee and Vernon	21
Frederick A. Douglass High School	23
Bass Reeves	27
Green I. Currin	29
Inman E. Page	31
Sidney D. Lyons	33
The Buffalo Soldiers	35
Wyatt H. Slaughter / J. D. Randolph	39
Zelia P. Breaux	41
Albert C. Hamlin	43
Roscoe Dunjee	45
George W. McLaurin	49
Jim Crow Laws / Black Codes	51
Walter J. Edwards / Carl Barclay	55
F. D. Moon	59
Amos T. Hall	61
Joseph J. Simmons, Jr.	63
Ira D. Hall, Sr.	65
Gravelly E. Finley	67
The Goodwin Family	69
Percy H. James	73
Charles N. Atkins	75
Rubye Hibler Hall	77
James E. Stewart	79
Booker T. Washington High School	81
Ralph W. Ellison	83
John Hope Franklin	85
Alfonzo L. Dowell	87
Juanita K. Stout	89
The Tulsa Race Riot / Greenwood	93
Clara Luper	99
Segregated Public Accommodations	105
Leslie Brown	108
Portwood Williams	110
Hannah D. Atkins	113
Ada Sipuel Fisher	115
Charles L. Owens	119
E. Melvin Porter	121
Maxine Horner	123
Hubert Ausbie	125
Willa Johnson	127
Russell M. Perry	129
Horace Stevenson	131
Al Downing	133
Don R. Ross	135
Lelia Foley Davis	137
Kenneth C. Watson	139
Judy Eason McIntyre	141
Susan Woodard Bragg	145
Leona P. Mitchell	147
Tom Colbert	149
The Original 12	151
Kevin C. Cox	155
Constance J. Johnson	157
The Selmon Brothers	159
Vicki Miles LaGrange	161
Opio Toure	163
Angela Z. Monson	165
David B. Lewis	167
Currie Ballard	169
Joseph C. Carter	171
Wayman L. Tisdale	173
Tammy Bass-LeSure	175
Anastasia Pittman	177
Michael Shelton	179
Ernest Lee Spivey, Jr.	181
Jabar Shumate & Tahrohon W. Shannon	183
Oklahoma Legislative Black Caucus	185

dedication

This book is dedicated to my late sister Sarita Stephney – Civil Rights worker, fighter for equality, trailblazer, mentor, and leader, and to my husband, Peter, Sr., and children Peter, Jr. and Stephney Roberson.

acknowledgments

First and foremost I would like to thank God. I simply can not thank my supporters enough, those who have assisted and encouraged me throughout the writing of this book. There are so many people out there and I would not want to leave anyone out, so thank you all! I especially want to give credit to my family – husband Peter, Sr., son Peter, Jr., and daughter Stephney. They have given me great support, patience, assistance and understanding. Thank you to my siblings, other family members, and friends for their support and guidance. Special thanks to Dr. Carl Holmes and his wife and Mr. Portwood Williams for inviting me into their homes and giving me interviews, information, and photos. Mr. Horace Stevenson, Mr. Russell Perry, Dr. Leon Bragg, The Walter Edwards family, Ms. Willa Johnson, and Mayor Lelia Foley Davis, Ms. Mae Neece Barclay and Mr. Bruce Fisher for their interviews, assistance, and time. Mr. James O. Goodwin and Mr. Ed Goodwin II for the help and tours throughout the city of Tulsa. The many attorneys, judges, legislators (present and past), musicians, sports players, civil rights workers, and historians who have in the past and present fought for equality. Linda Lynn at *The Oklahoman* gave great assistance in helping to locate many photos throughout this project. A final thanks to the staff of my first publishing company, Forty-Sixth Star Press for guiding me through the process of writing this book and making it all happen. You have all been wonderful.

preface

The reader should know that this resource book is nowhere near a complete history of black history in the state of Oklahoma. It is only the tip of the iceberg. There are many important African Americans who have made a huge IMPACT on this state who are not included. This is not because of their lack of importance or the amount or type of their contribution, but due to the fact that I simply had to have a cut off point for my research.

Throughout my many years of working in the public school system, I found that a large number of youth are not educated about the wonderful impact many African Americans have had on the state of Oklahoma as well as on the nation. This is not because students are not interested, but because there has simply not been a tool of this kind available. This book includes worksheets and activity pages for each section. Every available opportunity has been used to include information that relates to Oklahoma's Priority Academic Student Skills (PASS).

Many of the individuals who are still living and are featured in this book have provided me with actual interviews, photos, and biographical information about themselves in addition to information concerning their community service projects, organizations and civil rights activities.

The sequence of the book is in order of occurrence of events as much as possible. At the beginning of the book, there is information about things before statehood along with appropriate activities. Each section progresses through Oklahoma history, telling a story of things that were happening within the African American community from before statehood until the present. It is my hope that this book will not only be used to educate youth but to also enhance the knowledge of adults in our state and even the nation about this important African American chapter in Oklahoma history. It is full of wonderful, rich history.

A Note to Educators

The answer keys to the activities in this book are available by request from the author or publisher at www.thingswithimpact.com or booksofimpact@gmail.com

Oklahoma and Indian Territories

THE TRAIL OF TEARS

In the 1830's, many African Americans arrived as slaves of one of the Five Civilized Tribes. The tribes – Cherokees, Creeks, Choctaws, Chickasaws and Seminoles – were exiled from plantations at the order of President Andrew Jackson. The decision was made in hopes to clear the land for white cotton growers. Indian tribes traveled thousands of miles from the southeastern United States (U.S.) and relocated to Indian Territory using numerous routes, with one of the most famous one being the "Trail of Tears." The Trail of Tears is the relocations of thousands of Native American nations from southeastern parts of what is now known as the United States (their homelands) to Indian Territory, what is now eastern sections of present day Oklahoma. Some modern day historians describe this as an act of genocide, which is the deliberate and systematic destruction of a racial, religious, ethnic, or national group in part or in whole. Tribes suffered great hardships being forced from their ancestral lands by federal and state governments. Many suffered and died from disease, starvation, and exposure to harsh weather conditions. More than 4,000 of the relocated Cherokees died while enroute to their new destination. Many died from infection of the bacterial disease Cholera, which can be caused by contaminated food and water.

Survivors of the trip were forced to start over from scratch in unknown territory rich with virgin land. One Indian Tribe, the Choctaws, spread across over 5,000 acres in southeastern Oklahoma and owned 500 slaves. The Civil War lasted from 1861 – 1865. President Abraham Lincoln signed the Emancipation Proclamation on January 1, 1863, proclaiming freedom to over 3.1 million of the nation's 4 million slaves with the rest freed after the Union armies advanced. In February of 1865, Congress passed the Thirteenth Amendment which totally abolished slavery. The law was ratified and took effect by all states in December of 1865. The order for the five tribes granted freedom, tribal membership, and land allotments to each of their slaves. These former slaves became known as "Freedmen."

THE LAND RUNS

On April 26, 1879, President Rutherford B. Hayes issued a proclamation which forbade trespassing onto the land. Landless citizens and speculators began organizing groups demanding the opening of the land. One group wanted the land opened up for non-Indian settlement, they were known as "Boomers." They participated in the land runs. Another group called "Sooners," were those who illegally entered the territory before the official opening of the land.

The government gave in to pressure making a decision to open up the territory to settlers by holding five land runs. The First Land Run was held on April 22, 1889. The unassigned land was divided into 160 acre homesteads. Iowa, Sac, Fox, Pottawatomie and Shawnee Lands were opened up on September 22, 1891, when a estimated 20,000 settlers rushed to claim one of the 6,098 160 acre homesteads. Cheyenne and Arapaho Land runs were held on April 19, 1892. Settlers came by wagon, buggy, foot, race horse, and plow horse to claim homesteads. By April 1903, more than 100 homes had been established. The Cherokee Outlet opened on September 16, 1893. President Grover Cleveland penned this the "run" for 6,000,000 acres. Over 100,000 settlers arrived by wagon, train, horse, and foot hoping to stake claims. Some remained landless. In the fifth and smallest Land Run, Kickapoo Land was offered to land seeking citizens. It was held on May 3, 1895. Other claims for land included the "land lottery," which was held on August 1, 1901. Homesteads totaling three and one-half million acres was given out by a drawing called the "land lottery." In 1906, the Osage Allotment Act was passed, which was an auction process of dividing homesteads among the Five Civilized tribe members.

The number of blacks who participated in the land runs is still debatable, but the Territorial Census rolls of Oklahoma in 1890 listed approximately 3,000 black residents. Forty-two were recorded in April 1889 as filing claims of entry into the territory. There were between 50,000 and 60,000 blacks who participated in the land runs. President Theodore Roosevelt made a proclamation on November 16, 1907 making Oklahoma the forty-sixth state in the nation. Oklahoma was affectionately known as the "Sooner State."

OKLAHOMA TERRITORY
Answer the multiple choice questions below.

1. What United States President issued a proclamation which prohibited trespassing onto the unclaimed land in Oklahoma Territory?
a. President Rutherford B. Hayes
b. President Andrew Jackson
c. President Robert E. Lee

2. Why were one group of land seekers called "Sooners?"
a. Because they got to the land run sooner than any one else
b. Because they illegally entered onto the unclaimed land before the land was opened up
c. Because they were the first group to get to Oklahoma

3. What was the name of the bacterial disease that many died from on the Trail of Tears?
a. Mylaria
b. Cholera
c. Polio

4. What is the Emancipation Proclamation which was signed on January 1, 1863?
a. It was a law to give the Indian's food on their journey to Oklahoma Territory
b. It was a proclamation which freed over 3.1 million slaves
c. It provided homes to the homeless after they arrived to Oklahoma

5. What is the Thirteenth Amendment?
a. It allowed "Boomers" to participate in the land runs
b. Gave reparations to the Indians because so many of them died during their travels
c. It totally abolished slavery

6. Why did the Five Civilized Tribes leave the plantations in the southeastern United States?
a. Because Indians were paid more money in other places
b. Because President Andrew Jackson ordered them to leave
c. Because there were better living conditions than where they currently lived

7. On this date President Theodore Roosevelt named Oklahoma the 46th state:
a. April 16, 1889
b. November 16, 1907
c. April 26, 1879

8. President Grover Cleveland penned this the "run" for 6,000,000 acres:
a. The Cherokee Outlet
b. Cheyenne-Arapaho
c. Osage

9. Oklahoma is nicknamed
a. The Sunflower State
b. The Garden State
c. The Sooner State

10. When the slaves became known as Freedmen, the government ordered the Five Tribes to do this:
a. give the freedmen 2 cows and 10 acres of land
b. grant them freedom, land and tribal membership
c. help them build homes for their families

USING THE COLORS LISTED BELOW COLOR THE COUNTIES THAT ARE NOW WITHIN THE BOUNDARIES OF THE ORIGINAL INDIAN LANDS

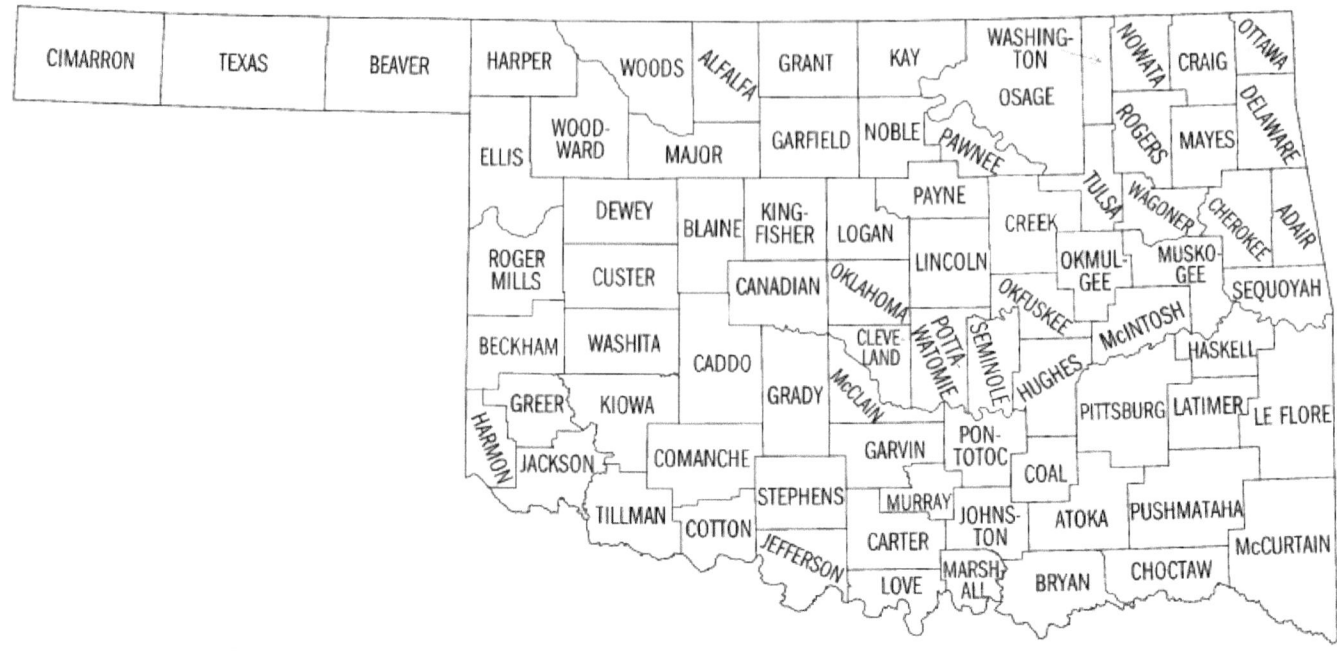

1. CHEYENNE – ARAPAHO * BLUE

2. SAC, FOX, IOWA, POTAWATOMIE, SHAWNEE * GREEN

3. CHEROKEE OUTLET * RED

4. KICKAPOO * YELLOW

5. FIRST LAND RUN IN 1889 * PURPLE

Existing All-Black Towns in Oklahoma

All-Black Towns

Oklahoma's all-black towns remain an important part of African American history. They reflect the struggle for freedom, equality and justice. Black towns offered hope for land ownership, self-governance, full citizenship, unity, and the American dream. After the Civil War, treaties enacted by the U.S. government forced Indian tribes to give up their lands and accept individual property allotments. There was even talk of using Indian Territory for settlement of African Americans recently emancipated from slavery.

African American history in Oklahoma is unlike any to be found in the United States. When southern blacks moved to Oklahoma, they found that Freedmen had established farms, served on tribal councils or as town chiefs. They could vote, study and freely move about. Blacks in southern states were urged through advertisements to join in land runs in the Indian Territory. Oklahoma was once considered the site of an all-black state. A New Hampshire Senator by the name of Henry W. Blair introduced a bill in favor of this proposal. In 1890, Edward P. McCabe, founder of Langston, Oklahoma visited with President Benjamin Harrison to convince him to allow the creation of black cities and perhaps an all-black state in Oklahoma. Many blacks hoped for creating towns and colonies where black people would be free to steer clear of interference and exercise their political rights.

Oklahoma boasts more all-black towns than any other state in the country. By 1891, 200 people lived in Langston, including a doctor, minister, and a teacher. Soon black farmers owned 1.5 million acres valued at $11 million. There were more all-black towns in Oklahoma than all the black towns in the rest of the country. Oklahoma produced some of the greatest musicians and led some of the nation's greatest civil rights battles. In all, 32 all-black towns formed in Oklahoma. Most were established by blacks for blacks on land formerly held by the Five Civilized Tribes.

These Oklahoma all-black towns no longer exist: Arkansas Colored, Bailey, Bookertee, Canadian Colored, Chase, Ferguson, Gibson Station, Liberty, Lincoln City, Marshall Town, North Fork Town, Old Vinita, Wellston Colony, Wybark.

Today, many of Oklahoma's original black towns are gone. Thirteen still exist.

BOLEY, OKLAHOMA was established in 1903. It's the most famous all-black town in Oklahoma. It is located on Highway 62 sixty-seven miles east of Oklahoma City. Boley was established by two white entrepreneurs – John Boley, a railroad manager and Lake Moore, a former federal officeholder and attorney – on 160 acres of land inherited by Abigail Barnett McCormick the daughter of Creek Freedman James Barnett. The town was first slated to be named Barnett, Indian Territory, but a town by the name of Barnett already existed. The incorporation of Boley, Creek Nation, Indian Territory was developed. It was later changed to Boley, Oklahoma when the state was formed in 1907. A black man by the name of Tom Haynes was hired to promote the community of Boley. Haynes publicly invited blacks to come and settle there and served as the town's first mayor. In its prime, Boley was the largest predominately black town in the United States, doting over 7,000 residents in its prime. It was seen as the Jewel of Black Towns with homes just as good as any major white community. There were both public and private schools, banks, fraternal clubs, and churches of every denomination. Boley had a post office, telephone company, power plant, jewelry store, livery stables, department stores, and a railroad depot. In addition there was a tuberculosis hospital for blacks. It had the first black-owned electric company and one of the first black-owned banks. Booker T. Washington visited Boley in 1908. The town, he wrote, "is striking evidence of the progress made in thirty years. . . . The westward movement of the negro people has brought into these new lands, not a helpless and ignorant horde of black people, but land-seekers and home-builders, men who have come prepared to build up the country. . ." Two years later, Boley's agricultural prices plummeted, crops failed, and in 1908 after Oklahoma gained statehood, the state legislature quickly adopted Jim Crow laws, segregating schools and accommodations. Today, its population remains mostly black with approximately 1000 residents. Its businesses include boarding schools, gas stations, grocery stores, a hardware store, community center, elementary, and high schools in addition to a town hall.

BOLEY TODAY
Boley's early beginnings included a training school for Negro boys. It started with one single story building, but its growth demanded for more educational institutions. At its peak, Boley's school district had the ability to populate up to seven hundred students. Today, it is one of the smallest school districts in the state. Some 30,000 people attend one of the oldest African American rodeos in the nation, The Boley Rodeo and Bar-B-Q festival, started in 1961. It is held each Memorial Day weekend. Families, friends, and visitors from all over the United States flock to this community each year to enjoy the parade, barrel racing, bull riding and other activities. A large array of food vendors are plentiful at this event. The actual rodeo begins at 8 PM each night of the festival.

Smokaroma pressure smokers are manufactured in Boley and sold all over the world. The company was founded in 1959 by Maurice Lee, Sr. The cooker uses wood and pressure to add a smoky flavor to vegetables and meat. Smokaroma's cooking technique can be used in the kitchen with claims to produce a delicious, tender, and juicy food with meat that falls off of the bone. The Smokaroma manufacturing company is still located in Boley, Oklahoma.

BOLEY, OKLAHOMA
Rewrite the sentences to make them into true statements

1. The Smokaroma pressure smokers are assembled in Boley. They are sold only in Oklahoma.

2. The Boley Rodeo is held each Labor Day weekend.

3. John (J.B.) Boley was the town's first mayor.

4. Abigail Barnett McCormick, was the daughter of Cherokee Freedman James Barnett.

5. The town of Boley began with 6,000 acres of land.

6. The Smokaroma cooker uses charcoal and pressure to add flavor to vegetables and meat.

7. People from all over the Creek Nation come to the annual rodeo.

8. Boley had the first black-owned telephone company and one of the first black-owned banks.

9. In its prime, Boley boasted a population of over 1 million residents.

10. A black man by the name of Booker T. Washington was hired to promote the town of Boley.

BROOKSVILLE, OKLAHOMA

Brooksville, Oklahoma was established in 1903. It is located in Pottawatomie County, four miles southwest of Tecumseh. The town was originally named Sewell, after a white doctor who attended to the residents living on the surrounding land that was owned by the doctor. The name was changed to Brooksville in 1912 in honor of A. R. Brooks, the first African American who moved to the area. Brooks was a cotton buyer and farmer. His son, W.M. Brooks, was the town's first postmaster. Rev. Jedson White organized the

town's first church in 1906, St. John's Baptist Church. The church still remains today. Rev. White traveled throughout the South, promoting the town and encouraging African Americans to move to Brooksville. The town of Brooksville had three hotels, two mills, two doctors and a Santa Fe Railroad station. A new school, Banneker School, was built in 1924 with the aid of the Rosenwald Fund. It was a rock school with a three-hundred seat auditorium, four large rooms, a library, and a science room. Due to a fire, the building was replaced by a wooden one and remained open until 1968. The former school building became the town's community center and is located next to city hall. The Great Depression and declining cotton market affected many residents. Many of them moved, but the town survived and has a population of approximately 90.

CLEARVIEW, OKLAHOMA

Clearview, Oklahoma is located in Okfuskee County. It was founded in 1903 along the tracks of the Fort Smith and Western Railroad, just 45 miles south of Tulsa, Oklahoma. The town had a two-story hotel, print shop, brick school building, a drug store, theatre, a general store, bakery, cigar factory, soft-drink factory, barbershop, beauty shop, cleaners, several gas stations, five general stores, a brick plant, sewing factory, canning factory, three cotton gins, and two churches. In 1907, the population was 618. In 2009, its population had decreased to 135 people. The people in Clearview's community still enjoy an annual rodeo.

GRAYSON, OKLAHOMA

Initially named Wild Cat, Grayson, Oklahoma is a town located in Okmulgee County. It is a community near the Tulsa metropolitan area and was named for George W. Grayson, an Indian tribal leader. The town has a total area of 1.1 square miles, mostly land. In 2003, the population was 136.

The old jail in Grayson, Oklahoma

BROOKSVILLE, CLEARVIEW & GRAYSON

Answer the true-false questions below. Write t or f on the line next to each sentence.

1. _____ Brooksville, Oklahoma is located in Okfuskee County.

2. _____ Clearview, Oklahoma is 45 miles south of Tulsa, Oklahoma.

3. _____ A.R. Brooks was the first African American to move to the Brooksville area.

4. _____ St. John Baptist Church was organized in 1908 and is located in Grayson, Oklahoma.

5. _____ The town of Grayson is named after Wild Cat Grayson, an Indian Tribal leader.

6. _____ Rev. Jedson White was the organizer of St. John Baptist Church.

7. _____ The town of Grayson was originally named Sewell, Oklahoma.

8. _____ Rev. White traveled the South to encourage blacks to move to Clearview, Oklahoma.

9. _____ The town of Brooksville consists of an area of 1.1 square miles.

10. _____ Clearview, Oklahoma was established in 1903.

11. _____ Banneker School was built in 1924 and is a large rock building.

12. _____ The former school in Brooksville was remodeled and is now used for the town's community center.

13. _____ Grayson, Oklahoma is a part of the Tulsa metropolitan area.

14. _____ The small town of Grayson still hosts a community rodeo each year.

15. _____ St. John's Baptist Church in Brooksville is now closed.

ALL-BLACK TOWNS

LANGSTON – "PARADISE OF EDEN AND THE GARDEN OF THE GODS"

Edward P. McCabe purchased 320 acres near Guthrie, Oklahoma. A supporter of all-black towns and an all-black state, he named the town in honor of John Mercer Langston, an African American Congressman and educator from Virginia. McCabe founded the town of Langston and urged Blacks to settle there, "The Only Distinctively Negro City in America." McCabe declared the territory of Langston, "paradise of Eden and the garden of the Gods." Blacks grew tired of segregation and lynching in the South. His newspaper, the *Langston Herald*, advertised the town's lots. He wrote "Negroes can rest from mob law; here he can be secure from every ill of the southern policies." The newspaper reached blacks in Kansas, Arkansas, Texas, Louisiana, Missouri and Tennessee. The McCabe Town Company used agents to travel into the southern states to attract blacks to the new town. The purchase of a lot included a railway ticket to Oklahoma. Blacks were inspired by McCabe's portrayal of Langston, it was portrayed as the land of milk and honey. E.P. McCabe described the town thus:

"Do you ask why? We will tell you. Langston City is a Negro city, and we are proud of the fact. Her city officers are all colored. Her teachers are colored. Her public schools furnish thorough educational advantages to nearly two hundred colored children. The country is as fertile as ever was moistened by nature's falling tears or kissed by heaven's sunshine. Here, too, is found a genial climate - about like that of southern Tennessee or northern Mississippi - a climate admirably adapted to the wants of the Negro from the southern states. A land of diversified crops, where there need be no such things as a total failure. A land of diversified crops, where every staple crop of both north and south can be raised with pride. One of the finest fruit growing countries in the union. A land where a few dollars judiciously invested in real estate will yield returns in the future that cannot be estimated. Do you want to build for the future? If so you can do no better than to invest a few dollars in Oklahoma soil. It does not matter whether you contemplate coming here at once or not. Real estate is the basis of all wealth. There is nothing in which money can be so safely invested. Do you wish to build for the future? If you do, you cannot do anything that will be more to your advantage than a small investment in Langston City property. This property combines everything that it needs to commend it to home seekers or investors, viz: Reasonable prices, easy payments, steady and rapid increase in value, sure returns, absolute safety, good society, church privileges, school privileges, and last but not least, absolute political liberty and the enjoyment of every right and privilege every other man enjoys under the constitution of the country. What more do you want? Young men, if you will save the money that many of you now squander and invest it in Langston City property, ten years from now you will be independent."

Edward P. (E.P.) McCabe was born in Troy, New York on October 10, 1850. He was the son of Elizabeth McCabe. E.P. was orphaned at an early age. In 1890 he married Sarah J. Bryant. They had three children: Lenore, Edwina and Edward "Eddie" Jr. E.P., a Kansas politician, moved to Oklahoma Territory in hopes of establishing an all-black community. In 1907 when Oklahoma gained statehood, the Republicans lost control of the legislature and McCabe lost his job. One of his daughters died and the other became deathly ill. In 1908, Edward sold his land in Langston and moved to Chicago to be with his family. At the age of 69, on March 12, 1920, Edward P. McCabe died in Chicago, Illinois. He is buried in Topeka, Kansas.

LANGSTON UNIVERSITY

Through the combined efforts of McCabe and white land owner, Charles Robbins, the town of Langston was officially formed on April 22, 1890. In 1892 the town had 25 retail businesses. Blacks were not allowed to attend institutions of higher education in Oklahoma Territory. Langston's black citizens petitioned the Oklahoma Industrial School and College Commission for a college. Territorial Governor William G. Renfrow agreed, and Langston was founded as a land grant college through the Morrill Act of 1890. Under this act, seventeen southern states were to establish schools for African Americans. Its purpose would be to instruct "both male and female Colored persons in the art of teaching various branches which pertain to a common school education and in the fundamental laws of the United States in the rights and duties of citizens in the agricultural, mechanical and industrial arts." The bill stipulated that the land the college would be built on had to be purchased by the citizens. Although many lived in tents and soddies, the black community was determined to provide higher education for their children. They held bake sales, auctions, and had picnics to raise the money. Mr. McCabe had set aside forty acres of land for the Oklahoma Colored Agricultural and Normal University. The school was founded in 1897 but opened its doors on September 3, 1898 in the city of Langston. The first school was built with a budget of only $5,000. The school was first opened as a high school and later added college level courses. The school's first president was Inman Edward Page. He served in this capacity from 1898 until 1915. During Inman's administration, the campus expanded to 160 acres, and the enrollment increased from only 41 students to over 650. The name Langston University was officially adopted in 1941. The university is a known leader in the field of agricultural research. It is the only historically black college in the state of Oklahoma, offering associates, bachelor's, master's and doctoral degrees in a variety of disciplines. Langston's choral programs are among the top in the nation. Its 150-piece band engages in performances across the nation and abroad for bowl games, parades, and marching competitions. Today Langston University has campuses in Langston, Tulsa and Oklahoma City. Together they educate over 4,000 students per year.

OKLAHOMA'S FIRST AFRICAN AMERICAN FEMALE PRESIDENT

In 2005, Langston University appointed the university's first female president. Dr. JoAnn Wright Haysbert was the university's fifteenth president. She is the first African American woman college president in Oklahoma. Dr. Haysbert went to Langston University after serving twenty-five years at Hampton University in Hampton, Virginia. There she served in key positions such as provost, acting provost, acting president, and assistant vice present. In addition, Dr. Haysbert has held positions at Auburn University, Virginia State University and Alexander City State Junior College. Under the guidance of Dr. Haysbert, Langston has developed a 10-year strategic plan: "from excellence to greatness." Dr. Haysbert has five children: Samaria, Jordan, Nazareth, Ninevah and Andre.

Melvin Beaunorus Tolson was born on February 6, 1898 in Moberly, Missouri. He was one of four children born to Reverend Alonzo and Lera Hurt Tolson. As a child, he enjoyed playing ball and playing the mandolin. Melvin's parents put great emphasis on education for their children. He attended high school in Kansas City, Missouri where he was named captain of the football team and named class poet. Melvin attended Fisk University and graduated with honors from Lincoln University in Kansas City. He later earned a master's degree in 1931 from Columbia University in New York City. In 1922, Melvin married Ruth Southall. They had four children: Melvin B. Jr, Ruth, Arthur and Wiley. In 1924, Melvin became an instructor of English and speech at Wiley College in Marshall, Texas. In 1947 he accepted the position as professor of English and drama at Langston University. Melvin retired from Langston in 1965. During that time he served as mayor of the city of Langston from 1954 and remained for four terms. In August 29, 1966, Melvin B. Tolson died in Dallas, Texas from cancer. In 1973, the Langston Creative Writing Club donated a stone monument erected in front of his former home. It says, "A Black Poet Lived Here." In 1962, his son Dr. Melvin B. Tolson, Jr. became the first full-time African American faculty member at the University of Oklahoma. He taught French at the University over thirty years.

RENOWNED POET

Melvin was a renowned poet in the 40's and 50's and was widely accepted as a teacher, drama director and debate coach. Prior to joining the staff at Langston, Melvin was an established debate coach and led Wiley College debate teams to ten national championships. By the 1930's his attention turned to drama and playwriting. He brought great recognition to the school of Langston through his poetic achievement and creativity. Melvin reportedly had a custom of waking after midnight devoting the night to writing poetry. After retiring, Melvin was in high demand for speaking engagements. He was honored at the White House, the Library of Congress and the Tuskegee Institute.

The Melvin B. Tolson Black Heritage Center was established in 1970 at Langston University. The Center's function is to provide research materials for anyone researching African and Afro-American Studies. The Tolson Collection of black literature and art can be found on the Langston campus in its library holdings. It is one of the most extensive collections of its kind in the country.

THE GREAT DEBATERS – THE MOVIE

The 2007 film *The Great Debaters* is a true story with a plot that revolves around the efforts, triumphs and struggles of debate coach Melvin B. Tolson and his team while he taught at the historically black Wiley College. Melvin's character is played by Denzel Washington. The film depicts the Wiley Debate team matching up against Harvard College and defeating them in the 1930's. In actuality, this match never occurred. The true history is that Wiley College debated against the University of Southern California, the reigning debate champions in the United States. The movie producers chose to use Harvard in the film, as they were a university of higher stature. The change in college in the movie was done to demonstrate the heights of achievement of Wiley College. Although Wiley did succeed in winning the match, they were not allowed to call themselves victors as black students were not allowed to become members of the debate society at that time.

LANGSTON
Answer the multiple choice questions below.

1. The town of Langston was named in honor of
a. Langston Hughes
b. John Mercer Langston
c. Langston L. Lyons

2. The McCabe Town Company agents traveled the United States to do this
a. Help black farmers to learn to milk cows
b. Teach blacks how to grow gardens
c. Encourage blacks to move to Langston

3. Langston University's first African American female president, Dr. JoAnn Haysbert, was employed in
a. 2005
b. 1980
c. 1941

4. Hollywood movie producers made a movie about Melvin B. Tolson. He was a debate instructor at Langston and also served four terms as Langston's mayor. Denzel Washington played Melvin. The name of the movie is
a. Remember the Titans
b. The Great Debaters
c. School Daze

5. In order to build a school to educate their children, the black community of Langston were required to pay for the land themselves. The money for the school was raised by
a. Having a car wash at the local restaurant
b. Selling candy bars door to door
c. Having bake sales, auctions and picnics

6. Seventeen schools for African American children were opened as a result of the passage of this act.
a. The Morrill Act of 1890
b. The Governor William Gary Renfrow Act
c. The United States Agricultural school act

7. Poet Melvin B. Tolson would often wake up after midnight and do this
a. Bake muffins for the next morning
b. Write poetry
c. Practice playing music on the Mandolin

8. Edward P. McCabe promised this to individuals who purchased a lot in the new town of Langston.
a. A new car
b. A railway ticket to Oklahoma
c. A job at the McCabe Town Company

9. In 2005, JoAnn Haysbert became Langston University's
a. fifteenth president
b. acting provost
c. assistant vice president

10. By 1892, the City of Langston had a population of approximately this many businesses
a. 5000
b. 25
c. 100

LIMA, OKLAHOMA

Lima was founded in 1904. It is located in Seminole County, 55 miles southeast of Oklahoma City. Although there is only one Lima on the map today, the original town was founded by all-black residents. During the 1920's a white settlement originated during the oil boom and it was given the name New Lima. They are less than a mile apart. Both towns had separate post offices and separate segregated schools. The schools were not integrated until 1957. The population was 239 in the 1930's. Lima had a hotel, sawmill, cotton gin, jail, several stores and a telephone company. It was considered a resort, where people from Oklahoma City could go on the weekends to enjoy picnics and ballgames. Today, the population is approximately 154.

THE ROSENWALD FUND

Julius Rosenwald was born in 1862 into a poor family in Springfield, Illinois. Although he did not have a high school diploma, Julius worked hard and succeeded in the clothing industry. Julius landed at Sears, Roebuck and Company, becoming the President, and earned a personal fortune. Julius became close friends with former slave Booker T. Washington, and was concerned about improving the condition of America's southern black population. The Rosenwald Fund was established in 1917. Its purpose was to provide facilities with grant money for black schools in the southern part of the United States. The fund required that local communities match money acquired through the program. Julius financed more than 5,300 school buildings and contributed close to $700 million. Through his program, he was able to build schoolhouses, vocational shops, and teacher-training facilities. Nearly 200 black schools in Oklahoma benefited from the fund. Rosenwald also funded construction to build YMCA's for urban blacks and help fund programs to train black doctors and nurses and provide medical care in black communities. Over one-third of the black children in the south attended a Rosenwald school. Many of these schools have disappeared. Although it is not in use, one of the last remaining Rosenwald schools in the state of Oklahoma still stands in Lima, Oklahoma. Built in 1921, Rosenwald Hall is listed on the National Register of Historic Places.

RED BIRD is in Wagoner County about twenty one miles northwest of Muskogee. The town's first post office opened in Red Bird, Indian Territory on June 21, 1902. It is located along the MKT (Missouri-Kansas-Texas) Railroad. Red Bird is laid out on an allottment owned by Creek Indian Fus Chata. His name meant Red Bird and the town took his name. The all-black town had a population of 400 in the 1920's. Red Bird served as a market center for black farmers in the region. Prior to 1913, the school children were forced to walk two miles a day to attend the McKellop school. Red Bird's "Main Street School," was a two room building with two teachers. At its peak, Redbird had a blacksmith shop, casket factory, several grocery stores, hotels, a soda pop factory, cement block factory, and cotton gins. Today, Redbird is one square mile in size. It has a population of approximately 170 with four churches, a post office, and city hall. Many homes are boarded up and there are no businesses.

RED BIRD INVESTMENT COMPANY

E.L. Barber helped form the Red Bird Investment Company. He instructed agents to travel throughout Arkansas, Mississippi, Louisiana and Texas to recruit "colored" families to move to the new town. On August 10, 1907, the town of Red Bird had its grand opening. Over 600 people attended. Businessmen from sixteen states were present. The visitors were enthused. The town drew entrepreneurs who started businesses of every imaginable kind. The above booklet was distributed by land agents to assist in the recruiting during the early 1900's.

THE VOTER REGISTRATION LAW

I.W. Lane had been a resident of Red Bird since 1908. He attempted to register to vote in 1934. The county register refused, stating that they were "instructed by highups not to register any colored person." The voter registration law was enacted by the Oklahoma legislature. I.W. filed a federal lawsuit, *Lane v. Wilson*. Both the trial court and court of appeals rejected Mr. Lane's claim of discrimination stating that the law barred whites as well as blacks and automatically qualified all persons who had voted in 1914. Individuals who had not voted in 1914 or who had been previously excluded from voting had only twelve days (April 30 to May 11, 1916) to register to vote. If they failed to register, their right to vote was lost forever. The United States Court later ruled that the statute was in conflict with the Fifteenth Amendment to the United States Constitution. It was declared unconstitutional. This step was an important victory to ensure equal voting rights.

ALL-BLACK TOWNS

LIMA and REDBIRD

Answer the following true or false questions by writing a t or f in the blank

1. _____ Lima was founded in 1940.

2. _____ Lima and New Lima had integrated schools.

3. _____ Red Bird took its name from the Creek Indian Fus Chata, which meant red bird.

4. _____ Today Red Bird is 100 square miles.

5. _____ E. L. Barber helped form the Red Bird Investment Company.

RENTIESVILLE AND HONEY SPRINGS

Rentiesville, Oklahoma was founded in 1903 just north of Checotah, Oklahoma. It was developed on 20 acres owned by William "Bill" Rentie and 20 acres owned by Phoebe McIntosh. The town had a population of about 1000. Its school had about five hundred students. There were many stores, a cotton gin, a doctor and attorney, post office and churches. Everyone in Rentiesville was black and blacks owned and operated all the businesses. This once-thriving community was devastated by The Great Depression and by the year 2000, its population was 102.

Troops like these fought at the battle of Honey Springs (seen today above)

The community of Honey Springs was named for the natural springs found there. In 1863 the bustling town consisted of a small church and a few one- and two-story buildings. Honey Springs had become the headquarters for Confederate Brigadier General Douglass Hancock Cooper during the Civil War in July 1863. While planning an attack on the Federal garrison at Fort Gibson, the Confederate General gathered supplies and troops. The goal was to take control of Fort Gibson so they could enjoy the rich natural resources found there. On July 15, 1863, Major General James G. Blunt led the march of over 3,000 Union soldiers south along the Texas Road. Marching from Fort Gibson to Honey Springs took two days. Their march was made with urgency in hope of preventing an attack on Fort Gibson from the 5,000 Confederate soldiers.

The first battle where blacks fought alongside whites and Native Americans was fought on July 17, 1863 – the Honey Springs Battle. The racial mix of soldiers fought the white and Indian Confederate soldiers. Blacks had previously served only as laborers, but the Union's need for armed men swayed their decision to allow blacks to fight. Honey Springs battle lasted four hours on a small field about 20 miles southwest of Fort Gibson. Once the battle was over, Union troops took control of Honey Springs. Confederate supplies were salvaged and Union soldiers buried the dead from both sides. Exhausted from the long march and battle, the Union soldiers did not pursue the fleeing Confederates but returned to their headquarters at Fort Gibson. Today, Honey Springs Battlefield is used as a state park. Every third year a reenactment of the battle takes place just one and a half miles from the all-black town of Rentiesville. The park is open to the public and tours can be arranged.

OKLAHOMA BLUES HALL OF FAME
Blues musician D.C. Minner was born in 1935. D.C.'s grandmother, Lura Drennan, opened the Kozy Korner in Rentiesville soon after he was born. Miss Lura operated many other businesses: a grocery store, a dance hall and a community center. She passed away in 1968 and the property, known as "home place," was rented while D.C. and his wife Selby traveled the country playing the blues. In 1988 the couple renovated the Kozy Korner, opening at 9 p.m. and closing at 5 a.m. the next morning. Business boomed and the couple expanded the facility and renamed it "The Downhome Blues Club." On Labor Day weekend 1991, the first "Dusk Til Dawn Blues Festival" was held. The event was so popular, it became an annual celebration. In 2003, the Friends of Rentiesville Blues (FOR Blues) was formed. Their goal is "to build community between musicians, artists, music lovers and art lovers." They seek to preserve and develop African American traditional music through education in addition to entertainment. Although D.C. died in 2008 at the age of 73, his wife Selby continues the dream. The doors of the Down Home Blues Club remain open and the annual events continue to expand.

SUMMIT was established in 1903 just south of Muskogee. In 2009 the town had a population of 232. St. Thomas Primitive Baptist Church was significant to the town's early development. It was built in 1922 and is the oldest remaining public building in the community. It served as a social and religious center for many years. The Summit Fire Department is all-volunteer and is one of few buildings remaining in the small town.

RENTIESVILLE AND SUMMIT
Circle the letter next to the statement that correctly completes the statement

1. Summit Oklahoma was established in 1903. The St. Thomas Primitive Baptist Church was built in
a. 1903 c. 1904
b. 1922

2. The forty acres that Rentiesville began on was donated by
a. Phoebe McIntosh and William "Bill" Rentie c. Checotah Rentiesville
b. Redbird Rentie

3. In 1988, blues musician D.C. Minner re-opened his grandmother's old club and named it
a. The Down Home Blues Club c. Rentiesville Railroad Rack
b. D.C. Minner's Kitchen

4. At its peak, Rentiesville, Oklahoma had a population of approximately
a. 100,000 c. 2,000
b. 1,000

5. The Dusk Til Dawn Blues Festival is held in Rentiesville, Oklahoma each
a. Easter weekend c. Labor Day weekend
b. Memorial Day weekend

6. In Summit, Oklahoma, the oldest remaining public building is
a. The Muskogee court House c. The Volunteer Fire Department
b. St. Thomas Primitive Baptist Church

7. In 2009 the town of Summit has a population of
a. 1922 c. 1903
b. 232

8. Miss Lura Drennan of Rentiesville owned the Kozy Korner and these businesses as well
a. Laundromat and car wash c. catering service and music store
b. Community center and grocery store

9. FOR Blues stand for
a. Friends of Rentiesville Blues c. Friends of Rock and Roll
b. Forever operating Rentiesville

10. D.C. Minner died in 2008, but his dream and blues tradition lives on thanks to
a. his step-father c. his wife Selby
b. his grandmother's sisters

TAFT The all-black town of Taft was founded in 1902. It is located in Muskogee County 8 miles west of Muskogee, Oklahoma. It was named in honor of President William Howard Taft. By 1907, Taft had approximately 250 residents. The Reaves Realty Company advertised Taft as the "fastest growing colored community in Oklahoma." The town of Taft had two newspapers: the *Enterprise* and the *Tribune*. Prior to 1910, the community had grown to enjoy a soda pop factory, a lumberyard, two hotels, a restaurant, a bank, one drugstore, a funeral home and three general stores. Taft now has a population of approximately 400 residents. It does not have any businesses. The mayor of Taft is Lelia Foley-Davis, the first African American female mayor in the United States.

EDUCATIONAL AND CORRECTIONAL FACILITIES

The town of Taft has been a host to several educational and state run facilities. During its existence the W.T. Vernon School, The Industrial Institute for the Deaf, Blind, and Orphans of the Colored Race, Moton High School and the State Training School for Negro Girls, The Taft State Hospital for the Negro Insane and the state of the art Junior High School have all been located in Taft at one time. Most of these facilities have been replaced by two state penitentiaries, Jess Dunn Correctional Facility and the Eddie Warrior Facility for Women. Both are located in Taft.

TATUMS is named for brothers Lee B. and E.G. Tatum. It is located in northern Carter County. Lee arrived in the county in 1894 and, envisioning a town, pitched a tent along Wild Horse Creek. He and his wife Mary promoted the would-be town and assisted families moving there. The town grew and opened a hotel, cotton gin, sawmill, blacksmith shop and motor garage. Oil wells drilled in the 1920's brought wealth to many black residents. In 1927, Norman Studios filmed a silent movie called "Black Gold." Lee B. Tatums played a role in the film but no copies of it exist. It is said that the script and camera have been preserved at the Gene Autry Museum of Western Heritage in California. The Great Depression crippled the town of Tatums. By 2003 the population was listed as 173.

Bethel Missionary Baptist Church is located in Tatums. The church is known as "Big Bethel" and was built in 1919. It is the oldest remaining public building in that community. Bethel Missionary Baptist Church was listed in the National Register in 1994. The congregation is still in existence, and the building is used as a fellowship hall and for Sunday school classes. In 1936 the Julius Rosenwald Fund helped to build a brick school there. A gymnasium was added in 1949. The building is still there.

"Big Bethel" Missionary Baptist Church at Webster and Lane streets in Tatums was built in 1919.

TAFT AND TATUMS
Use the words from the word bank to complete the sentences

Black gold	Great Depression	Wild Horse	fire
Eddie Warrior	businesses	Tatums	Reaves
Lee	E.G.	Jess Dunn	William Howard Taft

1. In 1880, a _____ devastated the Creek Indians. They later abandoned the town.

2. Marshal Lee B. Tatum played a role in the silent movie named _____.

3. The _____ proved to be crippling to the town of Tatums.

4. The church known as "Big Bethel" built in _____ is the oldest remaining building in this community.

5. The town of Tatums is named after these two brothers _____ and _____ Tatum.

6. Taft, Oklahoma was named in honor of this U.S. president: _____.

7. There are two correctional facilities now located in the town of Taft, they are _____ and _____.

8. The town of Taft does not have any of these: _____.

9. This realty company advertised Taft as the "fastest growing colored community in Oklahoma": _____.

10. Lee arrived in Carter County in 1894 and pitched a tent along this creek: _____.

20

TULLAHASSEE is located five miles northwest of Muskogee. It is considered the oldest of the surviving all-black towns in Oklahoma. The town was named in 1850. The Creek Nation created a town, established a mission and built a school along the Texas Road. The Creek freedmen grew in numbers while the Creek Indians' population declined. In 1880, a fire proved to be devastating to the Creek Indians. They later abandoned the town and left the remains of the Tullahassee Mission School to the former African slaves. In 1899, the town post office was established. In the early 1900's, the Mason brothers built and opened the A.J. Mason General Store. People traveled for miles to shop at Mason's. The store stands today as an historical landmark and is listed on the Oklahoma Landmarks Inventory. Tullahassee was incorporated in 1902. Its name means "old town." Tullahassee's population was nearly 200 in 1920. By the year 2008, the population was 104.

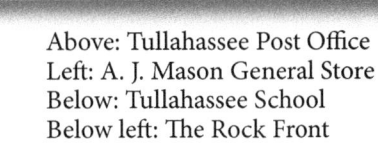

Above: Tullahassee Post Office
Left: A. J. Mason General Store
Below: Tullahassee School
Below left: The Rock Front

VERNON was established in 1911 in McIntosh County in the Creek Nation. It was founded by Edward P. McCabe, who was instrumental in the black town movement. Thomas Haynes was largely responsible for securing much of the land to form the town. The town was named in honor of Bishop W.T. Vernon. The forming congregation held church under a tree. Mrs. Louise Wesley established the first school, using her home to conduct class. One of the first Rosenwald schools built in the state of Oklahoma was constructed in Vernon. The town's grocery store, known as "The Rock Front," served as a recreational center and dry goods store. The Rock Front once housed the town's post office. It was built in 1920 and was listed on the National Register of Historic Places in 1985.

TULLAHASSEE AND VERNON
Answer the true false questions below.

1. _____ Vernon, Oklahoma was founded in 1911 by Edward P. McCabe.

2. _____ In 1880, a tornado devastated the Creek Indians. They later abandoned the town of Tullahassee.

3. _____ Tullahassee is the oldest of the surviving all-black towns in Oklahoma.

4. _____ A.J. Mason General Store was built and opened in Tullahassee, Oklahoma. People traveled for miles to shop there.

5. _____ One of the first Rosenwald schools built in the state of Oklahoma was constructed in Vernon, Oklahoma.

6. _____ The slaves took over the Tullahassee Mission School after it was abandoned by the Creek Indians.

7. _____ "The Rock Front" served the community of Tullahassee as a multi-use building for groceries, recreation and dry goods.

8. _____ The A.J. Mason General Store still stands. It is listed on the Oklahoma Landmarks Inventory.

9. _____ The name Tullahassee means "old soil."

10. _____ In the year 2008, the population of Tullahassee is listed to be over one million.

11. _____ When the first school was established in Vernon, classes were held at the home of Mrs. Louise Vernon.

12. _____ The "Rock Front" in Vernon once housed the town's post office.

13. _____ The town of Vernon was named in honor of United States President William Vernon.

14. _____ The congregation of Vernon, Oklahoma's first church held church under a tree.

15. _____ Thomas Haynes was instrumental in gaining land for Vernon, OK.

DOUGLASS HIGH SCHOOL

BIOGRAPHICAL PROFILE

Frederick Augustus Washington Bailey, better known as Frederick Douglass, was born in Talbot County, Maryland in February 1818. He was born into slavery and became separated from his mother, Harriet Bailey when he was only a baby. It is speculated that Frederick's father was a white slavemaster. Frederick was raised by his maternal grandmother, Betty Bailey. His mother died when he was seven years old. Although it was against the law to teach slaves to read, at the age of twelve Douglass began learning the alphabet under the tutelage of his slave owner's wife. He later learned to read from the white children in the area and learned to write by observing the white men he worked with. He secretly progressed with his reading and writing skills saying 'knowledge is the pathway from slavery to freedom." Frederick would teach other slaves to read during weekly Sunday school. This went unnoticed for over six months until the slavemaster became aware. Frederick was whipped and beaten on a regular basis, being sold from one slave master to another. After several failed attempts to escape, in 1838, Frederick dressed in a sailor's uniform and escaped slavery. Carrying identification papers he received from a free black seaman, he boarded a train in Havre de Grace, Maryland and rode to New York City, finally a free man. He died February 20, 1895.

THE BEGINNING

The Board of Education made a decision on January 5, 1891 to establish a "colored school" for the black children of Oklahoma City. They hired two staff members – a principal, Mr. J.D. Randolph and one teacher, Mr. Lewis S. Wilson. The school was a two-story frame building which was long and barn-like. The little elementary school was located in 400 block of East California.

The First Brick Douglass School Opened in 1903

THE FIRST GRADUATING CLASS

By 1898, the "colored school" children were ready for high school. A new building, principal and a faculty of eight teachers were hired for Oklahoma City's first black high school. Mr. J.W. Sharp was the newly elected principal. He requested that the children choose a name for the new high school. They chose the name Douglass, named after Frederick A. Douglass, the great Negro leader. The name was recommended and approved by the Board of Education. The first graduating class of Douglass was in 1903. The graduating class consisted of eight young men and women. The old frame building which had once housed Douglass students, burned and the students were moved.

THE EXPANSION

In 1903 new principal J. S. A. Brazelton was charged with the leadership of Douglass. The brick building was located at 200 E. California Street. Brazelton organized and was first president of the Oklahoma Association of Negro Teachers. Art, Music, Home Economics, Industrial arts, and Athletics were offered to the students at Douglass. High standards were maintained for the students at the school. In 1921, Dr. Inman E. Page, former president of Langston University served as principal of Douglass and supervising principal of separate schools. The school's enrollment continued to grow. Dr. Page's daughter, Mrs. Zelia N. Breaux headed the music department at Douglass. The school's music abilities ranked among the best in the country.

Douglass High School Football Team about 1910

A NEW SITE FOR DOUGLASS

In 1934, Douglass moved to a new site. It was located at 600 N. High Street in Oklahoma City. This was the third school for the blacks in Oklahoma City. It was later named Page Woodson fifth year center.

DOUGLASS HIGH SCHOOL SWAPS LAND WITH STATE FAIRGROUND

In June of 1940, Dr. F.D. Moon was chosen to become the principal of Douglass. A new school was needed. The present school superintendent first suggested Washington Park at Fourth and High Streets. Great opposition came from the black community and the idea was soon abandoned. The first Oklahoma State Fairgrounds site was eventually selected for the new Douglass. It was located on N.E. 10th and Eastern streets in Oklahoma City. The school would be built on a forty acre site to house 1200 students, grades 10 - 12. The school would include a gymnasium which would seat 2300, outdoor and indoor swimming pools, library, football field, cinder track, tennis courts, baseball and softball diamonds, a 1300 seat auditorium and a cafeteria to seat 500 people. It was completed in 1954.

Copyright, The Oklahoma Publishing Company

FIRST HIGH SCHOOL IN OKLAHOMA COMMEMORATED ON A LICENSE PLATE

House Bill 2708 was passed by both Oklahoma House and Senate and was signed by governor, Brad Henry. This bill gave way for "The Pride of the East Side" to be represented with a specialized license plate. Frederick Douglass High School alumni and friends were given the opportunity to purchase the specialized license plate to honor one of the oldest high schools in Oklahoma.

DOUGLASS DEMOLISHED — AND REBUILT

On April 8, 2006, the official grand opening celebration was held. The brand new state-of-the-art Douglass High school would be the first new high school built in the Oklahoma City Public School district in 50 years. The 202,000 square foot facility, built on 36.3 acres, came at a cost of $27.7 million. It was designed to accommodate 1,200 students for grades 7-12. The school housed a 1200 seat auditorium, 30 classrooms, 8 science laboratories, a courtroom classroom, 24 specialty classrooms for music, drama, art and special education. In addition a new football and track stadium was built with a 6,000 seat capacity.

DOUGLASS HIGH SCHOOL

1. Discuss facts about Frederick Augustus Washington Bailey and his life.

_____

_____

_____

2. Write facts about the first "colored" school established in 1891.

_____

_____

_____

3. Write about Frederick's escape from slavery. How did he accomplish it?

_____

_____

_____

4. When a new school was needed in 1940, what were some of the challenges and opposition about?

_____

_____

_____

5. Describe some of the features of the new Douglass school which was built in 2006.

_____

_____

_____

BASS REEVES

BIOGRAPHICAL PROFILE

Bass Reeves was born a slave in 1838 in Crawford County, Arkansas. He took the surname of his master, Colonel George R. Reeves. In the 1860's, Bass beat his master in a fight over a card game. He became a fugitive slave. He knew hanging was the penalty for striking his master so Bass found refuge in Indian Territory (modern-day Oklahoma) among the Creek and Seminole Indians. Bass worked for thirty-two years as a deputy marshal in the Indian Territory in Oklahoma. Later, he became a policeman in Muskogee where his reputation was praised often. After he retired a newspaper wrote, "in the early days when the Indian country was overridden with outlaws, Reeves would herd into Fort Smith, often single-handed, bands of men charged with crimes from bootlegging to murder." Bass Reeves died of a kidney ailment called Bright's disease in Muskogee, Oklahoma in 1910.

A UNITED STATES MARSHAL

Bass ran a family farm until he become a deputy United States (U.S.) marshal in 1875. Marshal James F. Fagan had heard of Bass Reeves' reputation and skills. Bass could speak several Indian languages and was skilled with pistols or rifles, shooting accurately using his right or left hand. He was a legend at catching criminals under trying circumstances. Boasting that he knew the Indian Territory "like a cook knows her kitchen," Bass never feared any man. At six feet, two inches tall and weighing 180 pounds, Bass, some settlers claimed, could whip two men at once using his bare hands. Bass looked spiffy in his favorite wide brimmed hat and boots polished to a glossy shine. He was sometimes forced to wear disguises in order to catch a criminal. Bass dressed as a cowboy, drover, outlaw, or gunman, whatever the situation required. In efforts to earn a $5,000 reward, Bass dressed as a tramp, wearing an old pair of shoes, carrying a cane and a beat up old hat. He then walked twenty-eight miles in his disguise to the home of the outlaws' mother. She fed him and invited him to sleep at their home for the night. Once the outlaws were asleep, Bass handcuffed them and escorted them back on the twenty-eight mile walk. The *Chickasaw Enterprise* reported that Bass had arrested over three thousand men and women for federal law violations. Bass was never shot during any of his arrests, but had his hat and belt shot.

Clay model of the Bass Reeves statue created by sculptor Harold Holden in Fort Smith, Arkansas

BOTH BASS AND SON CHARGED WITH MURDER

Bass was devoted to his wife, Nellie, and his ten children (five boys and five girls), but he was also devoted to his duty. He once arrested his own son, Bennie for murder. Bennie was accused of shooting and murdering his own wife. He was later convicted and spent time in the federal prison in Leavenworth, Kansas. Bass had killed fourteen men duing the course of his work as a deputy. He was proud that he never shot a man unless it was necessary to save his own life. In 1887, though, Bass Reeves himself was charged with murdering a trail cook. A witness testified on Bass' behalf and he was later acquitted and freed, but most of his life savings had been used for his defense during the trial.

BASS REEVES MEMORIAL BRIDGE

In 2008, a bridge on U.S. Highway 62 was named in Bass Reeves' honor. It crosses the Arkansas River and connects Muskogee with Fort Gibson, Oklahoma. In 2011 Gov. Mary Fallin authorized permanent markers placed on the bridge bearing Bass Reeves' name.

BASS REEVES
fill in the blanks to complete the sentences

1) Bass was a _____ before he was offered the job as United States Marshal in 1875.

2) Bass wore disguises to do his job. He once dressed as a tramp to earn _____

3) Bass became a fugitive slave after beating his _____ in a fight stemming from a card game.

4) Bass had ten children, _____ girls and _____ boys.

5) Bass arrested Bennie, his _____ for murder.

6) Bass was charged for murdering his _____. He was later acquitted because it was ruled self defense.

7) In _____ Bass died of a kidney ailment called Bright's disease.

8) Governor _____ signed an act in 2011 which instructed the Oklahoma Department of Transportation to install markers on the Bass Reeves Memorial Bridge which would bear his name.

9) After working as a deputy marshal for thirty-two years, Bass took a job at the _____ police department.

10) Bass was able to speak several _____ languages.

BIOGRAPHICAL PROFILE

Green I. Currin was born on October 20, 1842 in Williamson County, Tennessee, near the town of Franklin. Green and his wife Caroline had five children; Winsor, Thomas, Henry, Janie and Rosie. After emancipation, Green moved to Nashville. He relocated to Kansas by the year 1877 and became a lawman in Topeka. In 1889 Green and his family staked out a claim in the Land Run. Their homestead was near Union Township in Kingfisher County, Oklahoma Territory. The family made a living farming. Green died on October 21, 1918 at his home in (Dover), Kingfisher, Oklahoma. He is buried in Burns Cemetery.

FIRST BLACK LEGISLATOR

Green began showing an interest in politics while in Topeka. He campaigned as a Republican nominee and ran for the position of police judge. Green lost the election. In 1890 Green I. Currin was elected in Kingfisher County District 5. He along with four other delegates were voted into the House of Representatives. He served as a member of the first Territorial Legislative Assembly. The day after the election, three white men clubbed and seriously injured an African American man. Due to the increase of violent racial attacks against blacks, Green saw the need for legislative action to protect the African Americans in his territory. During Green's term in the legislature, he introduced two bills, neither of them passed. House Bill 119 was a civil rights bill. It was the first to be introduced into the new territory. The proposed law included penalties for racial violence. It failed to become law by one vote. Green served only one term in the assembly. After his time in the legislature, Green served as a deputy United States marshal. In 1887, he was appointed to serve on the Board of Regents at the Colored Agricultural and Normal College (Langston University).

THE 15th AMENDMENT

The 15th Amendment, ratified February 3, 1870, gave blacks the right to vote. It states "The right of citizens of the United States to vote shall not be denied or abridged by the United States or by any State on account of race, color, or previous condition of servitude." This did not guarantee blacks or women the right to hold office and it did not address the fact that many states, North and South, required the ownership of property, payment of poll taxes and literacy as a condition to vote. In 1910, Oklahoma legislators fought to keep blacks from voting. The use of the grandfather clause was one tactic. The grandfather clause stated that if your grandfather or father voted on January 1, 1867, you were allowed to vote. This disqualified all blacks from voting. Green Currin testified that his grandfather, an Irishman named Tommy Currin, had previously voted. He argued that being a former legislator and a United States Deputy Marshal should qualify him to vote. Since he could read and write and his grandfather voted, he should have been allowed to vote, but was not. In 1915, the United States Supreme Court ruled against the grandfather clause. I.W. Lane filed a lawsuit against the state of Oklahoma in 1939. The U.S. Supreme Court ruled in Lane's favor and demanded that all states allow blacks to vote.

GREEN I. CURRIN

Answer the following questions by filling in the blanks.

1. Green Currin and his wife Caroline had _____ children.

2. In 1890 Green Currin was elected to serve in the House of Representatives in _____ County.

3. Green introduced House Bill 119. It was a _____ _____ bill.

4. Green served on the Board of Regents at this college in 1887 _____.

5. After statehood, Oklahoma legislators fought to keep _____ from voting.

6. While living in Topeka, Kansas, Green ran for this political office but lost. _____

7. The 15th Amendment gave blacks the right to _____.

8. Tommy Currin was Green's _____.

9. Green made a living doing this _____.

10. His family's homestead in Kingfisher County is a result of the _____ in 1889.

11. After his term as a legislature, Green became _____.

12. Green I. Currin died on _____ in Kingfisher, Oklahoma.

13. During his term in the legislature, Green wrote _____ legislative bills.

14. Green I. Currin was born in_____.

15. States sometimes used these requirements in order to vote_____.

16. Green wrote legislative bills to protect _____ after violent racial attacks increased.

17. After Green located to Topeka, Kansas in 1877, he became a _____.

18. The _____ clause stated that if your grandfather or father voted on January 1, 1867, you were allowed to vote.

19. Currin Green served as a member of the first _____ _____ _____.

20. Green was appointed to serve on the Board of Regents at _____ _____.

BIOGRAPHICAL PROFILE

Inman Edward Page was born into slavery on December 29, 1853 in Warrenton, Virginia. His parents are Horace and Elizabeth Page. Inman and his parents worked on a plantation during the Civil War. They managed to escape and moved to the Washington D.C. area where Inman began his education. He attended a private school for African American students and later enrolled in Howard University, later becoming the first African American to be admitted to Brown University in Providence, Rhode Island. Inman graduated from this prestigious university in 1877. Inman married Zelia R. Ball in 1898. The couple had three children, Zelia N., Mary and Inman E. Page Jr, who died at the age of seven. Inman became the first president of the Colored Agricultural and Normal University (Langston University), at the all-black town of Langston, OK. During his eighteen year tenure, Inman traveled Oklahoma recruiting students and transformed the University by significantly increasing its enrollment. In 1922 Inman accepted the position of principal at Oklahoma City's Douglass High School, later accepting a position as supervisor of all the separate schools in Oklahoma City. Inman retained this position for 12 years, retiring in May of 1935. On December 21, 1935, at the age of 81, Inman E. Page died at the home of his daughter Zelia N. Breaux in Oklahoma City, OK.

INMAN PAGE GRADE SCHOOL

The Inman Page Grade School was named after Inman. Formerly known as Bryant School, it was located at 317 N. Geary in Oklahoma City, Oklahoma. In 1948 a devastating fire severely damaged the school. Its cause was believed to be a leaking gas boiler in the school. Damage to the school proved to be extensive. The school has since been demolished.

PARK NAMED TO HONOR EDUCATOR

A new "negro park," Page Park was constructed at Northeast Second and Stiles streets in Oklahoma City, Oklahoma. It was built in honor of Inman E. Page. Construction began in 1937 after his death. The funds were a combination of funds from the Oklahoma City Board of Education and the city of Oklahoma City. The funding was approximately $6,000.00. It was constructed on an area of seven acres of land. The park was adjacent to the school grounds of the Inman Page school.

INMAN E. PAGE

INMAN E. PAGE
Make each false sentence true. Cross out the false word and write the correct one in the blank.

1) Inman and his family worked in a (factory) during the Civil War.

_____

2) Inman was one of the first African Americans to be admitted to the (University of Oklahoma).

_____

3) Inman became the first president of (Douglass High School).

_____

4) The Inman Page grade school was closed and later demolished due to damage from a (tornado).

_____

5) The "negro park" was built in honor of Inman E. Page. Its construction began after Inman's (speech and protest).

_____

Answer the true/false statements below

6) _____ Inman had two children, they are both girls.

7) _____ Inman was buried on the campus of Brown University.

8) _____ One of Inman's daughters, Zelia, took care of her father at his death.

9) _____ Langston University's first president was Inman E. Page.

10) _____ The Page Park was funded by donations and funding from the City of Oklahoma City and Oklahoma City Public Schools.

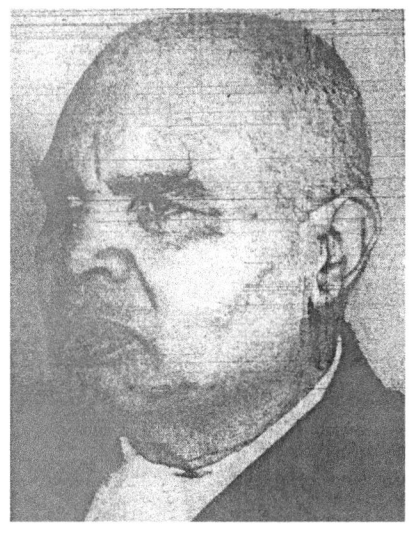

BIOGRAPHICAL PROFILE

Sidney Daniel Lyons, was reportedly born in December 1860 near Hugo, Oklahoma in Choctaw Nation, Indian Territory. His parents, Reuben and Emily Lyons raised him in Lamar County, Texas. Sidney married Mary and was stepfather to Melvin F. Luster. Sidney moved to Oklahoma City from Guthrie, Oklahoma in the early 1900's, Sidney died in Oklahoma City, OK, on April 9, 1942 from heart disease.

ENTREPRENEURS

Sidney amassed a fortune through his entrepreneurship. His ventures included a restaurant and grocery store in Guthrie. He was the owner of Lyons Hotel, rental homes, and commercial property in Oklahoma and Texas. Lyons' property included a block of businesses and buildings on Northeast Second Street in Oklahoma City. In the 1930s he invested in the oil business. Mary Lyons was one of the wealthiest women in the city. She owned numerous oil and gas properties across the United States. During the late 1930's and early 1940's, members of the black community traveled to Lyons Park near Arcadia. The segregated park owned by Mary Lyons featured swimming, dancing, and carnivals. She funded the construction of many buildings in the Deep Deuce area. Sidney's daughter, Ruby, married into the Luster family. Ruby was owner of the Lyons Den and Ruby's Grill.

EAST INDIA TOILET GOODS

In 1918 Sidney opened a factory, "East India Hair Grower." It produced a hair product that was second only to Madame C.J. Walker, one of the largest African American hair product companies in the world. The oil was to be used for straightening and dressing the hair and came at a price of 50 cents. From this small building, the Lyons family also produced face powder, soap, toiletries, hair tonic, perfume, and rouge. Sidney advertised and marketed his products to customers coast to coast and gained national and international recognition due to the fine quality of his products. The East India toiletries plant was located at 316 North Central Ave. in Oklahoma City, one-half block from the family residence. The plant closed in 1935.

THE LUSTER FAMILY

Melvin F. Luster was the son of Mary Lyons and the stepson of Sidney Lyons. Melvin married Ernestine and they started a very successful hair product company known as "The Sunray." Melvin and his wife were also owners of Luster's Motel located at 3402 NE 23 in Oklahoma City. This was the only luxury motel built for African Americans. The Lusters also owned the Wishing Well, another motel property also on NE 23rd. The Lusters were one of the largest property owners in the Oklahoma City area.

SIDNEY D. LYONS

THE MELVIN F. LUSTER HOUSE

Mr. Lyons' family residence was known as the Melvin F. Luster House. It was the first brick house built among blacks and was referred to as "The Mansion." It is listed in the National Register of Historic Places and still remains at 300 NE 3rd St. in Oklahoma City, OK. The elegant two-story brick and wood home was built in 1926 with a Spanish tile roof, and a porch that extends across the entire front of the house. It was completed with fine furniture, canvas walls (painted in oils), sculptured ceramic tile, beveled glass French doors, stone fireplaces, oriental rugs, and carpets.

ANSWER THE TRUE FALSE QUESTIONS BELOW.

1. _____ The Lyons Den was a playhouse at the Oklahoma City Zoo.

2. _____ Melvin Luster was Sidney's son from his first marriage.

3. _____ Sidney opened many stores and businesses in Guthrie, Oklahoma after moving to Oklahoma City.

4. _____ The home that Sidney Lyons had built was referred to as "The Mansion."

5. _____ The Sunray was a place where some blacks went to get sunglasses.

6. _____ The Luster Motel was a luxury hotel, built from the ground up for African Americans.

7. _____ The East India Hair Grower was the number one hair grower in the entire world.

8. _____ Ruby's Grill was a place most blacks went to when they had picnics. They would grill their food.

9. _____ Sidney married Emily Daniels in 1942

10. _____ The East India Toilet Goods and Manufacturing Company sold toiletries, soap, perfume and food.

Congress approved the Militia Act on July 17, 1862 which allowed black soldiers to participate in the armed forces. The black soldiers were so successful in battle they were used even more. On January 1, 1863, President Abraham Lincoln signed the Emancipation Proclamation, freeing the slaves. By law, blacks were not allowed to serve in the regular peacetime U.S. Army until July 28, 1866. Congress formed six regiments of black army soldiers, four units as infantry (soldiers who marched or fought by foot) and two as cavalry (soldiers who fought on horseback). Although these regiments had white commanders, blacks saw this as an opportunity to better their lives by learning to read and write and learn other skills of trade. These soldiers served under harsh conditions. Their treatment was lower than whites. Blacks were paid $10 regardless of their rank, while the lowest ranking white soldier was paid $13. After long debates the pay was made equal. Black soldiers were faced with many obstacles – finding presentable uniforms, shoes, equipment, weapons, and supplies. They were issued pitiful equipment and sometimes crippled, discarded, Civil War horses. Black soldiers were subjected to having food thrown from moving trains which was sometimes spoiled and unfit to eat. For survival they sometimes ate plants and grazed the land for food and fashioned other items to use as weapons. The soldiers faced prejudice from many citizens. One injured soldier on his way to the hospital by train reportedly went for 48 hours without food because he was refused service on the train and at the train station. The soldiers endured, having the lowest desertion rate of any unit in the U.S. Army. The Native Americans began calling the soldiers "Buffalo Soldiers" because of their tightly curled hair which resembled the roaming buffalo of the great plains. They accepted this name as a token of honor, respect, braveness, and strength. During the land runs of Oklahoma, the Buffalo Soldiers acted as a protective force to keep "Boomers" off of land not assigned to them. The Buffalo Soldiers acted as protectors of settlers as they moved westward and were peacemakers during threat of war. The Buffalo Soldiers helped to fight off bandits and cattle thieves and assisted in catching outlaws. They constructed thousands of miles of roads and telegraph lines and built and renovated numerous posts, forts, and camps. They also protected the mail routes and railroad surveyors. These brave men opened new roads, pinpointed water holes, mapped out new parts of land, escorted stages, protected river crossings, and guarded supply wagons. The 10th Cavalry unit was the first to be called "Buffalo Soldiers." Later other regiments got the name.

FORT GIBSON

Fort Gibson was the first fort established in Indian Territory. The tenth cavalry soldiers were headquartered in Fort Gibson, serving from 1867 until 1869 and from 1868 until 1873. At the time the fort was completed, it consisted of seven large stone buildings and ten frame buildings. Its purpose was to keep peace between the Osage and Cherokee Indians. Soldiers there laid out a network of military roads and attempted to control illegal liquor trafficking. It was also the center of trade and travel. The fort was developed on low ground and was subject to flooding. The stagnant water gave constant threat to malaria. In 1936, the state of Oklahoma used the Works Progress Administration (WPA) grant to complete a 55 acre tract, reconstructing the original log stockade. The fort was designated a national historic landmark in 1960. Fort Gibson Historic Site is now a museum.

FORT RENO

Fort Reno, which is located in the vicinity of El Reno, Oklahoma was established in 1874. It was designed to provide security to the Cheyenne and Arapaho land. Fort Reno was home to members of both the 9th and 10th Calvary at some point. The Buffalo Soldiers used this facility until approximately 1909. Later it was converted into a U.S. Army remount station. By 1949, the fort was being used as an agricultural research station.

FORT SILL

In 1866 a site near the base of the Wichita Mountains was established. The fort was named Camp Wichita. It was later changed to Fort Sill. In January of 1869, soldiers staked out a site at Fort Sill in Lawton, Oklahoma. They were the Ninth Cavalry. Their motto was, "We can. We will." The Buffalo Soldiers were there at the establishment of Fort Sill. Buildings of sturdy rock and stone were constructed by the troops of the 9th and 10th Calvary. On March 21, 1856, Henry Ossian Flipper was born into slavery in Thomasville, Georgia. At the age of 21, Henry became the first black graduate of the United States Military Academy at West Point. In 1879 he was assigned to serve as Captain and Second Lieutenant at Fort Sill. While there Henry also served as the post's engineer and created and supervised the construction of a new drainage system eliminating many stagnant ponds and other bodies of water which were deemed responsible for the spread of malaria. In 1977, his first engineering success was named "Flipper's Ditch." It has now been designated a National Historic Landmark.

SENATE BILL 659 – LAW TO HONOR BUFFALO SOLDIERS

African American soldiers served in the Civil War, World War I, Plains Indian Wars, and land runs. On May 18, 2005, Governor Brad Henry signed Senate Bill 659 into law. Senator Judy Eason McIntyre was the principal author of the legislation. The law creates the "Buffalo Soldiers Heritage Corridor." The heritage district will extend from Boley to Vinita, Oklahoma. A five member advisory committee consisting of the Oklahoma Historical Society, a representative from the Greenwood Cultural District, a member from the All-Black Town and another member from the public in conjunction to the Tourism and Recreation Department will oversee the project. It is hoped that the Buffalo Soldiers Heritage Corridor will further education of history in addition to stimulating economic development for the towns and cities along the Corridor. Twenty-two African Americans earned Congressional Medals of Honor for their heroism during the Civil War.

BUFFALO SOLDIERS SCHOLARSHIP

The Ninth and Tenth Cavalry Association offers an annual college scholarship through the Lawton-Fort Sill Chapter. Seniors attending Eisenhower High School, Lawton High School, MacArthur High School, or Lawton Christian Secondary School can apply. Students who have either been accepted or enrolled in college of university are eligible to apply, other qualification criteria apply to interested individuals.

WRITE ABOUT SOME OF THE POSITIVE THINGS THE BUFFALO SOLDIERS ACCOMPLISHED

_____
_____
_____
_____
_____
_____
_____
_____
_____

BUFFALO SOLDIERS

Find the following hidden words in the word search puzzle below.

MILITIA ACT
CAVALRY
FORT SILL
FORT RENO
BRAVERY

BUFFALO
REGIMENT
FLIPPER
ARMY
CHEYENNE

SOLDIER
GIBSON
SCHOLARSHIP
BOOMERS
ARAPAHO

```
A C T E H E H W N A V S G P O M
C N R P E D D O S G L T E A D O
L Z M F R K D R E P P I L F I C
N O A N U A A I O I O Y R P G R
S E F S T T T D H B M A G D K T
T W B O U O Y S H R P I I G F O
R I J R L Y R L A V A C B J E T
E M T C A A I T I L I M S E A E
I M R N L V B A S G C E O E R X
D D L O E N E O A I E T N B A E
L N H I U M R R O A L N Y H P M
O C V Q Q N I A Y M E L G R A P
S E N L V B D G N Y E L X A H T
B U F F A L O N E R T R O F O G
P Z S G P N E H B R C O S P W S
M S S R S Y C L T Y L R G C H F
```

WYATT H. SLAUGHTER

BIOGRAPHICAL PROFILE

Wyatt H. (W.H.) Slaughter was born in the state of Alabama around 1873. He was orphaned at the age of five years old and was raised by his aunt, a former slave. In 1903, Wyatt moved to Oklahoma City. He was one of the first black doctors to move there, he often served patients who were without money. W.H. married Edna Randolph in 1907. The couple had two children, Wyatt Jr. and Saretta. In 1935, Saretta married Dr. Gravelly E. Finley, Wyatt Jr. who followed in his father's footsteps also became a physician. In addition to being a medical doctor, W.H. was a skilled architect and builder. W.H. was very generous and financed many of the buildings and businesses on the northeast side of Oklahoma City. W.H. was also the first African American west of the Mississippi to own his own airport. It was located near what is now I-35 and 63rd in Oklahoma City. The former airport is now being used as a construction business. W. H. died in 1952.

THE SLAUGHTER BUILDING

The Slaughter Building was located on the northwest corner of NE 2nd and Stiles in Oklahoma City. Randolph's Drugs on the first floor had a soda fountain where customers could purchase banana splits and milk shakes. As a boy, Ralph Ellison worked at the soda fountain and as a delivery boy. The second floor was used for professional offices of physicians, dentists, and attorneys. The third floor was called "Slaughter's Hall" and hosted conventions, musical events, and dancing. Popular local bands and others from out of state played there nightly. Above the third floor was a rooftop garden. This establishment was the hub of the community. It was demolished in 1992.

Wyatt H. Slaughter built this mansion in 1937. The 4,400 square foot home was built on 8 acres at 3101 NE 50th St. in Oklahoma City.

UTOPIA HOSPITAL

William Lewis (W.L.) Haywood was five years old and his brother three when both of their parents died. Orphaned, they were raised by their aunt. In 1908, W.L. Haywood graduated from Meharry College, a medical school in Nashville, Tennessee. While traveling by train to California, he became ill and stopped in Guthrie, Oklahoma. He visited Dr. Slaughter who convinced him to relocate. The two doctors worked together to improve medical care for blacks in Oklahoma. Their care consisted of house calls due to blacks being barred from white hospitals. Dr. Slaughter and Dr. W.L. Haywood were co-founders of the Great Western Hospital. The hospital was later renamed Utopia Hospital. It was established January 26, 1910. This facility was located at 415 N.E. 1st Street in Oklahoma City. It was the first hospital for blacks. Dr. Wyatt H. Slaughter was the first black doctor to have authority to practice at Oklahoma City's St. Anthony hospital. In 1945, Dr. Haywood became the first black physician allowed to practice at the University Hospital, (OU Medical Center), in Oklahoma City, Oklahoma. The area for treating black patients was called the South Ward or "Negro Unit." Haywood died at the age of 88 in 1971.

JEFFERSON DAVIS (J.D.) RANDOLPH was born in Adarville, Kentucky on October 19, 1862. J.D. grew up in Gallatin, Tennessee, where he received private tutoring. He moved to Oklahoma in 1898 with the other Boomers. J.D. served as the first principal of the "colored school" which was established in Oklahoma City, 1881. During his principalship, J.D. earned $60.00 per month, which was equal to the amount of other white instructors in the area. After leaving the education field, J.D. opened a drugstore and real estate business, partnering with his son-in-law, W.H. Slaughter. J.D. worked at the state capitol building as a custodian from 1927 – 1934. The white legislators referred to him as "Uncle Jeff." J.D. had a daughter, Edna, who married Dr. Wyatt (W.H.) Slaughter. His son T. J. was the territory's first black dentist. Dr. T.J. Randolph opened his dentistry practice on the 2nd floor physicians area of the Slaughter Building. T.J. Randolph was the first black dentist in Oklahoma City.

DR. WYATT H. SLAUGHTER

Identify each sentence below as true/false

1. _____ Wyatt H. Slaughter was born in the state of Oklahoma around 1873.

2. _____ Slaughter was the first African American west of the Mississippi to own his own airport.

3. _____ As a boy author Ralph Ellison worked at the soda fountain of Randolph's Drugs on the first floor of the Slaughter Building.

4. _____ The Slaughter Building was located on the northwest corner of NE 2nd and Stiles in Tulsa, Oklahoma.

5. _____ Dr. Slaughter and Dr. W. L. Haywood were co-founders of the Great Western Hospital, later renamed Utopia Hospital.

ZELIA N. BREAUX

BIOGRAPHICAL PROFILE

Zelia Page was born in Jefferson City, Missouri in 1880. She was the daughter of Inman Edward and Zelia Ball Page. In 1898 Inman Page moved his family to Oklahoma Territory and served as president of Langston University for 17 years. Zelia received a bachelor's degree in music from Lincoln Institute in Jefferson City, later going on to earn a master's degree in music from Northwestern University in Evanston, Illinois. On December 6, 1905, Zelia married Armogen Breaux. The couple had one son, Enimen. He later became vice president at Langston University. To some she was considered the "mother" or "mentor" of several Deep Deuce greats. Zelia was a genius in that she was able to teach students both band and orchestral instruments. Her pupils included Charlie Christian, Jimmy Rushing and Ralph Ellison. Zelia died in Guthrie, Oklahoma on October 31, 1956 at the age of 76. She was inducted into the Oklahoma Bandmasters Association Hall of Fame in 1991 and the Oklahoma Women's Hall of Fame in 1983.

ZELIA'S ENJOYMENT OF MUSIC

Zelia began her teaching career at Langston University in 1898 as head of the music department. She was only 18 years old. Zelia implemented a three year vocal program, where her student's received both voice and piano instruction. Zelia required her student's to play Bach, Chopin, Liszt and Mozart. She spent 20 years at Langston University. In 1918, Oklahoma City public schools were segregated. Zelia accepted the position of supervisor of music for the African American schools, and she placed a music teacher in every grade school. In 1923 she organized the Douglass High School band with twenty-six students. It became one of the most outstanding bands in the United States, appeareing all over the nation. In 1933 Zelia took the band to the Chicago World's Fair where they performed on national radio. In 1937 she organized the Black State Band Festival which began with seven bands and later expanded to eighteen. The Douglass band also attended and participated in the Texas Centennial celebration in Dallas, Texas in 1936. Zelia retired from Douglass in 1948.

SEGREGATED PARADES

Prior to 1924, African Americans were not allowed to participate in the annual Downtown Boys Day Parade. Zelia prepared Douglass students for this event, practicing each day on the football field with precision and decorum. Everyone enjoyed their performances.

ALDRIDGE THEATER

Zelia and F.E. Withrow were co-owners of the Aldridge Theater, which opened in 1919 and was located at 303-305 NE 2nd St. in Oklahoma City. It was one of the first theaters built in the black community. Patrons enjoyed music, drama, comedy, and live performances in addition to motion pictures. Many young musicians performed at the Aldridge. These included music legends Billie Holiday, Count Basie, Cab Calloway and Duke Ellington. In 1983, Zelia was inducted into the Oklahoma Women's Hall of Fame. She was also named one of Oklahoma's "100 Notable Women of Style."

African Americans always had a presence in movies, but when movies began to use sound, African Americans began to make their own films that showed more positive depictions. For example, Oscar Micheau, remade popular movies like *The Exile*, *The Girl from Chicago* and *Swing* for black movie audiences. During the 1930s, some African American filmmakers joined with their white counterparts and made movies and musicals that voiced specific African American concerns. Directors like Marc Connelly and actors like Paul Robeson became famous figures in the African American film industry. The Aldridge brought all these to Oklahoma City.

ZELIA PAGE-BREAUX
Identify each sentence below as true/false

1. _____ Zelia is the daughter of Inman E. Page.

2. _____ Zelia had sixteen children.

3. _____ Zelia's music pupils included Charlie Christian, Elvis Presley, Nat King Cole, and Ralph Ellison.

4. _____ The Aldridge Theater was one of the first theaters built in the black community in Oklahoma City.

5. _____ Patrons enjoyed music, comedy and drama performances at the Aldridge theater.

6. _____ Zelia was co-owner of the Aldridge Theater in Oklahoma City.

7. _____ Prior to 1924, blacks were always allowed to participate in the Downtown Boys Day Parade.

8. _____ With twenty-six students, Zelia organized the Douglass High School band. It was one of the most outstanding bands in the United States.

9. _____ Zelia organized the Black State Band Festival which began with over 50 bands.

10. _____ Zelia Breaux never attended college.

11. _____ Zelia was the supervisor of music for African Americans in Oklahoma City Schools.

12. _____ Zelia died in Langston Oklahoma in 1983.

13. _____ Douglass' band has appeared all over the United States.

14. _____ Zelia married Armogen Breaux. They had one child.

15. _____ Zelia was named one of Oklahoma's 100 Notable Women of Style.

ALBERT C. HAMLIN

BIOGRAPHICAL PROFILE

Albert Comstock Hamlin (A.C.), was born February 10, 1881 in Topeka, Kansas. A.C.'s parents, Andrew Jackson and Fanny Hamlin were former slaves from Tennessee and later moved to Kansas in 1880. The Hamlins moved to Oklahoma when Oklahoma Territory opened in 1889. They staked a claim and settled on a farm in Guthrie, Oklahoma. When A.C. was just a child, he took on the responsibility as head of the household after his father died. A.C. continued his education and after graduation he married Katie Weaver in 1899. The couple had five children. A.C. died on his farm on August 29, 1912, at the age of 31.

MAKING HISTORY IN 1908

Albert became active in politics as a young adult. In 1908, he became the first African American to be elected to the Oklahoma state legislature. Being the only African-Amercan legislator, Albert faced many challenges and prejudices. While completing his term, Albert worked hard and introduced many important bills. He was able to successfully obtain $35,000 with the passage of a bill which created a state school for blind, deaf, and orphaned black children in Taft, Oklahoma. In addition, Albert sponsored legislation that made equal facilities for black and white railroad passengers. Albert sought stricter observance of the Sabbath, amending a bill preventing activities such as theatrical performances and baseball games on Sundays. By 1910, a white legislature had created laws that prohibited blacks from voting, A.C. was not reelected.

VOTING CHALLENGES

Albert served on the local school board and was also successful as trustee of the Springvale Township in Logan County where he lived. Albert, a Republican, won election to the Oklahoma House of Representatives in 1908 but lost his bid for re-election in 1910. Fearing a rise in black political power, the white majority in the legislature passed several laws to make it difficult for most blacks to vote. The "grandfather clause" stated that "no person shall be registered as an elector in the state of Oklahoma, or be allowed to vote in any election held unless he be able to read and write any section of the Constitution of the State of Oklahoma." This clause also prevented individuals who had never voted prior to January 1, 1866 from voting.

> The Hon. A. C Hamlin of Logan county has filed as candidate for re-election Hamlin was the only negro in the last legislature, but there will be several negroes in the next legislature—provided the "grandfather clause" should fall to become a law Arch Jones of Muskogee, H L. Storms of Wagoner and G A Garrett of Okfuskee—all negroes—have already filed for representatives Others are threatening to break into the race. Thus the menace of negro ascendancy on the east side passes the boundary and threatens every citizen of the west side Six weeks will determine finally whether Oklahoma is to be Negroid or Anglo-Saxon The democratic party will fill the political morgue with negroes or the republican party will fill the legislature of Oklahoma with them.

This clipping from an Oklahoma newspaper in 1910 boldly and unashemedly describes the efforts white politicians made to prevent blacks from voting.

ALBERT C. HAMLIN

Unscramble the words to get the facts about Albert then complete the paragraphs.

1. Albert was born in 1881 in Topeka, S N A S K A _____

2. Albert's parents; Andrew Jackson and Fanny Hamlin, were former L E S V A S _____

3. Albert sponsored legislation to form a school for Disabled and Orphaned children. It was located in F T A T, Oklahoma. _____

4. Albert wrote legislation to make equal facilities for white and black A I O D A R L R passengers. _____

5. Albert died at the age of T T E N H O I R Y. _____

6. When Albert was nine years old, he and his family moved to a farm in T E I R H U G, Oklahoma. _____

7. Albert D D E I on his farm, _____

8. Laws prevented S B L C A K from voting. _____

9. Albert and Katie Weaver were married in 1899, they had V E F I children. _____

10. Albert was the T I F R S African American elected to the state legislature. _____

11. Write about how Albert felt being the only African American on the legislature and some of the challenges he probably faced. _____

12. Discuss some of the responsibilities Albert had when his father died. _____

13. When Albert authored legislation to make railcars equal, what types of things would need to be addressed? _____

14. What is the grandfather clause? _____

15. Describe how Albert probably felt when he made history in 1908. _____

ROSCOE DUNJEE

BIOGRAPHICAL PROFILE

Roscoe Dunjee was born June 21, 1883 in Harper's Ferry, West Virginia. Roscoe was one of five children. His parents were Rev. John William Dunjee and Lydia Ann Taylor Dunjee. Rev. Dunjee was a prominent Baptist minister and was appointed general missionary over the Baptists of Oklahoma. His father was also a financial agent for Storer College and published the Harper's Ferry newspaper. Roscoe claimed his father was the son of President John Tyler. After moving to Oklahoma, Roscoe's family first lived in a dugout in Choctaw. His father died in 1903 and the family moved to Oklahoma City.

SELF-TAUGHT EDITOR

At the age of 15, Roscoe enrolled in the Oklahoma Colored Agricultural and Normal University (Langston University) elementary department. He completed one year. Until age thirty-two, Roscoe raised and sold vegetables in order to support his mother and two siblings. Roscoe bought a small printing plant from Olivia J. Abby, a teacher in Oklahoma City Public Schools, and the first issue of the weekly *Black Dispatch* was printed on November 5, 1914. He was a self-taught publisher-editor and read extensively from books he inherited from his father. From 1915 to 1954 Roscoe Dunjee was editor of Oklahoma City's only African American newspaper. Roscoe sold the paper to his nephew John Dunjee in 1955. It remained in the family until 1982. The *Black Dispatch* had a motto "The paper that tells the truth." Roscoe used the newspaper as an avenue of communication in the struggle for civil rights in the black community and the state of Oklahoma. Roscoe used the newspaper to train black journalists. He insisted on high standards of journalism. At its peak, the newspaper had more than 26,000 subscribers. Roscoe was devoted to civil rights and worked to change discriminatory practices in Oklahoma and the nation until his death in 1965 at the age of 82.

ROSCOE'S EDITORIALS

Roscoe wrote editorials attacking Jim Crow laws. During the 1921 race riot in Tulsa, the *Black Dispatch* provided complete coverage of the destruction of Greenwood, a black community. Dunjee raised money for thousands of homeless, black, Tulsa residents. The riot claimed hundreds of lives. Roscoe reported that white businessmen hired agitators to start the riot to gain access to the valuable real estate in Greenwood area.

DUNJEE INDUCTED

The Oklahoma Journalism Hall of Fame is located on the campus of the University of Central Oklahoma in Edmond, Oklahoma. Since 1971, they have recognized journalists who have made outstanding contributions to Oklahoma for at least 10 years. This recognition chooses as many as nine individuals to add to the Hall of Fame each year. Roscoe Dunjee was inducted into The Oklahoma Journalism Hall of Fame in 1971. He was later joined in the Oklahoma Journalism Hall of Fame in 1997 by his friend and colleague James E. Stewart who had a regular column in the *Black Dispatch* entitled "Jimmy Says..."

HOUSING SEGREGATION

Housing for blacks in Oklahoma City was terrible. An imaginary line drawn down NE 8th Street prevented blacks from living north of the line. Attempts by blacks to purchase, rent or lease property in the area designated "whites only," resulted in arrest. The majority of blacks lived in West Town, Walnut Grove, South Town, and Sandtown. But the North Canadian River would often flood these black communities. Roscoe was very instrumental in breaking this discriminatory practice. In 1936, he financed a habeas corpus action which was filed in the Oklahoma State Supreme Court. The favorable decision ended government-supported residential segregation in the state of Oklahoma.

SANDTOWN – In 1884, a group of Chickasaw freedmen settled in what would become a rural area of Oklahoma City. The community, soon known as Sandtown, was established in a nook of the North Canadian River. Nearby, the Army set up a sawmill at Council Grove where timber was cut for the use of Fort Reno. The Sandtown residents also used the wood from the grove to build plantation style homes. Removing the trees reduced the land to just a sandy patch. The townspeople used the wood to sell or trade, but after becoming more financially stable most moved away to higher ground. There were many types of housing in Sandtown from three story brick houses to houses made of crate material. The old Sandtown became known as "The Bottoms." In 1884, when Sandtown was founded, the area that would be Oklahoma City was filled with Boomers hoping to gain squatters' rights. Later came the '89ers who had a legal claim to the land. They were from all walks of life. Most Boomers strongly disliked blacks, but the '89ers were tolerant to black settlers. John F. Marrow claimed the quarter section on which Sandtown was located and sold it to Peter F. Doffing, who later sold it to D.M. Hadlock.

In 1910, the Morris & Company packing plant (later Armour) opened. The company hired many blacks, giving the Sandtown residents a cash economy. In 1911, Schwartzchild and Sulzbeger (later Wilson) opened a packing plant, providing more work for the black community.

In 1911, the Antioch Baptist Church built a new church at Noble and Doffing Streets. Next to it was the Sandtown schoolhouse. The school served students to 10th grade until it burned down in 1943. The community once had five churches and when the Sandtown school burned, the Antioch Baptist Church became home to the school until George Washington Carver Elementary was built. The church rang its bell each time an important event needed to be announced – sometimes in the wee hours of the night residents would come from their beds to hear the news. Today, the whereabouts of the bell are unknown.

After statehood, many parts of Oklahoma City denied services to blacks. Numerous segregated neighborhoods formed as the growing number of whites grew, threatening Sandtown's residents. One group organized more than once to "clean out" Sandtown. The Sandtown men lined up to protect their families and property. Black residents from nearby Southtown migrated to the Eastside or Sandtown.

The population grew to over 1000 residents by the 20th century. Sandtown was basically established on worthless soil. The area suffered regular flooding, the trees had been removed and the sandy

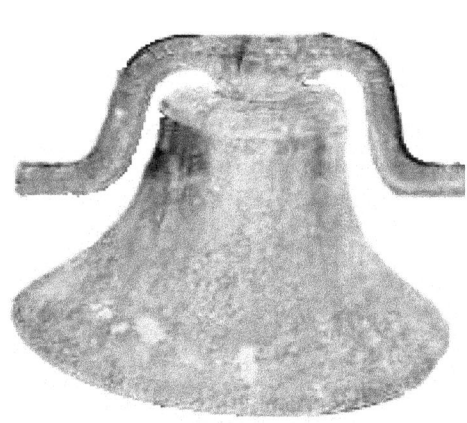

The bell of Antioch Baptist Church rang in Sandtown for 88 years.

worthless soil had no substance to support vegetation. The 1923 floods proved devastating to the community, leaving the area with floating homes, destroyed bridges and roads submerged in water and waste. The plantation style homes and crate houses were often washed away each spring and rebuilt when the river receded. The flooding problem was later resolved with the help of the Corps of Engineers who redirected the river's course.

Sandtown was a close-knit, loving family. In the 1950s the Oklahoma City Chamber of Commerce designed a new urban highway system, which cut straight through the heart of this community. In 1960, the Armour packing house closed its doors. Wilson downsized in 1980. This devastated the community's way of living. Property values declined and residents were offered $1700 to leave. Many of them relocated to the John F. Kennedy area and other homes and apartments on the East-side. By 1997, Sandtown had only a handful of residents left. Today, the Doffing Neighborhood Association consists of community members revitalizing the neighborhood. Many residents who lived or grew up in Sandtown still hold a lot of history and sentiment for Oklahoma City's first Negro settlement.

Entrance to the
Doffing Neighborhood

ARRESTS MADE FOR ATTEMPTS TO GO HOME

Roscoe was aware of the stranglehold on blacks to keep them in unlivable housing situations. He became the motivating force behind breaking this practice. Shoemaker William Floyd had purchased a home in an area near 2nd and Central in Oklahoma City. William was arrested a total of four times in one day for attempting to occupy his property. Each time he was arrested, Roscoe would bail him out with instructions for him to go back and try again. William Floyd's case was finally won in federal court. He was then able to move into and enjoy his home. He even established a business on his property and remained there until his senior years. In another instance, a gentleman by the name of Sidney Hawkins purchased a home on N.E. 8th Street. Each time he attempted to occupy his property, he was arrested. Sidney was arrested three times in one day. Each time he was bailed out. Finally in 1936, the Oklahoma State Supreme Court ended government supported residential segregation. An Oklahoma County District Judge struck down a case concerning real estate restrictions which banned blacks from areas in which whites lived. In October of 1948, white residents sought to have the courts rule that blacks would not be allowed in their block, the 1100 block of N.E. 9th St. The judge stated that the Supreme Court had ruled that such a covenant is unconstitutional and that he would follow the ruling.

Pretend you are Roscoe Dunjee and you are writing an article about your life, family, struggles and accomplishments. Remember he is writing this to be published in his newspaper.

_____

_____

_____

_____

_____

_____

Fill in the blanks below to answer the questions correctly.

1. Roscoe Dunjee was one of _____ children born to Rev. John and Lydia Dunjee.

2. When moving to Oklahoma, Roscoe and his family first moved to this city _____.

3. The Black Dispatch newspaper provided coverage about this event in 1921 _____.

4. Name the four communities blacks were forced to live in while in Oklahoma City
   _____   _____   _____   _____

5. Peter F. Doffing purchased portions of Sandtown from _____.

6. After Sandtown's schoolhouse burned, the name of the new school was _____.

7. The purpose of the church bell was to _____.

8. Roscoe Dunjee was very instrumental in helping to break this discriminatory practice _____.

9. The Old Sandtown community is known as _____.

10. Roscoe would help blacks by bailing them out of jail when they would try to go to their _____ in a segregated neighborhood.

BIOGRAPHICAL PROFILE

George W. McLaurin was born in 1887. He held a master's degree from the University of Kansas. He taught at Langston University for 33 years, retiring in 1948. That year 61 year-old George McLaurin applied to the doctoral program in the College of Education at the University of Oklahoma (OU). All three of McLaurin's children had already earned master's degrees. At the time of his application, state laws prevented blacks and whites from attending the same school.

The law mandated blacks would attend Langston and whites could choose to attend Oklahoma A&M (now Oklahoma State University) or OU. If Langston did not offer the program, the individual would qualify for state funding to attend a school in a nearby state that allowed blacks. The law was challenged by McLaurin, and by court decision he became the first African American student to be admitted to OU. He enrolled in four courses in 1948. All of his classes were assigned to the same room, 104. Although he could attend the same classes as whites, he was still segregated. McLaurin's classes were in a small room (described as a broom closet by some) adjacent to the major classroom. Black students were instructed to enter the cafeteria through a side door and sit at designated folding tables in a corner. Their eating area was surrounded by heavy iron chains and armed guards. Black students were only allowed to eat when no whites were present. There was special seating in the library and sporting events and separate restrooms were created. By the end of McLaurin's first year at OU, approximately 20 other blacks had enrolled at the university. They were all subject to the same discriminatory conditions. McLaurin later challenged these conditions. With the continued help and support of NAACP attorney Thurgood Marshall, Oklahoma attorney Amos T. Hall and *Black Dispatch* newspaper editor Roscoe Dunjee, McLaurin's case was filed in the Supreme Court, *George W. McLaurin v. Oklahoma Board of Regents for Higher Education*. He argued that humiliation and segregation "handicapped him in his pursuit of effective graduate instruction" and violated his Fourteenth Amendment rights. In 1950 the Supreme Court ruled that universities must provide the same treatment for blacks as they do other races and that the courts would not tolerate separate treatment due to race. George McLaurin left the university after completing only two semesters.

GEORGE W. McLAURIN
Draw lines to match the word on the left that goes with the one on the right.

DOCTORAL	TWENTY	1950
FOURTEENTH	1948	OKLAHOMA A & M
ARMED GUARDS	104	AMOS HALL
MASTER'S	33	BROOM CLOSET
THURGOOD MARSHALL	TWO	STATES

1. McLaurin argued that humiliation and segregation "handicapped him in his pursuit of effective graduate instruction" and violated his _____ Amendment rights.

2. The law mandated blacks would attend Langston and whites could choose to attend _____ or OU.

3. McLaurin later challenged discriminatory conditions with the continued help and support of men like NAACP attorney _____ .

4. _____ and Roscoe Dunjee were black Oklahomans who assisted McLaurin.

5. The black students eating area was surrounded by heavy iron chains and _____.

6. By the end of McLaurin's first year at OU, approximately _____ blacks had enrolled at the university.

7. McLaurin applied to the Education _____ program at the University of Oklahoma.

8. All of George McLaurin's classes were assigned to Room _____.

9. In _____ the Supreme Court ruled that universities must provide the same treatment for blacks as they do other races.

10. McLaurin taught at Langston University for _____ years.

11. All three of McLaurin's children had already earned _____ degrees when he applied to graduate school.

12. George McLaurin retired from Langston University in _____.

13. Some described McLaurin's classroom as a _____ _____.

14. In all, McLaurin George attended the University of Oklahoma _____ complete semesters.

15. If Langston did not offer a program, black students could qualify for state funding to attend school at nearby _____ that allowed blacks.

JIM CROW LAWS

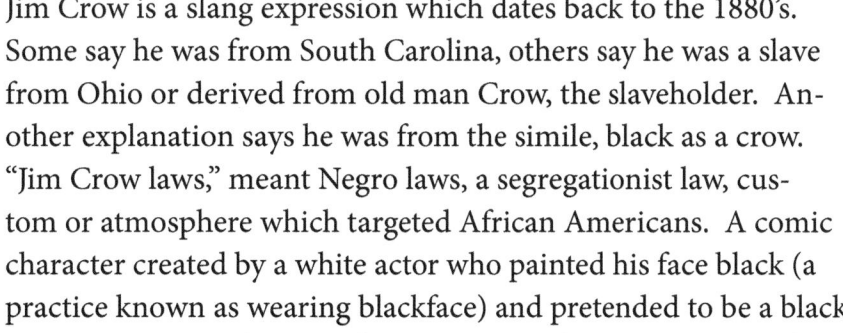

Jim Crow is a slang expression which dates back to the 1880's. Some say he was from South Carolina, others say he was a slave from Ohio or derived from old man Crow, the slaveholder. Another explanation says he was from the simile, black as a crow. "Jim Crow laws," meant Negro laws, a segregationist law, custom or atmosphere which targeted African Americans. A comic character created by a white actor who painted his face black (a practice known as wearing blackface) and pretended to be a black man. These performances were known as minstrel shows. They included jokes, songs and skits which made fun of blacks. This comic routine behavior was popular among prejudiced whites. Oklahoma strongly supported separation of races and between 1890 and 1957, passed numerous Jim Crow laws. The first Jim Crow law was passed in Oklahoma Territory on December 4, 1890. None of these laws were passed without opposition through every available legal means by blacks. Hoards of blacks tried to keep the laws from being passed, having them repealed or declared unconstitutional. Many Oklahoma blacks were politically knowledgeable and effective in spite of many objections from whites. There were numerous black newspapers that were instrumental in this fight. Their editors were blunt and outspoken, willing to tell the truth as they knew it, regardless of the consequences. Some of the state's black newspapers were: *The Boley News, Church and State, The Muskogee Cimeter, Langston City Herald, Western Age, Twice A Week Sun, The Black Dispatch, The Tattler, Boley, Bookertee, The Tulsa Eagle, The Muskogee Star, The Peoples Elevator, The Oklahoma Guide, Clearview Tribune, The Southwesterner, The Dispensation, Castle, Clearview Patriarch, Oklahoma Safe Guard, The Muskogee Lantern* and *The Saturday Evening Tribune*.

EXAMPLES OF JIM CROW LAWS

1890 – Education (Statute) – School elections were held every three years. Electors would vote for or against having separate schools for white and black children.

1897 – Education (Statute) – It is unlawful for a black child to attend a school intended for white students, (or vice versa). Wherever there are at least eight black children, a separate school district will be established.

1903 – Mining bath facilities (Statute) – The baths and lockers for the blacks shall be separate from the white race, but may be in the same building.

1904 – Education – Teaching (Statute) – Any instructor who teaches in a school, college or institution where members of the white and colored race are received and enrolled as pupils for instruction shall be deemed guilty of a misdemeanor, and upon conviction thereof, shall be fined in any sum not less than ten dollars nor more than fifty dollars for each offense.

1907 – Education (Constitution) – The legislature will provide separate schools for white and black children.

1907 – Funerals (Statute) – Blacks were not allowed to use the same hearse as whites.

1907 – Voting (Statute) – Needy people who live in poorhouses paid for by the public will not be allowed to vote.

1907 – Voting rights (Statute) – This statute required electors to be able to read and write any section of the Oklahoma state Constitution. Those who had a right to vote on January 1, 1866 and their lineal descendants will be exempt. Although this statute was declared unconstitutional in 1915, the literacy provision was upheld. SPECIAL NOTE: The Amendment allowed people of Indian descent to vote.

1908 – Voting (State Code) – In 1907 inmates of institutions are excluded from voting. "Any person kept in a poorhouse at public expense, except federal, Confederate, and Spanish-American ex-soldiers or sailors."

1908 – Railroads (Statute) – This statute easily passed through Oklahoma's first legislature. It was also known as the Senate Bill One or the coach law. It stated that "every railway company, urban or suburban car company, street car or interurban car or railway company . . shall provide separate coaches or compartments as hereinafter provided for the accommodation of the white and negro races, which separate coaches or cars shall be equal in all points of comfort and convenience." It also stated that each depot must have separate, adequately signed waiting rooms for each race. disobeying the law had penalties ranging from $100 to $1000 for companies. Individuals who failed to comply after being warned by the conductor faced a fine ranging from $5 to $25 and charged with a misdemeanor. Conductors failing to enforce the law could be fined $50 to $500. All fines were designated to go to the common school fund.

1908 – Miscegenation (Statute) – It is unlawful for any person of African descent to marry any person not of African descent. The fine would be a felony punishable by imprisonment from one to five years and a fine up to $500.

1908 – Education (Statute) – Public schools will operate under a plan of separation between white and black races. The penalty for teachers who failed to comply was a fine between $10.00 and $50.00, and face the cancellation of their teaching certification for a period of one year. Corporations who operated schools not in compliance of the law would be guilty of a misdemeanor and could face paying fines between $100 and $500. In addition, white students who attended black schools could be fined between $5 and $20 daily.

1915 – Public accommodations (Statute) – Telephone companies are required to maintain separate booths for black and white patrons.

1921 – Miscegenation (Statute) – Marriages between Indians and blacks were prohibited.

1921 – Education (Statute) – Teachers were forbidden to teach white and black students in the same school. The penalty was cancellation of the teacher's certificate for the period of one year.

1921 – Public accommodations (Statute) – In cities with a black population of 1,000 or more, separate accommodations for blacks in public libraries were required.

1925 – Entertainment (City Ordinance) – Oklahoma City prohibited black and white bands from marching together in parades. In addition, white Golden Glove boxers were prohibited from sparring against black boxers.

1928 – Recreation – Fishing, Bathing and Boating (Statute) The Conservation Commission shall have the right to make segregation of the white and black races as to the exercise of rights of fishing, bathing and boating.

1937 – Public Carriers (Statute) – Black public carriers were required to be segregated from white public carriers.

1949 – Health Care (Statute) – Required for consolidation of a black institution to care for the deaf, blind and orphaned.

1954 – Public accommodations (Statute) – Separate restrooms, baths and lockers were required for black and white workers in mines.

1955 – Miscegenation (Statute) – Blacks were prohibited to marry anyone of the white race. The penalty for breaking this law would be a fine up to $500 and imprisonment of one to five years.

1957 – Adoption (Statute) – All adoption petitions must state the race of the petitioner and the child.

BLACK CODES – In 1865 the Thirteenth Amendment to the United States Constitution abolished slavery throughout the country. Following emancipation some whites feared retaliation from blacks due to the inhumane and harsh treatment some slave owners dealt out. States in the South sought to regain what the Thirteenth Amendment had destroyed. Black Codes are laws created by southern states after the Civil War. They were created to regain control over freed slaves, maintain white supremacy and protect the cheap labor supply. Black codes regulated the newly freed slaves and stripped their basic rights. Black Codes existed in many southern states: Alabama, Arkansas, Florida, Georgia, Kentucky, Louisiana, Mississippi, North Carolina, Oklahoma, South Carolina, Tennessee, Texas, and Virginia. The codes differed from state to state, but the result was the same – limited civil rights and civil liberties and control of the labor, activities, and movement of African Americans.

Blacks were free but not allowed to vote, own full rights to property or to marry interracially. They were not allowed to carry weapons or meet in large groups. They were not allowed to hold office, serve on a jury or receive a public education. Blacks were not allowed to testify in courts against whites, to travel, or enter into contracts.

Blacks fought for justice and full citizenship against overwhelming odds. Many only stopped when their lives ceased, then others stepped in to fight the battle. The Civil Rights Act of 1866 made it illegal to discriminate against blacks or expose them to inferior legal and economic status. The Fourteenth Amendment guaranteed "equal protection of the laws" to residents of all states in 1868.

Raymond Dancel Gary was born on a farm near Madill, Oklahoma on January 21, 1908. Raymond worked nine years in public schools then fourteen years as an Oklahoma State Senator. Governor Raymond Gary was inaugurated as Oklahoma's fifteenth governor on January 10, 1955. He served from 1955 – 1959 and was the first state governor born in Oklahoma. He led the state through a difficult integration era. Upon taking office, he ordered the "whites only" and "colored only" signs to be removed from the capitol's restrooms. He was adamant that the state was in compliance with the 1954 Supreme Court decision *Brown v. Board of Education*, which deemed segregation as unconstitutional. In a statewide radio address, Gary said, "I feel sure that defiance of the Supreme Court mandate will not be tolerated. School boards which might entertain such ideas will find themselves on their own. Certainly the State of Oklahoma cannot possibly defend such action." He also won passage of an amendment to the state Constitution ending separate schools for whites and blacks. Governor Raymond D. Gary died in December of 1993 at the age of 85.

The family of former governor Raymond D. Gary donated funds to form a scholarship in his honor. The African American Studies Department of the University of Oklahoma offers three scholarships each year to students of any race who have excelled in black studies and show financial need. The scholarship fund began in 2008. It is the family's goal to expand the program to offer at least ten scholarships each year.

OKLAHOMA JIM CROW LAWS AND BLACK CODES
Write T for true and F for false next to each sentence.

1. _____ Jim Crow is the name of the Oklahoma State bird.

2. _____ Jokes, songs, and skits which made fun of blacks were known as minstrel shows.

3. _____ Black children were allowed to go to schools with white children as a result of an education statute in 1897.

4. _____ Teachers were not allowed to teach black and white students in the same school.

5. _____ Telephone companies had to provide separate telephone booths for whites and blacks.

6. _____ Black and white bands were not allowed to march together in parades.

7. _____ Black Codes were created after emancipation to restore the master-slave relationship.

8. _____ Blacks and whites were not allowed to ride in the same train car. Separate but equal accommodations were required.

9. _____ Governor Raymond Dancel Gary was the first Oklahoma governor born in Oklahoma.

10. _____ Once taking office at the state Capitol, Governor Gary ordered the removal of "white only" and "colored only" signs.

BIOGRAPHICAL PROFILE

Walter James (W.J.) Edwards was born in Maston, Mississippi on March 23, 1892 on a plantation. He was one of seven children. His father J.E. Edwards, a tenant farmer, moved his family from Mississippi to Wellston, Oklahoma in 1907. At the age of twenty-two Walter secured a job at a local junk yard, where he earned nine dollars a week. From his salary, Walter saved part of his earnings which enabled him to open a baggage company, complete with a horse and a wagon. From there, he opened a carpet cleaning business and a ice cream plant. He owned the Blue Bird Taxi Cab Line, several pharmacies, and an auto garage. By the age of 54, Walter had made a fortune in Oklahoma City, but never ventured far from the junk business. Unfortunately, Walter lost everything in the Stock Market Crash of 1929. He started a business selling scrap iron from his junk yard during World War II. He named it Edwards Scrap Iron and Junk Yard. Walter met Frances Gilliam Waldrop. She was one of eleven children born in 1898 in South Carolina. Frances was a qualified bookkeeper, teacher, and real estate dealer. The couple was married in 1930. Together they raised three sons and seven daughters. In April of 1949, *Ebony Magazine* listed Walter Edwards as one of the "10 Wealthiest Blacks in America." W.J. owned over $1,000,000 in real estate, but the majority of his money was made dealing scrap metal.

EDWARDS HOUSING ADDITION

From 1907 through 1930, the city of Oklahoma City enacted an ordinance which restricted African American residents to a small area. In 1933, Governor, "Alfalfa Bill" Murray recommended two invisible boundaries be drawn. The recommendation stated that the southern area of NE 8th be exclusively black and the northern area be exclusively for white housing. The residents on the north side were concerned about being "invaded" by blacks. Although the black population reached more than 20,000 in the 1940's, they were forced to live in a section which lacked adequate housing, educational, recreational and medical facilities. The ordinance was declared unconstitutional in 1936 but was still enforced. In the northeast area of Oklahoma City, the Edwardses found an area of semi-wooded land. The 33 acre tract of land extended north from NE 10th to NE 16th streets and from Page Street to Grand Boulevard. The land was owned by a white man of Tuttle, Oklahoma, C.T. Hassman. An arrangement between Hassman and Edwards was made for the current owner Hassman to have the city council to approve the platting of the area for developing the area prior to Edwards completing the purchase transaction. Edwards said "We knew there might be a fight if we

WALTER J. EDWARDS

tried to get it platted after we bought." In 1937, the Edwards Real Estate Investment Company purchased the land for $15,000 from C.T. Hassman. The director of the Federal Housing Administration (FHA) listened to the Edwards' real estate plan and felt the idea would never work. "Negroes," he said, "will never work hard enough or save enough of what they do earn, to pay off the loans. I know; I've had them working for me." Walter replied "perhaps my people have never had the right opportunity. We think they can do it." The Edwardses ran water, sewer and gas lines, paved streets and built three homes before securing financing from FHA. The Edwardses financed loans to prospective buyers and sold primarily to black homeowners. This was the end of residential segregation in Oklahoma City. The Edwards' decision to finance prospective buyers came as a result of the FHA's refusal to loan funds to African Americans. In 1939, the FHA approved the project. This was the first FHA-approved housing project ever received by blacks. The Edwardses struggled with finding skilled African American construction workers. There were shortages of bricklayers, electricians, and carpenters. As a solution, Edwards hired a white foreman to supervise young blacks who had a desire to train for these skilled jobs. Many of these trained workers went on to open their own businesses. The single-family homes were constructed of brick, stone and wood. Each had kitchens with modern appliances, bathrooms and neat yards planted with trees and shrubs. House payments ranged from $16.00 to $24.00 per month for up to 25 years. Altogether, the Edwardses are responsible for construction of approximately 800 homes. These homes were built by blacks for blacks and in 1951 the Edwardses could boast that "no Edwards-built home has yet been repossessed for delinquent payments."

The Edwardses either gave or loaned money to others so the community would flourish. Their donation of land made it possible for the community to enjoy a public park, school, and two churches. Edwards Elementary School (left) and Edwards Park (above) remain in the addition.

EDWARDS MEMORIAL HOSPITAL

Frances Edwards became critically ill and was taken to a nearby hospital where she was placed in a basement room. Doctors informed Walter that she needed to get proper hospitalization and rest. They visited the Mayo Clinic in Rochester, Minnesota where Mrs. Edwards had surgery, spending seven weeks regaining her health. The Edwardses realized their wealth allowed them to get the medical care that Frances needed. They thought about the other 30,000 blacks in Oklahoma City, where the majority could not afford to seek medical care in another city. On their return trip from Minnesota, the Edwardses began making the plans for a new hospital in Oklahoma City, as at that time, there were only eighty-nine hospital beds to meet the needs of the black community. The hospital would be one that would serve the needs of the African Americans in their community in grand fashion. They believed that "if you give your best to life, life will give its best to you." In the fall of 1945, the couple obtained the necessary land and construction work began. On April 18, 1948, the Edwards Memorial Hospital opened; it was the first hospital of its size and caliber in the South, which was completely owned and operated by African Americans. The three story modern facility included 105 beds, two operating rooms, a delivery room with nursery, an examination room, ear, eye, nose and throat clinic, x-ray room, modern laboratory, pediatric ward, physical therapy room and kitchens. The hospital cost the Edwardses more than $400,000 of their own life savings. They refused to raise outside money. The hospital trained African American doctors, nurses and lab technicians. The leading white physicians in Oklahoma City were totally cooperative with the opening of the new hospital. Twenty-six of them joined thirteen black physicians to make the first interracial staff in the South. The hospital closed in 1960 and was later sold. The new owners transformed the property into Edwards Redeemer Nursing Home. It was named in honor of the Edwards family.

Frances Edwards

CARL A. BARCLAY was born in Maryland in 1922. He graduated from Howard University Medical School in 1947. Carl married Mae Neece Hodge and moved his family to Oklahoma City where he became the first staff physician at the newly established Edwards Memorial Hospital. After three years as resident physician at the Edwards Memorial Hospital, Carl entered general practice and opened an office in the Finley Building at 324 NE 2nd in Oklahoma City. He had many long-time patients. They referred to him as a caring doctor who would "go the extra mile" and make housecalls. His care for patients outweighed his fee. He later moved his practice to Walnut Street. It became something of a clinic, a veritable sanctuary for the needy who were suffering but could not afford to pay. Dr. Barclay cared for them. The author recalls: "I remember his office only opened in the evenings around 4:00. There was no receptionist; patients entered the unlocked waiting area and sat quietly. I remember the quiet. There was never any ruckus; everyone knew their turn when he called 'next,' one by one. His desk was extremely messy and I wondered how he found anything. There was no nurse and he charged the same each time whether you got a shot or not. I remember it was $5.00. Doctor Barclay took good care of our family, he was always kind and he always made us well."

WALTER J. EDWARDS
Use the word bank to correctly complete the sentences.

WORD BANK

hundreds	finance	Edwards Memorial Hospital	best
stock market crash	three	wealthiest	land
money	bookkeeper	Minnesota	eleven
going the extra mile	first	Howard University Medical School	construction

1. In 1949, *Ebony Magazine* listed W.J. Edwards as one of the 10 _____ blacks in America.

2. Although W.J. earned a fortune, he quickly lost most of it in the 1929 _____ .

3. W.J. loaned _____ to others so that the community would flourish.

4. Housing restrictions forced the black population to live in a section of Oklahoma City which lacked adequate housing, medical and educational facilities. The Edwardses made a decision to _____ loans to allow blacks to purchase homes.

5. Blacks were placed in the basement of local hospitals to receive their medical care. Most white physicians refused to serve blacks. _____ was built to allow blacks to receive adequate medical care. The Edwardses used $400,000 of their own _____ to build the facility.

6. It was a struggle to find skilled _____ workers to build the homes for the Edwards addition.

7. The Edwardses believed in helping others. They lived by the motto, "if you give your _____ to life, life will give its best to you."

8. In 1948, the new Edwards Memorial Hospital opened. The facility had _____ stories.

9. Frances Edwards, was a qualified _____. She helped straighten out W. J.'s financial records.

10. The Edwards family donated _____ for a public park, two churches and a school.

11. Mrs. Edwards traveled to _____ in order to get needed medical care.

12. Frances Edwards was born in South Carolina. She was one of _____ children.

13. Dr. Carl Barclay was the Edwards Memorial Hospital's _____ staff physician.

14. Many of Dr. Barclay's patients praised him for _____.

15. Dr. Carl Barclay graduated from _____ in 1947.

BIOGRAPHICAL PROFILE

Frederick Douglass (F.D.) Moon was born on May 4, 1896 in Fallis, Oklahoma Territory, approximately fifty five miles from Oklahoma City. Frederick was born on the family farm. He was the son of former slaves Henry Clay and Pollie Twiggs Moon. Frederick was one of nine children. The family moved to Oklahoma from Pine Bluff, Arkansas in 1892. F.D.'s family raised crops, vegetables and cotton. The family worked hard together, and the nine children were provided for well. They were poor people but always had food and fun. He attended the segregated schools in Lincoln County, Oklahoma. He and his brother E.C. attended Langston schools in the eighth and ninth grades. The room and board was six dollars a month, twelve for both brothers but they worked their way through school. The school required all students to do farm work. He and his brother worked at the little hospital in addition to milking cows. F.D. entered the Oklahoma Colored Agricultural and Normal University (now Langston University), and graduated in 1929, with a bachelor of science degree. He also received a master of arts degree in 1938 from the University of Chicago and an honorary doctorate from Langston University in 1961. F.D. received his life certificate to teach in Oklahoma schools. He enjoyed history and reading books, magazines and newspapers. F.D. married Leoshia Harris in 1935.

THE DEAN OF AFRICAN AMERICAN EDUCATION

Frederick served in many towns as an educator and principal. These include Crescent, Wewoka, and Oklahoma City, Oklahoma. It is a strange coincidence that every school he served included the name "Douglass" – named for the same Frederick Douglass after whom Frederick was named. In 1940, Frederick became the principal of Douglass High School in Oklahoma City, Oklahoma. He served as the principal of that school until 1961. He was known as the "dean" of African American education. In 1972, Frederick was elected to serve on the Oklahoma City Board of Education. In 1974 he was chosen to serve as the board's president.

FREDERICK'S ASSOCIATIONS

Frederick and his wife Leosha were proud Langston alumna. In 1925, Negro educators created the Langston Alumni Association. F. D. was president from 1926 until 1940. He was also president of the Oklahoma Association of Negro Teachers. They lobbied for many important improvements such as stronger libraries and higher salaries for faculty members.

F. D. MOON

FREDERICK DOUGLASS (F.D.) MOON

Unscramble the words to complete the facts about F.D. Moon.

1. Every School that F.D. served included the name _____.
   G D L S S O U A

2. F.D. was born in this Oklahoma town. _____.
   S I L A F L

3. African Americans fondly called F.D. the _____ of education.
   N D A E

4. F.D. was elected to serve on the Oklahoma City Board of Education in _____, making him the first African American president of this district's board.
   7219

5. F.D. was the son of former _____.
   L A S E V S

6. F.D. was born on the _____ _____.
   M L I F A Y   R F M A

7. F.D. received his bachelor's degree from _____
   _____ .   A G N L S N O T
   I N I V U R T E S Y

8. Frederick was the principal of Douglass High School in Oklahoma City for _____ years.
   R T E N E F U O

9. F.D. was an educator and principal in the following Oklahoma towns.
   _____, _____, and _____ _____.
   W K W E A O   S E R C N T E   O A K M L A H O   Y C T I

10. F.D. was one of _____ children born to Henry Clay and Pollie Twiggs Moon.
    E I N N

AMOS T. HALL

BIOGRAPHICAL PROFILE

Amos T. Hall was born on October 2, 1896 in Bastrop, Louisiana. Amos attended Bastrop schools and graduated from Rust College in Holly Springs, Mississippi. He also graduated from Gilbert Industrial College in Baldwin, Louisiana. Amos moved to Tulsa, Oklahoma in 1921. He married his wife Ella. They had one daughter, Adelle Hall Gibbs. Amos worked as a church janitor and found an old set of law books. He began reading them and developed an interest in law. He studied his law books at night and was admitted to the Oklahoma Bar in 1925.

AMOS' CAREER IN LAW

Amos was one of the most significant civil rights attorneys in Oklahoma. He served as the attorney who fought for equal salaries for teachers in the case of *Freeman v. Oklahoma City School Board* (1948). He also represented Ada Lois Sipuel in the landmark "separate but equal" case of *Sipuel v. Board of Regents of University of Oklahoma* (1948). Amos T. Hall was the first African American to be elected judge in Oklahoma. In 1969, Amos was appointed special judge of the District Court of Tulsa County in Oklahoma. In 1970, Amos was elected associate district judge of Tulsa County and served in that capacity until he died of a heart attack on November 12, 1971.

EQUALITY IN TEACHER PAY

In 1943 the constitution of Oklahoma said that schools for the state shall be "separate and equal." Then School Board Superintendent H.E. Wrinkle told board attendees the average teacher salary in white schools was $1,640.92 while black teachers' salaries were $1,347.66. Emma Lee Freeman was a teacher at Douglass High School for twelve years. She held a Bachelor of Science degree from Kansas State Teachers' College with a lifetime teaching certificate in Oklahoma. In April of 1947, attorney Amos T. Hall who represented Emma and the National Association for the Advancement of Colored People (NAACP) filed a court petition, *Freeman v. Oklahoma City Board*. The petition stated that the school board's actions violated Emma's 14th Amendment rights, depriving her of property which she was entitled to. In October of 1948, U.S. District Judge Edgar S. Vaught ruled that teachers who were equally qualified must draw equal pay. The plaintiffs agreed to dismiss the lawsuit. The 14th Amendment prohibits deprivation of life, liberty, or property.

Emma Lee Freeman fought for equal pay and won

AMOS T. HALL
Answer the true/false questions

1) _____ Amos Hall was one of the most powerful civil rights attorney's in Oklahoma.

2) _____ Amos worked as a church janitor. He found an old set of law books and studiied them, later becoming a lawyer.

3) _____ Amos was born in Tulsa, Oklahoma.

4) _____ Amos was once an attorney for the NAACP.

5) _____ Amos fought to hard make sure everyone received equal pay.

6) _____ In 1969, Amos was the first African American to be elected judge in Oklahoma.

7) _____ Amos was once married to Emma Lee Franklin.

8) _____ Freeman v. Oklahoma City School Board, was the divorce case Amos filed against his wife.

9) _____ NAACP stands for National Allegiance to the Colored People.

10) _____ Amos' second wife was Ada Lois Sipuel Fisher.

11) _____ The 14th Amendment means that everyone has 14 days to file a lawsuit if they are discriminated against.

12) _____ Emma Lee Franklin received her Bachelor of Science degree from the University of Oklahoma.

13) _____ Amos became a lawyer but never studied any law books.

14) _____ Ada Lois Sipuel's landmark case was "separate but equal." It was against the Oklahoma City Public School system.

15) _____ Amos was born in Bastrop, Louisiana.

16) _____ In 1948, Judge Edgar S. Vaught ruled teachers who were equally qualified must draw equal pay.

17) _____ Judge Amos T. Hall died from a car accident in 1971.

18) _____ Amos T. Hall was funeralized in October 2, 1896, in Oklahoma City, Oklahoma.

19) _____ Emma Lee Freeman was a teacher at Douglass High School in Oklahoma City.

20) _____ Amos was admitted to the Louisiana Bar association in 1925.

JOSEPH J. SIMMONS, JR.

BIOGRAPHICAL PROFILE

Joseph Jacob (Jake) Simmons Jr. was born on January 17, 1901 in Haskell, OK. Jake was the ninth of ten children. Jake's great-grandfather was a slave of the Creek Indian tribe. He later became a chief and leader for the freed Creek slaves. Jake was personally recruited by Booker T. Washington to attend Tuskegee University. In 1919 Jake received his degree from Tuskegee and married Melba Dorsey. The brief marriage ended in divorce. He later married Willie Eva Flowers. Jake fathered four children: Joseph III, Donald, Kenneth, and Blanche. Jake died in Tulsa, Oklahoma at the age of 80 on March 24, 1981. Jake "rose above humble beginnings to become the most successful and most recognizable black entrepreneurs in the history of the petroleum industry."

"I WANT TO BE AN OIL MAN"

Jake's father owned a 500 acre ranch in the Haskell area. Jake repaired fences and worked cattle as a child. As early as the age of ten, Jake knew what he wanted to do in life. He told his father, "I want to be an oil man." Being a member of the Creek Nation, Jake received 160 acres when tribal property was allotted to each citizen. Oil flowed on his land, and in the 1920's he became an oil broker and entrepreneur. His dream came true. He began buying and selling oil leases and started a real estate business. He turned to real estate, selling farmland to African Americans during the Great Depression of the 1930's. In the 1960's, Jake worked multi-million dollar deals between American oil companies and other countries in Africa, including Nigeria, Ghana and Liberia. He worked with oil barons such as Henry Sinclair and Frank Phillips (the founder of Phillips Petroleum). In 1969 he became the first black to be appointed to the National Petroleum Council. Jake built the Simmons Royalty Company with the help of his sons and L.W. Thomas of Summit, Oklahoma. By the 1930's, Jake was operating in Kansas, Arkansas, Texas, Louisiana and Oklahoma. At the time of his death in 1981, Jake Simmons was the nation's most prominent African American oilman.

NO VICTIM OF BIGOTRY

Jake became the president of the Oklahoma National Association for the Advancement of Colored People. (NAACP) He strongly believed in fighting for civil rights and had a huge sense of racial pride. Refusing to be a victim of bigotry, he told his children, "You are equal to anyone, but if you think you're not, you're not." Jake would help blacks gain skills in his business and then help them find employment with other businesses. He believed that "It is a waste of time for a man to fail to achieve when he has the opportunity." He felt it was just as important to achieve in order to help others as it was to achieve to help yourself.

WHAT DOES AN OILMAN DO?

An oilman is a person who owns or operates oil wells or is an executive in the energy industry. From finding oil deep in the ground, to setting up drilling wells, and even distributing the oil to refineries, an oilman is an important part of America's use of oil products and petroleum. Oil can be found in nearly every part of the world and an oilman employs geologists and other earth scientists to help him locate oil and gas deposits deep underground or even deep underwater in the case of offshore drilling. Oilmen can become very wealthy in the process of owning and operating drilling rigs. Some of the world's richest men are, in fact, oil men.

JOSEPH J. SIMMONS, JR.

Rewrite the misspelled words below to spell them correctly.

1. entraprener _____

2. Tuskejee _____

3. patrolium _____

4. assoshiation _____

5. endeuun _____

6. hasskil _____

7. akkers _____

8. bizznes _____

9. mploymint _____

10. kattll _____

11. Amarikan _____

12. Cinklar _____

13. rollty _____

14. Oaklahoma _____

15. millun _____

16. nijeeria _____

17. sugsessful _____

18. sivul right _____

19. skeels _____

20. eequel _____

BIOGRAPHICAL PROFILE

Ira DeVoyd Hall, Sr. was born on August 25, 1905 in Colbert, Oklahoma. Ira was the youngest of five children born to Carrie Williams and Claude DeVoyd Hall. He and siblings Jural, Lola, Belfry, and Bertrand lost their father when Ira was just two months old. Their mother died when Ira was only fourteen years old. Ira received a small award to allow him to begin his college education at the Oklahoma Colored Agricultural and Normal University (now Langston University). His education was interrupted five times so that he could earn money to pay his tuition and living expenses. Ira was employed as a waiter, bellhop, car salesman, ad taker, packing house worker, and Pullman car porter. In 1932 Ira was one of the first to graduate from Langston with a bachelor of science degree in Business Administration. Ira was later admitted to the University of Oklahoma (OU), and earned a master of science degree in Education Administration. He married Rubye Maie Hibler on July 20, 1930. Six children (four daughers and two sons) were born to this union. He was later employed as principal of the separate school (a racially segregated school), in Colbert, Oklahoma. Ira made many academic improvements and achievements in Colbert and was offered the position of School Superintendent in Clearview, OK.

HALL FIDELITY REAL ESTATE COMPANY

Ira Hall and his family were forced to leave the home they had purchased in Oklahoma City. By 1944, the Halls had spent three years in court battling a restrictive covenant that prohibited African Americans from occupying homes in certain areas of Oklahoma City. In the early 1960's, Ira started a real estate company named Hall Fidelity Real Estate and began to sell homes to African Americans in many Oklahoma City neighborhoods.

What is a Restrictive Covenant?

A restrictive covenant is a legal obligation written in a deed by the seller of the real estate saying the buyer can or cannot do something. The restrictions frequently "run with the land" and are enforced on subsequent buyers of the property. Residential covenants are common in the United States and are generally harmless. They can prevent owners or tenants from painting the outside of their home a particular color or from removing healthy shrubs or trees. They can dictate how many trees can be planted in one's yard or where one's cars can be parked. Before the 1960's racially discriminatory deed restrictions were common. The covenant may include a promise that members of a certain race could not live in or own the property. In the court case of *Shelley v. Kraemer*, the United States Supreme Court ruled that it was unconstitutional to enforce racially restrictive covenants and those covenants can no longer be enforced.

ASSISTANT DIRECTOR OF SECONDARY EDUCATION

In 1947, Dr. Oliver Hodges was elected to be state superintendent of public education in Oklahoma. Dr. Hodges appointed Ira D. Hall, Sr. as assistant director of secondary education for separate schools. Ira was the first African American to hold this position. Some of Ira's duties included overseeing all ninety-seven African American high schools in the state, improving teacher qualifications, class curriculum, science materials, and library holdings.

CLOSE RELATIONSHIP WITH LANGSTON UNIVERSITY

Ira was a proud Langston alumnus and maintained a close relationship with the school. He served as an instructor there for a short period. Ira spent over 12 years on the Langston University Alumni Association Board raising over $100,000 for the Langston University Development Foundation. In 1979 Ira was elected National President of the Langston University Alumni. For over 55 years he fought for the survival and expansion of Langston and the development of a graduate program, which began in 1988.

IRA D. HALL, SR.
Write T for true and F for false next to each sentence.

1. _____ Ira was an instructor at Langston University.

2. _____ Ira was ophaned by the age of 14 years old.

3. _____ Ira was the youngest of ten children.

4. _____ Ira was the first African American to become the assistant director of secondary education for separate schools.

5. _____ Separate schools kept boys and girls separated from one another.

6. _____ Ira was married to Rubye M. Hibler in 1930.

7. _____ Ira earned a master of science degree from the University of Oklahoma.

8. _____ Ira worked as a bellhop, car salesman, construction worker, and baker.

9. _____ Ira was born in Clearview, Oklahoma.

10. _____ Ira and his family were forced to leave their home because of a restrictive covenant.

11. _____ Ira and Rubye had six children.

12. _____ Ira received a small scholarship to study at Colbert College.

13. _____ Ira helped to raise over $100,000 for Langston University.

14. _____ Ira, his wife, and children were forced to leave their home in Oklahoma City.

15. _____ Ira was a Langston University alumnus. He worked for over 100 years for its survival and expansion.

GRAVELLY E. FINLEY, SR.

BIOGRAPHICAL PROFILE

Gravelly Eugene Finley, Sr. (G.E.), was born on March 20, 1908 in Batesville, Arkansas. G.E. was one of seven children born to Samuel and Bessie Finley. He and his siblings were forced to attend high school 111 miles away from their home. Segregation forced blacks to attend high school in Little Rock or Hot Springs, Arkansas, the only places in the state with high schools that accepted blacks. The Finley children would have to stay with a relative in Little Rock during the school year. They weren't able to go home during Christmas. They would work odd jobs to help pay their way and would return home during the summer months. All of the Finley children persevered, graduating from high school and college. G.E. graduated from Gibbs High School in 1926. He went on to attend Wilberforce University in Ohio, graduating from Meharry Medical School in Nashville, Tennessee. G E. met his future wife, Saretta Slaughter, while in medical school. They married in June of 1935 in Oklahoma City, Oklahoma. They had one son, Gravelly E. Finley, Jr. Dr. G.E. Finley died on May 30, 2008 at the age of 100 years old.

A CHANGE OF PLANS

After graduation, G. E. rented an office in Columbus, Ohio intent on beginning his medical practice there. His plans were changed after his father-in-law, Dr. W.H. Slaughter announced his retirement in 1937. G.E. moved to Oklahoma City and began his practice. Black doctors were in high demand as most white doctors refused to extend medical care to blacks. G.E.'s first office was located at 324 NE 2nd Street in the Deep Deuce area. He moved to a cream-colored brick building at NE 2nd and Walnut in 1951. It would be known as the Finley Building. In addition to his practice, G.E. made house calls. He made his way to many residents' homes working from 7 a.m. until noon each day. G.E. treated many cases of the airborne tuberculosis disease, yellow fever, and polio. Immunizations for these diseases were not available yet and the diseases ran rampant in the black community. He and other black physicians used Edwards Memorial Hospital and Western Hospital as neither black patients nor black physicians were allowed access to other hospitals in the area. G.E. processed black soldiers for the United States Government, giving them physical exams for the Selective Service. In 1946 he became on of the first black physicians to practice at St. Anthony Hospital. At the age of 90 years old, G.E. was still a practicing physician.

The Finley Building was located on NE 2nd and Walnut in Oklahoma City. The building was donated for the purpose of housing an Oklahoma African American museum. Several attempts were made to condemn this historical building. In August of 2010, the Finley building was demolished to make way for the modern Aloft Hotel to include a mixture of restaurants and shops. Although the historic building could not be saved, the City of Oklahoma City reconstructed the old Walnut Avenue bridge (above) and named it in Dr. Finley's honor.

GRAVELLY EUGENE FINLEY, SR.

Circle the letter next to the statement that correctly completes the statement

1. After medical school, Gravelly opened his doctor's office in Oklahoma City, Oklahoma because
    a. the rent for doctor's offices were cheaper in Oklahoma City.
    b. his father-in-law announced his retirement.
    c. his new wife was pregnant

2. The Finley Building in Oklahoma City was demolished in 2010 to make way for a new
    a. Doctor's office
    b. Bricktown hospital
    c. Aloft Hotel with a mixture of restaurants and shops

3. Gravelly met his wife, Saretta Slaughter, while in
    a. high school
    b. Army boot camp
    c. Meharry Medical School

4. Gravelly and his siblings attended high school over one hundred miles from their home because
    a. This was the closest high school to them
    b. Arkansas only had two high schools that blacks were allowed to attend
    c. The high school close to their home burned down

5. In addition to his office practice, Gravelly also helped the community by
    a. keeping the area around his office free of debris
    b. tutoring at the area schools
    c. making house calls from 7 a.m. to noon each day

6. Diseases like tuberculosis, yellow fever and polio were high in the black community because
    a. immunizations for these diseases were not available yet
    b. the United States government refused to treat blacks for these diseases
    c. the needles for the immunizations were too expensive and were not affordable to most people

7. Gravelly married the daughter of
    a. Dr. Martin Luther King
    b. Dr. W. H. Slaughter
    c. Dr. Inman Page

8. Gravelly treated his patients at Edwards Memorial and Western Hospital because
    a. The others were too far for him to drive
    b. black physicians were denied access to other hospitals in the area
    c. his medical license only allowed him to treat at these hospitals

9. Through hard work and perseverance, all seven of the Finley children
    a. graduated from high school and received college degrees
    b. became millionaires
    c. became medical doctors

10. The former Finley Building was donated by Gravelly for the purpose of opening a
    a. school
    b. African American clinic
    c. African American museum

THE GOODWIN FAMILY

JAMES H. GOODWIN

James Henri (J.H.) Goodwin grew up in Water Valley, Mississippi. He grew tired of the humiliations of the south and its degrading customs. Impressed by the promotional advertisements of O.W. Gurley, he moved to Tulsa, Oklahoma in 1909. Upon arriving in Tulsa, J.H. began working at S.D. Hooker and Company, a variety store. He once was a fireman on the Rock Island Railroad putting coal in the engines. Due to his keen sense of business, J.H. earned a sizeable fortune. He was a self-made man. J.H. married Carlie Osby. They had four children: Lucille, James, Anna and Edward Lawrence. He and Samuel Jackson (brother of Joe Jackson, of the Jackson Five) are founding partners in the Jackson Undertaking Company, known as one of the oldest surviving businesses in North Tulsa. His property, the Goodwin Building, housed the Union Grocery and the Duncan-Clinton Restaurant. It was valued at over $30,000. J.H. was a fairskinned man–part Cherokee Indian and white–he sometimes used this to his advantage as some business opportunities were afforded him because he was assumed to be white. During the Tulsa riots, many of the Goodwin properties were destroyed but the home was saved. One

Edward L. Goodwin

newspaper reported that J.H. hired white men to stand in front of his home and directed the rioters away. Another report stated the fair-complexioned J.H. stood outside his home and the mob assumed he was white as he steered them away. The Goodwin family were spared from the warfare and concentration camps because of J.H.'s heroism. J.H. died in 1958.

EDWARD L. GOODWIN

Edward Lawrence (E.L.) Goodwin Sr. was born in Water Valley, Mississippi to James Henri and Carlie Goodwin in 1902. He was the grandson of a slave. Edward graduated from Booker T. Washington High School in 1921. He was voted most likely to succeed by his classmates. Edward later went to Fisk University in Nashville, Tennessee, where he played football and graduated with a business administration degree. E.L. married Jeanne Bell Osby. The couple raised eight children: Edwyna, JoAnn, Onetha, Jeanne, Carlie, James O., Robert Kerr and Edward L. II. In 1941, then Governor Robert S. Kerr appointed E.L., Sr. as Superintendent of the Death, Blind and Orphan School in Taft, Oklahoma. He served in this capacity until 1945. In 1946, Edward purchased a 160 acre farm in Alsuma, where he built a 19-room rock home to raise his large family. All eight of the Goodwin children obtained college degrees. Due to segregation, minorities were denied access to white only accommodations; the Goodwin family routinely opened their home to famous minorities who traveled through the Tulsa area. Lena Horne, Joe Louis, George Washington Carver, among others, enjoyed the Goodwin family hospitality. Thirty years after Edward graduated from Fisk University, he went back to school and attended the University of Tulsa, graduating with a law degree. After retirement from his law practice and newspaper, E.L. opened an eleven acre catfish farm in the Alsuma district. The elder Goodwin passed away in 1978 at 76.

THE GOODWIN FAMILY STORE IN GREENWOOD

After graduating from college, E.L. Sr. purchased the S.D. Hooker variety store. The store lost $25,000 in inventory in the riot. He changed the name to Greenwood Haberdashery, selling high fashion men's clothing. In the early 1930's E.L., Sr. was the youngest entrepreneur in Tulsa's Black Wall Street.

THE OKLAHOMA EAGLE NEWSPAPER

In 1935 E. L. Goodwin, Sr. purchased an African American newspaper called *The Star*. The newspaper was later renamed *The Oklahoma Eagle*. Edward Sr. was publisher of the newspaper from 1936 until 1978. E.L., Sr. and son James halted urban renewal bulldozers from destroying the last block of Greenwood. Credit is given to them for saving the last remnants of the business district. Working together with a group of other developers, they made the decision to purchase the Greenwood property from the City of Tulsa which was later renovated in the late 1970's. The original Oklahoma Eagle Building was the last business to abandon the famous boulevard. Today, it remains a service to the black community in Tulsa, OK. On each edition of the family-owned newspaper's masthead, prints the words "We Make America Better When We Aid Our People." The newspaper has been in publication for over ninety years. Today the two Goodwin brothers, James O. and Edward L. II, are co-publishers of the thriving newspaper. It is now located on Archer street in Tulsa, Oklahoma.

THE GOODWIN FAMILY

THE *OKLAHOMA EAGLE* TODAY

The newspaper that was purchased by E.L. Goodwin, Sr. in 1935 is now run by two of his sons: Edward L. II and James O. The *Oklahoma Eagle* is the first and only newspaper to serve the black community in Tulsa, Oklahoma. The newspaper has been family owned since 1935 and remains a strong presence in North Tulsa.

Edward L. (Ed) Goodwin, II was born on December 7, 1935. He is married to Johnnie Mae. Ed has four children; Regina, Sabrina, Gregory and Eric. Ed is an editor at the family owned newspaper and stays active in the community. His days are spent working on the newspaper, volunteering for the elderly and shut-ins and helping to keep the Greenwood memory alive.

Edward L., Jr. and James O. Goodwin

James O. Goodwin was born on November 4, 1939, he is married to Vivian Palm-Goodwin, the couple has five children. Joseph, Jerry, Jeanne, Anna Marie and David. James is an attorney in Tulsa and practices all types of law. James is a member of the Tulsa County and Oklahoma Bar Association and American Bar Association. He is the former chairman of the Tulsa City-County Board of Health and in 2003, the east regional health center was named in his honor. It is named the James O. Goodwin Health Center.

HONORING THE GOODWIN FAMILY

Jeanne B. Osby-Goodwin was born in 1902. Although she died in 2006 at the age of 102, she continues to be remembered each day. Jeanne became an elementary school teacher. She taught in Bixby, Alsuma, and Booker T. Washington Elementary in Tulsa. The lifelong educator and literacy champion's legacy is honored with a storytime room located at the Rudisill Regional Library in Tulsa, Oklahoma. Children visiting The Jeanne B. Goodwin storytime room are greeted with ocean-themed décor and walls brightly painted with starfish, sharks, lobsters, turtles and other underwater wonders. In addition, the Tulsa Library Trust has created the Jeanne B. Goodwin Fund. Proceeds from the fund allow the Rudisill Library to feature performers and interactive storytellers cultivating an appreciation for reading and art. A gallery was named for Edward L. Goodwin Sr. It is located in the Greenwood Cultural Center in Tulsa. The Goodwin/Chapelle Gallery houses a wide display of historical photographs and artifacts from the 1921 Tulsa Race Riot.

Jeanne B. Osby-Goodwin

THE GOODWIN FAMILY

Unscramble the words below to give clues to the Goodwin Family. Use the Word Bank for assistance.

WORD BANK

entrepreneur	segregation	Fisk University
family store	James Goodwin	catfish farm
hospitality	Tulsa, Oklahoma	law
Booker T Washington High	Alsuma	Oklahoma Eagle
eight	Jeanne Bell	variety store
school teacher	Rudisill Library	Greenwood
Haberdashery	Goodwin Gallery	

_____   _____
s u a l a m   kreboo t shtonwaign ghih

_____   _____
y m a f i l   s t r o e   r e t r u e e r n p n e

_____   _____
r e s g o n i g a t e   k l m a o h a o   g a e l e

_____   _____
w l a   f i t s c h a   m f r a

_____   _____
m s a j e   o o w n i d g   f k s i   t r e v i y i u n s

_____   _____
s p l i t h o y t a i   n e n e a j l e l b

_____   _____
e g h i t   u t s l a   a m a l h o k o

_____   _____
e e o o g r w d n   hooscl   hcteare

_____   _____
wnoogdi   llagery   rybaeerashdh

_____   _____
llirisud   yrarbil   tyariev   ertso

72

PERCY H. JAMES

BIOGRAPHICAL PROFILE

Percy Harold (P.H.) James was born in Opelousas, Louisiana. As a young man, he traveled to Oklahoma to attend Colored Agricultural and Normal University in Langston. While there, Percy married another student, Hathyel L. James (Hattie). Percy and Hattie had three children: Jewel, Percy Jr., and Roland. They divorced in 1940. He later married Arvella Gamble and together they had a daughter also named Arvella. This marriage also ended in divorce in 1948. Percy H. James became a respected member of the black business community in Oklahoma City. On November 2, 1965, he died in Oklahoma City, Oklahoma.

JAY-KOLA BOTTLING WORKS

When Percy first came to Oklahoma City, he worked at the big Huckins Hotel in Downtown. Soon after that, Percy went to work for the Oklahoma City Coca-Cola Bottling Plant. At the time, the Coca-Cola company, based in Atlanta, would not sell their products to the black community due to segregation. Percy became good friends with his plant manager, Virgil Brown, who was also from Louisiana. Brown encouraged him to open his own bottling company. In 1918 Percy and his wife Hattie opened up the Afri-Cola Bottling Company. The name was later changed to Jay Cola. In 1935 it was named Jay-Kola. The company started in Percy's garage, which was located near NE 4th and Lottie in Oklahoma City. Later it moved to 925 NE 9th St and finally to Success Street near NE Grand Blvd. At first Percy's plant delivered his drinks to shops and restaurants in the local area. But soon his popular product was transported across the state, and by 1930 the company was described as using the region's most modern bottling process. In addition to cola, they produced many flavors of soda, to include root beer and fruit flavors. Into the 1940s, Percy's plant was one of only two in the country owned by blacks. He owned several buildings containing stores, hotels, and other businesses in the community on NE 4th. In 1963, Percy retired due to health reasons. The franchise closed soon after.

JEWEL THEATER

Percy worked hard in developing the Deep Deuce area in Oklahoma City. In July 1931 he and his wife Hattie built and opened the first movie theater for blacks, naming it after his daughter, Jewel. The success of the theater led Percy to open other theaters for African American communities in Amarillo, Texas and Ardmore and Wewoka, Oklahoma. He named these theaters Jewel also.

PERCY JAMES
Circle the correct letter to answer the multiple choice questions.

1. P. H. James was born in
a. Langston, Oklahoma
b. Opelousas, Lousiana
c. Tulsa, Oklahoma

2. Percy and his wife Hattie opened up the Afri-Cola Bottling Company in
a. 1945
b. 1999
c. 1918

3. The Afri-Cola Bottling Company name was later changed to
a. Jay-Kola
b. Coca-Cola
c. Sonic

4. The Jay-Kola plant was one of only _____ in the country owned by blacks into the 1940s
a. fourteen
b. seven
c. two

5. The Jewel Theater was located in
a. Deep Deuce
b. Sand Town
c. Springlake Amusement Park

6. The Coca Cola company, based in Atlanta, would not sell their products
a. to children under 21
b. to the black community
c. to consenting adults

7. The _____ Theater was the first movie theater for blacks.
a. Jewel
b. Opal
c. Hattie

8. Plant manager, _____, encouraged Percy to open his own bottling company.
a. Lloyd Jensen
b. Sidney Lyon
c. Virgil Brown

9. On November 2, 1965, Percy James died in _____.
a. Gnome, Alaska
b. Lawton, Oklahoma
c. Oklahoma City, Oklahoma

10. The Deep Deuce community contained stores, hotels, and other businesses on _____ in Oklahoma City.
a. NE 4th
b. NW 23rd
c. Lincoln Blvd

CHARLES N. ATKINS

BIOGRAPHICAL PROFILE

Charles Nathaniel Atkins was born in 1911 in Trinidad, West Indies. He graduated in 1950 from Meharry Medical College in Nashville, Tenn. He specialized in family medicine. The Medical Service Society of Oklahoma City surprised Charles by naming him Doctor Of the Year in May of 1972 – the first African American to receive the award. He was selected because of his contributions to the community, his civic involvement, and the contributions he has made to his profession. Charles married Hannah Diggs on May 24, 1943. They had three children: Edmund, Charles II and Valerie. In 1967, Charles became the first African American to be appointed to Charles died December 30, 1988 in Oklahoma City.

HELPING OTHERS HELP THEMSELVES

Charles served as Chairman of the Board of the Opportunities Industrialization Center (OIC). OIC is a government financed agency whose purpose is to provide services to economic and socially deprived individuals. There are over 130 cities throughout the United States who have OIC services. The Oklahoma OIC opened in October 1966. Their goal is to motivate, train, develop and utilize technical skills of the community. OIC helps everyone regardless of race, creed, color or sex. "OIC has contributed," remarks Charles, "in that many of those who've graduated from our programs were welfare recipients beforehand. . . Now they're earning salaries and wages and, thus, contributing to their communities. . . We're helping people help themselves." The current OIC facility in Oklahoma City is located at 400 N Walnut.

OKLAHOMA CITY'S FIRST AFRICAN AMERICAN BANK

Charles was chairman of Medical Center State Bank, Oklahoma City's only minority-owned and controlled bank. Now defunct, it was located at NE 13th and Lottie in Oklahoma City.

OPPORTUNITIES GARDENS

Through the efforts of the local OIC and the federal Department of Housing and Urban Development, a loan in the amount of $3.5 million allowed for construction of the Charles N. Atkins Opportunities Gardens, located in Oklahoma City. The three-story center opened in May 1987. It houses 29 efficiency apartments and 89 one-bedroom apartments. It also features a garden area, laundry, library, lounge area, and multi-purpose room with adjacent kitchen. The facility was built to house senior citizens and handicapped residents. The housing rent will be subsidized under a federal program. Eligible tenants will not pay more than 30 percent of their income. Rent includes utilities.

Charles N. Atkins Opportunities Gardens in Oklahoma City.

CHARLES N. ATKINS
Use the word bank to correctly complete the sentences

WORD BANK

Oklahoma City Council   themselves   socially deprived   1987
Trinidad, West Indies   Doctor of the Year   Hannah Diggs   89
Medical Center State Bank   family

1. Opportunities Industrialization Center (OIC) is an agency that provides services to _____ _____ individuals.

2. The Charles N. Atkins Opportunities Gardens opened in _____ in Oklahoma City.

3. Oklahoma's first minority owned and operated bank was called _____.

4. In 1967, Charles became the first African American to be appointed to _____.

5. The Charles N. Atkins Opportunities Gardens was built to house senior citizens. It has 29 efficiency apartments and _____ one bedroom apartments.

6. Charles was licensed to practice this type of medicine _____.

7. Charles Nathaniel Atkins was born on October 11, 1911 in _____.

8. Charles and _____ were married on May 24, 1943.

9. The motto of OIC is they help people help _____.

10. In May of 1972, Charles became the first African American to receive this award _____.

RUBYE M. HIBLER HALL

BIOGRAPHICAL PROFILE

Rubye Maie Hibler was born in Eufaula, Oklahoma on February 27, 1912 to Reverend Lamar Hibler and Jessie Green Hibler. Rubye attended Langston University where she met and married Ira DeVoyd Hall, Sr. They were married in July 1930, later having six children: Iris Marie, Carole, Janice, Jessilyn, Ira D. Jr., and John. Rubye earned her bachelor's degree in English, graduating in 1932. She attended the University of Oklahoma (OU) and earned a master of arts degree in English/Speech in 1959. She began teaching in 1932 and spent 43 years in public education. Her long-time service includes employment with Oklahoma City, Muskogee, Colbert, Clearview and Kingfisher schools. Rubye's years of service include speech pathologist, psychometrist, counselor, diagnostician, and teacher of English, music and mathematics. Rubye's first year of teaching included teaching geography, spelling, opera and coaching the boys' football team. She also studied speech pathology and neurology at the OU Health Sciences Center. Rubye died November 9, 2003.

FIRST BLACK APPOINTED TO STATE REGENTS OFFICE

In 1974, Rubye Hibler Hall was the first African American appointed to the board of the Oklahoma State Regents for Higher Education. She served as chair 1978-1979. What does the Oklahoma State Regents for Higher Education department do? It was created in 1941. It forms academic standards for students who wish to further their education past grade 12. They determine the functions and courses of study for state colleges and universities. They grant degrees and propose budgets to the state legislature for universities and colleges. The State Regents operate the Oklahoma Guaranteed Student Loan Program, which guarantees loans students wish to apply for so that they can attend college. They also manage 23 scholarships and other special programs.

Copyright, The Oklahoma Publishing Company

FACING OBSTACLES

Rubye was prohibited from enrolling in the University of Oklahoma's (OU) graduate program due to segregation laws. Soon, the Oklahoma State Legislature passed laws that allowed African Americans to enroll in graduate programs. Although she was allowed to enroll, Rubye was confronted with other obstacles. The dean of the College of Arts and Sciences tried to persuade Rubye to change her major. She persevered and has always remembered a quote from her father, "When they build a road and can't go over a mountain, they go around it." Rubye became the first African American to complete a master's degree from the department of English at OU.

GRANDPARENT'S ACADEMY

Affectionately known as "Miss Rubye," she spearheaded the Grandparent's Academy in 1996. The purpose of this program is to match "grandparent" mentors with children 5-18 years of age who are not achieving in school and who do not have help at home. The grandparent volunteers help reinforce self-esteem, love of learning, and other values.

RUBYE M. HIBLER HALL
Answer the questions below.

1. What is Grandparent's Academy? _____
_____
_____

2. What is the Oklahoma State Regents for Higher Education? _____
_____
_____

3. Who operates the Oklahoma Guaranteed Student Loan Program? _____
_____
_____

4. Rubye was the first black to complete her master's degree in this subject. _____
_____
_____

5. Due to segregation, Rubye was not permitted to enroll in this University's graduate program. _____
_____
_____

6 – 10. Write about Rubye's upbringing, her education and family. Also, discuss some of the obstacles she faced and how she persevered by remembering her father's quote, "When they build a road and can't go over a mountain, they go around it." _____
_____
_____
_____
_____

BIOGRAPHICAL PROFILE

James "Jimmy" Edward Stewart was born on September of 1912, in Plano, Texas. He was the son of Zena T. Stewart and Mary Magdeline Fegalee Stewart. He had one brother, Alfred, and two sisters, Ella and Johnnie. Jimmy moved to Oklahoma in 1916 and attended Orchard Park Elementary school in Oklahoma City, Oklahoma. He played in the band with his childhood friend Ralph Ellison. Jimmy's father was a Baptist minister who died when Jimmy was eight years old. At age 14, Jimmy and his family moved to Wichita, Kansas where he completed high school in 1931. Jimmy entered the Oklahoma Colored Agricultural and Normal University (now known as Langston University). He attended there one year. He later married Mae Belle Hayes. This marriage ended in divorce. Jimmy married Mae Lois Layne in 1942. He had three children, Don Gilbert, Zandra, and James E. Stewart, Jr. He donated the Black Chronicles of History to the Ralph Ellison Library located in Oklahoma City. The collection consists of over 30 years of black history, civil rights activities, and other related material. He died in Oklahoma City on April 13, 1997.

JIMMY VS. OKLAHOMA NATURAL GAS

After attending Langston University for a year, Jimmy moved to Oklahoma City where he began managing the Jewel Theater on NE 2nd Street. Jimmy waited tables at country clubs and was promoted in the banquet service at the Biltmore Hotel in Oklahoma City. During his work at the Biltmore, Jimmy became friends with Oklahoma Natural Gas official Thomas H. Sterling. Jimmy's fight for racial justice included a complaint lodged against ONG. Jimmy believed there were not enough black employees and managers at the company. The district manager of ONG, Thomas Sterling, was so impressed with Jimmy that he hired him. Jimmy was employed at ONG as a janitor in June of 1937 and worked his way up to be appointed Vice President in 1976. Jimmy's relationship with corporate leadership allowed him to promote ONG with the African American community in Oklahoma. Jimmy worked for ONG during the day but spent his evenings and weekends waging a war against racism.

JIMMY'S STRATEGY

In the 1930s, Jimmy became active in the National Association for the Advancement of Colored People. He rose to president for the Oklahoma chapter in 1942. Through hard work and cooperation with other civil rights activists, he helped dismantle racial discrimination in public facilities across the state. Jimmy's strategy of carefully balancing confrontation, creating workable compromise, and negotiation helped to destroy decades of racial segregation and discrimination across the state of Oklahoma.

JAMES E. STEWART GOLF COURSE

In 1999 the Oklahoma City Parks and Recreation Department named a golf course after James Stewart. The golf course is at NE 10 and Martin Luther King Jr., Avenue. The popular nine-hole course is enjoyed by people of all ages and races. The First Tee program is offered at the golf course to allow youth to be introduced to golf. In 2000 Tiger Woods held a junior clinic at the James E. Stewart golf course. Youth had the opportunity to hit the ball with Tiger in addition to ask questions.

JIMMY STEWART
Rewrite the sentence to make it into a true statement

1. James Edward Stewart was born in September 1912, in Oklahoma City, Oklahoma.

2. Both of Jimmy's parent's died when he was only 14 years old.

3. Jimmy credited his success in bringing racial change to Oklahoma with using firearms.

4. The Jimmy Stewart Golf Course is for people over 65 years old.

5. Jimmy had six brothers and two sisters.

6. Jimmy waited tables at Furrs restaurants.

7. Jimmy once worked at ONG as a customer service representative.

8. In 2000, Barack Obama held a junior clinic at the Jimmy Stewart Golf Course

9. The Tower movie theater hired Jimmy as part of their managing staff.

10. The Black Chronicles of History consisted of over 30 years of history of the presidents of the United States of America and their staffs.

BOOKER T. WASHINGTON HIGH

BIOGRAPHICAL PROFILE

Booker Taliaferro Washington was born into slavery April 5, 1856 in Hale's Ford, Virginia. He was the son of a slave mother and white father. He graduated from Hampton Normal and Agricultural Institute in 1875 and taught there for six years. At 25, Booker T. the first president of the Tuskegee Institute in Alabama. He remained in that position the rest of his life. He was heavily involved in black politics with great support of blacks and rich Northern whites. Booker T.'s work helped many blacks gain a better understanding of the legal system and achieve higher education and financial power. He was an American educator, author, political leader, and orator. He was author of fourteen books. His first publication, *Up From Slavery*, still remains popular today. Booker T. once said, "I have learned that success is to be measured not so much by the position that one has reached in life as by the obstacles which he has had to overcome while trying to succeed." Booker T. died in 1915.

A WORLD-CLASS HIGH SCHOOL

Tulsa's Booker T. Washington High School was named for the great African American educator. A four room frame building was built at 407 E Easton Street in 1913, designed by Leon B. Senter. The school only served African American students. This school became too small so a larger school was built at the same location in 1920. That three story brick building served the African American community until a third Washington High School was built at 1631 E Woodrow Place in 1958. Tulsa Public Schools chose Booker T. as their vehicle for desegregating the school system. Most African Americans lived in north Tulsa and most Caucasians lived in south Tulsa. A method called "desegregation busing" was used. Caucasian students were bused to the school while continuing to allow neighborhood students to attend there.

Washington (also called "The T") later became a magnet school. All students had to apply for admission and this attracted students from across the school district. The school now serves students from every racial, religious, socio-economic, and ethnic group. In 2003, on the 90th anniversary of Booker T. Washington High, a new 250,000 square foot school, 23 million dollars was dedicated. The new school was built using the front section of the previous school to retain its historical significance. The school offers a variety of foreign languages. These include Chinese, Japanese, Latin, Spanish, Italian, and Russian. They offer TV/radio/film production and a number of college-preparatory courses. BTW school has an active exchange program with Japan, China, Germany, Mexico, India, Russia, and many European countries. The school has a nationally-ranked academic bowl team, physics team, robotics team, forensics team and a competitive cheerleading team. They continue to pride their championship basketball, football, and soccer teams. The success and excellence of the school is due to its dedicated staff, continued community support and gifted student body. There continues to be a long waiting list of applicants who have a desire to attend the school because of its reputation of success. BTW is now known as a magnet school. Acceptance to the school is based on test scores, grades, recommendations, and community service participation. The 1,250-student academy serves as a cornerstone of Tulsa's African American community. Booker T. Washington High School is considered one of the top public high schools in Oklahoma and one of the top-rated schools in the United States.

HIGH STEPPIN' BAND

Booker T. Washington High School's annual school-wide talent show, "Hi-Jinks" claims to be the longest continuously running variety show west of the Mississippi. Though the school's mascot is the Hornet, the nationally known marching band is the "High Steppin T-Connection."

BOOKER T. WASHINGTON HIGH SCHOOL
Answer the true false questions below.

1. _____ Booker T. Washington was born on April 5, 1856 on the campus of Tuskegee Institute.

2. _____ Tulsa's first Booker T. Washington school was built in 1913.

3. _____ The new Booker T. Washington High School in Tulsa, Oklahoma was built in 2009.

4. _____ The High Steppers is Booker T. Washington High School's nationally known band.

5. _____ Part of the first school was used to build the current Booker T. Washington High School.

6. _____ The second Booker T. Washington High School was built in 1920. One of its unique features was that it had a foreign exchange program.

7. _____ The "Homestead Hornets" is the name of the school-wide talent show.

8. _____ In 2003, Tulsa's Booker T. Washington High School celebrated its 100th anniversary.

9. _____ Booker T. Washington High school is one of the top-rated high schools in the entire world.

10. _____ Booker T. Washington High School's mascot is the "Bumble Bee."

RALPH W. ELLISON

BIOGRAPHICAL PROFILE

Ralph Waldo Ellison was born on March 1, 1914 in Oklahoma City, Oklahoma. His parents were Lewis Alfred Ellison and Ida Millsap. Ralph had one brother, Herbert. He was the grandson of a slave who was owned by Mary Ann Ellison. Ralph's father named him after the great writer Ralph Waldo Emerson in hopes of sealing his success. Ralph's father was a construction worker and died when Ralph was only three years old. This left the family quite poor. His mother worked hard doing domestic work to support her family. She was also a stewardess at the Avery Chapel Afro-Methodist Episcopal Church in Oklahoma City. The family eventually moved into the church parsonage, and Ralph had the minister's library available to him. His mother would bring home books, record albums, magazines, in addition to a typewriter, chemistry set and desk from households that discarded these items. These tools encouraged Ralph to write and practice his musical talent. He attended Douglass schools and was under the tutelage of Zelia Breaux. Ralph played the trumpet in the Douglass High School band until he graduated in 1932. Ralph married Fanny McConnell in July 1946. He died of cancer on April 16, 1994 in New York City.

DREAMS OF WRITING

In 1933 Ralph left Oklahoma City to attend Tuskegee Institute in Alabama. His dream of writing a symphony was put on hold. There was a mix-up in his scholarship and Ralph chose to move north in order to work and save money for his college tuition. He found it hard to find work and even more difficult to find work as a musician. He worked various jobs; these included a file clerk and receptionist. During this time he met writers Langston Hughes and Richard Wright. Wright encouraged Ralph to be a writer instead of a musician. From that point on, Ralph focused on his writing, which earned him many awards.

INVISIBLE MAN

In 1952, Ralph's first book was released. He spent seven years writing the book *Invisible Man*. This book spent 13 weeks on the New York Times best-seller list. The novel is about a nameless young black man from the south, suffering from numerous humiliations he experienced from campus life to street riots. The character's illusions were shattered one after another. Ralph wrote several short stories, and two nonfiction collections, *Shadow and Act*, which was published in 1964, and *Going to the Territory*, published in 1986. He worked on a second novel, but it was destroyed in a fire that burned his summer home. Ralph died while trying to reconstruct this book. It was published posthumously as *Juneteenth*.

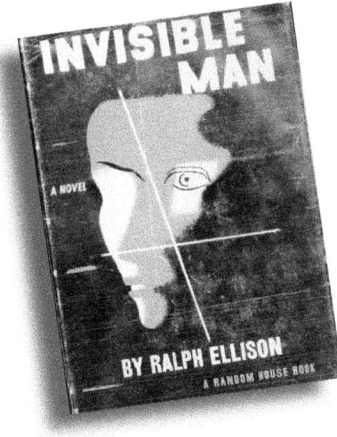

Ralph Ellison's novel, *Invisible Man*, won the National Book Award in 1953. The book was very experimental for its time and was influenced by jazz music he'd heard in Oklahoma City's Deep Deuce.

An episcopal priest in Oklahoma City challenged segregation of public libraries. In 1975, the Metropolitan Library System built the Ralph Ellison library in the predominantly African American area on Martin Luther King, Jr. Boulevard. The library has several collections which feature prominent African Americans.

RALPH W. ELLISON
Rewrite the misspelled words below to spell them correctly.

1. trumpit _____

2. aarthur _____

3. Alabaama _____

4. inviisable _____

5. slaav _____

6. freen _____

7. libreery _____

8. Walldoe _____

9. puur _____

10. shadoe _____

11. metrapoliton _____

12. Tuskige _____

13. Hues _____

14. mushishun _____

15. nu york siity _____

16. riter _____

17. Lanstun _____

18. beest sellur _____

19. novil _____

20. tiperiter _____

JOHN H. FRANKLIN

BIOGRAPHICAL PROFILE

John Hope Franklin was born on January 2, 1915 in Rentiesville, Oklahoma. He was the son of Mollie Parker, a school teacher, and Buck Colbert (B. C.) Franklin an attorney who practiced in Rentiesville and Tulsa, Oklahoma. B.C. was an attorney, postmaster, farmer, justice of peace, and president of the Rentiesville Trading Company. In 1931, John graduated from Booker T. Washington High School in Tulsa, Oklahoma. He enrolled in Fisk University, intending to earn a law degree and join his father in practicing law. He took classes with Professor Theodore S. Currier, chairman of History at Fisk. His interest in History grew intensely. After Fisk, John received a master's degree from Harvard University in 1936 and a doctorate in 1941. John married Aurelia E. Whittington on June 11, 1940. She was a librarian. They had one child, John Whittington Franklin. John was an avid fisherman. He loved to travel the world and was an orchid grower. His custom-built greenhouse held more than 1,000 flowers. John died on March 25, 2009, in Durham, North Carolina at the age of 94.

HIS WORK IN HISTORY

In 1956, John was the first black historian to have a full-time position at Brooklyn College. He also taught history at Duke, Cambridge, Harvard, Cornell, Fisk, Howard, Chicago, and California Universities as well as in New Zealand and Australia during his career. In addition, John received more than 130 honorary degrees. He wrote over a dozen books on various aspects of history. His book *From Slavery to Freedom: the History of African Americans*, has sold more than three million copies.

USE OF HISTORY FOR CIVIL RIGHTS

John helped prepare the legal research material for attorney Thurgood Marshall and the National Association for the Advancement of Colored People (NAACP). This assisted the legal defense team's victory in the landmark case of *Brown v. Board of Education*. In 1995, President Bill Clinton awarded John with the Medal of Freedom. It is the highest civilian award available.

The John Hope Franklin Reconciliation Park, pictured left, is located in downtown Tulsa. The park was opened in 2010. It pays homage to Tulsa's most recognized scholar. It commemorates the 1921 riot and tells the story of African Americans' role in building the state of Oklahoma.

JOHN HOPE FRANKLIN
Circle the correct letter to answer the multiple choice questions.

1. President Bill Clinton awarded John this honor. It is the highest award available to a civilian.
    a. The Purple Heart
    b. The Medal of Freedom
    c. The Nobel Peace Prize

2. The John Hope Franklin Reconciliation Park is located in this Oklahoma town.
    a. Rentiesville
    b. Muskogee
    c. Tulsa

3. John's book *From Slavery to Freedom: the History of African Americans,* has sold _____ copies.
    a. three million
    b. ten thousand
    c. six hundred

4. John has taught all over the world. In each of his assignments he taught this subject.
    a. Calculus
    b. World Geography
    c. History

5. In addition to traveling the world, John enjoyed growing flowers. His custom-built greenhouse had over 1,000 flowers. His favorite flower was the
    a. rose
    b. petunia
    c. orchid

6. John's historical knowledge helped this attorney in the case of Brown v. Board of Education.
    a. Thurgood Marshall
    b. Buck Colbert Franklin
    c. Johnnie Cochran

7. John received over _____ honorary degrees.
    a. 3000
    b. 130
    c. 600

8. John was the first black historian to teach full time at this college.
    a. Cornell University
    b. Duke University
    c. Brooklyn College

9. When John enrolled in Fisk University he intended to obtain a law degree and go into practice with his father, instead a professor who headed this department help steer him differently.
    a. History
    b. Horticulture
    c. Agriculture

10. The John Hope Franklin Reconciliation Park, located in Tulsa, commemorates this event.
    a. The Rentiesville Trading Company from John's hometown
    b. The Tulsa riot of 1921
    c. John's custom-built greenhouse

BIOGRAPHICAL PROFILE

Alfonzo Lewis (A.L.) Dowell was born in 1917. He grew up in a West Virginia coal-mining town. Alfonzo moved to Oklahoma City in 1948 after World War II, where he began his career as an optometrist in 1953. He and his wife Vivian had three children; Robert, Alfonzo N., and Consuelo. Vivian was the first African American female dentist in Oklahoma City. They both practiced their professions in a clinic named The Dowell Clinic. It was located in Oklahoma City and was built in 1956. The clinic was located at 934 NE 8th St., in Oklahoma City. Alfonzo Dowell died on November 6, 2001 at the age of 84.

THE FINGER PLAN

By 1910, Oklahoma laws prohibited African American students from attending the same schools as white and Indian students. In 1961, A.L. Dowell and his wife Vivian were dissatisfied with the Oklahoma City school system. Their son Robert planned to study medicine and take Latin, but the classes were offered at Northeast and not the all-black Douglass he attended. Robert was denied a transfer. In 1963 Dr. Dowell and other parents filed a federal lawsuit which led to desegregation of the Oklahoma City Public Schools. The lawsuit also sought to do away with the school board's policy that forced African American educators to only teach in all-black schools. Meanwhile, white educators were allowed to work in any school. United States District Court Judge Luther Bohanan found that Oklahoma City's residential patterns were heavily segregated due to restrictive covenants and laws which mandated residential segregation. It was found that segregated housing practices forced nearly all of the black population of the city to live in the "central east" area. In February 1972, Judge Bohanon ordered the school board to begin a desegregation plan known as the Finger Plan, authored by Dr. John A. Finger. The Finger Plan said that all kindergarten students could continue to attend their present schools and that parents of these students would be permitted to send their child to the school of their choice. The majority white elementary schools would reorganize to serve grades 1-4 of both races; black students would be bused from their neighborhoods to attend these elementary schools. The majority black schools would become "fifth grade centers," which would serve both black and white students; the white students would be bused for one year. Middle and high school students would be desegregated through new attendance zones and feeder patterns. The Finger Plan also made provisions for "stand alones," elementary schools located in neighborhoods already integrated. These schools would be exempt from the busing obligations and could serve students in kindergarten through fifth grades. As legal barriers to integrated housing were removed, many blacks in Oklahoma City were able to leave the east inner city area to which they had previously been confined. On June 2, 1975, after receiving evidence that the Board had "operated the Plan properly," Judge Bohanon issued an "Order Terminating Case." He felt the Finger Plan was no longer needed to keep racial equality within the school system. Dowell felt his children faced rejection because of his stand to stop segregation. His family received threatening telephone calls and mail. Vivian Dowell, deeply devoted to the cause, died in December of 1980.

FIRST BLACK CITY COUNCIL MEMBER

Serving Ward 7, Dr. A.L. Dowell was the first African American to be elected city councilman in Oklahoma City, Oklahoma. He served from 1967 to 1971. During that time he fought for many improvements in his ward. These included tougher open housing ordinances.

The Dr. A.L. Dowell Bridge is located over Interstate 35 and N.E. 23rd Streets in Oklahoma City, Oklahoma. A dedication ceremony for the bridge was held on February 4, 2000.

ALFONZO DOWELL

Answer the true - false questions by writing T or F on the line next to each sentence.

1. _____ Alfonzo Dowell Sr. was married to Consuelo.

2. _____ A dedication ceremony for the Dr. A.L. Dowell Bridge was held in Oklahoma City, Oklahoma on February 28, 1999.

3. _____ Alfonzo Dowell moved to Oklahoma City in 1953.

4. _____ The Finger Plan was named after one of the elementary schools which was located in Wetumka, Oklahoma.

5. _____ Alfonzo Dowell was appointed to the Oklahoma City council in 1967.

6. _____ In 1975 Judge Luther Bohanan issued an "Order Terminating Case" because the Finger Plan was no longer needed.

7. _____ As part of the Finger Plan, the majority black schools would become fifth grade centers.

8. _____ Alfonzo's son Robert was denied a transfer from Douglass High School to Booker T. Washington High School.

9. _____ Oklahoma City's residential patterns were segregated.

10. _____ Alfonzo's wife Vivian passed in 1970.

11. _____ Alfonzo grew up in a North Carolina coal-mining town.

12. _____ Vivian Dowell was a licensed physical therapist.

13. _____ The Dowell children were met with rejection because of their stand against segregation.

14. _____ Alfonzo was elected to serve Ward 2.

15. _____ The Dowell family received threatening letters and telephone calls.

BIOGRAPHICAL PROFILE

Juanita Kidd was born on March 7, 1919 in Wewoka, Oklahoma. She was the only child of schoolteachers Henry and Mary (Chandler) Kidd. Juanita's father had a college degree and her mother completed two years of college with an exceptional gift for math. She came from a family of professionals and likely college-educated people in Wewoka. They were heavily involved in Juanita's education and pushed her to succeed. She admired her parents' hard work and adopted these qualities in life. Juanita could read by the time she was only three years old and at the age of six started her first year of school in the third grade. She began to study piano at the age of five and graduated from high school at the age of 16. She attended a segregated school, traveling ten miles into town each day. During the school week Juanita lived with her aunt, who also taught at her school, and her uncle, who was a pharmacist. She spent time with her parents on weekends and holidays. Juanita feared algebra but her mother tutored her during the summer months. When school started, Juanita's algebra teacher thought she was brilliant. After graduating from high school, Juanita found it impossible to find an accredited college in Oklahoma that would admit African Americans. She moved to Missouri and later transferred to the University of Iowa, receiving her bachelor of arts degree in music in 1939. Juanita died on August 21, 1998 in Philadelphia, Pennsylvania. Her funeral services and burial were held in her birth town, Wewoka.

HENRY G. BENNETT AWARD

In 1980 Juanita won the Henry G. Bennett Distinguished Service Award. The award is given through Oklahoma State University (OSU) in honor of former president Bennett. President Bennett made noteworthy contributions to higher education that benefited humankind. This is the highest humanitarian award given by Oklahoma State University. "The recipient of this award may be an alumnus of the University, a citizen of the state or nation, or a distinguished world citizen. His/her record of achievement and qualities of leadership and service must be truly outstanding and merit this high award of recognition given by the University. He/she should possess the high ideals of citizenship and service and those qualities of character which exemplify the life of the OSU President in whose name this award is made. The person should have had a distinguished career in a professional field, some phase of business or industry, government service or humanitarian concern."

CAREER AS A TEACHER

Juanita moved to Seminole to begin her teaching career. She taught music for two years then moved to Sand Springs, a suburb of Tulsa, where she met her future husband, Charles Otis Stout. The couple married on June 23, 1942, but did not have any children. Juanita and Charles both taught in Sand Springs. At 5 feet 3 inches high and weighing only 88 pounds, she was often smaller than her students. When faced with unruly students she would often send them to her future husband, and soon the problem students were few.

MAKING A DIFFERENCE

Juanita made a difference in many lives as a result of her sternness and caring attitude. One youthful offender later went back to school and ended up becoming Judge Stout's law clerk. He went on to become an attorney.

LOVE OF LAW

Juanita began her legal studies at Howard University in Washington, D.C., later transferring to Indiana University, earning her law degree in 1948. In 1954 Juanita earned a law degree and passed the Pennsylvania bar exam the same year. Juanita wanted to be a lawyer from an early age and was fascinated with law. She stated, "I cannot understand how a person can work eight hours a day or more at a job that they do not like. I love my job. I love the law. I enjoy it." Juanita and her husband seldom took vacations because she stated, "There isn't anything I'd rather be doing than what I am – practicing law. If I were born again 10,000 times I'd want to be a lawyer. In September 1959 Juanita was appointed judge of a municipal court, becoming the first African American woman to sit on the bench in Philadelphia, Pennsylvania. Two months later, she was elected to that same position making her the first African American female judge elected in the United States. Juanita became the first African American woman to serve on a state supreme court (Pennsylvania) in January of 1988. Her husband Charles passed away that same year. Juanita was inducted into the Oklahoma Hall of Fame in 1981.

Artist Susan Schary's portrait of Judge Kidd-Stout hangs in the Pennsylvania Supreme Court
Copyright © 2000 - 2010 Susan Schary

JUANITA'S SPECIAL INTEREST IN YOUTH

Although Juanita was childless, she appointed herself as a stern, loving mother on the bench. Sitting on the bench, she had to bring along three pillows so that she could see over the top of it. She remained first and foremost an English teacher. She often stopped attorneys and corrected their grammar and chastised them for misspelling words when filing motions and other documents in court. Juanita lectured constantly about the dangers of declining literacy and stated that some high school graduates could not even read their diplomas. She noticed a common characteristic among the defendants who engaged in violent behavior – their inability to read. "A child who cannot read cannot succeed," she once said. Juanita received many death threats in the mail and by phone. These threats did not intimidate her. She complained that offender's grammar and misspellings were atrocious. Juanita would try her cases and hand out sentences swiftly and sternly. She received a threat from a member of a gang – Black Bottom – instructing her not to send any more of their gang to jail. She had law enforcement round them up and bring them before her. Once there was even a bomb threat which resulted in every employee of the court house being sent home. She began ordering everyone that entered her courtroom to be searched. On the first day deputies confiscated seven pairs of scissors, an 18-inch dog chain, seven files, two knives, two razor edged twine cutters, and a pair of tweezers. Juanita received so many threats on her life she was forced to have round-the-clock police guards. They drove her to work each morning and home every night.

JUANITA KIDD STOUT

Answer the true - false questions by writing t or f in the space provided

1. _____ Juanita instructed the deputies to search everyone entering her courtroom.

2. _____ Deputies confiscated knives, files, razors, and a dog chain upon searching people who entered Judge Stout's courtroom.

3. _____ Juanita was the first African American woman to sit on the bench in Philadelphia, Pennsylvania.

4. _____ Juanita was a very tall woman, measuring 6 feet 2 inches.

5. _____ Juanita's husband would drive her to work each day because of the constant threats on her life.

6. _____ Juanita wanted to become an attorney at an early age. She stated that she loved her job and she loved the law.

7. _____ The Henry G. Bennett Distinguished Service Award is the highest humanitarian award given by Oklahoma State University.

8. _____ One youthful offender turned his life around after being in Judge Stout's courtroom. He went back to school and eventually became a prominent attorney in Pennsylvania.

9. _____ Because of segregated schools, Juanita lived with her aunt and uncle during the week and went home to her parents on the weekend.

10. _____ Juanita was able to read by the age of 3 and her first year of school she was put in the third grade at the age of 6.

11. _____ After graduating from high school, Juanita moved to New York City because she could not find an accredited college in Oklahoma that would allow blacks to enroll.

12. _____ While in high school Juanita had to travel ten miles to go to school each day.

13. _____ Juanita married Henry Otis Stout in 1942.

14. _____ Juanita's motto was "A child who cannot read cannot succeed."

15. _____ Juanita earned her law degree from Indiana State University.

Circle the correct letter to complete the multiple choice questions.

1. As a judge, Juanita received numerous threats on her life, she was forced to
a. get round-the-clock police bodyguard protection
b. carry a concealed weapon
c. have her husband escort her to and from work each day
d. take an attack dog to court with her each day

2. The Henry G. Bennett Distinguished Service Award recognizes
a. African Americans who have boycotted restaurants
b. anyone who has attended Langston University
c. individuals who have made noteworthy contributions to higher education
d. individuals who have worked at any college in Oklahoma

3. When Juanita received threats by mail, she would complain because of
a. the white powder that would get on her clothing when she opened the letter
b. the misspelled words and bad grammar
c. the number of threatening pieces of mail occupied too much of her day
d. the paper cuts she normally received from the letters

4. The number of children Juanita and her husband had
a. two
b. eight
c. zero
d. four

5. Juanita was born in this town in Oklahoma
a. Pauls Valley
b. Little River
c. Wewoka
d. Boley

6. Once graduating from college, Juanita began her working career as a
a. law clerk
b. restaurant owner
c. teacher
d. nurse

7. At the age of five, Juanita began taking lessons to learn to play
a. the saxaphone
b. the guitar
c. the piano
d. the flute

8. Juanita died on August 21, 1998 in this town
a. Oklahoma City, Oklahoma
b. Wewoka, Oklahoma
c. Philadelphia, Pennsylvania
d. Sand Springs, Oklahoma

9. Juanita graduated from high school at the age of
a. eighteen
b. ten
c. sixteen
d. twenty-one

10. Juanita feared this subject while in high school. Her mother tutored her.
a. reading
b. algebra
c. social studies
d. science

FORMING A COMMUNITY – "BLACK WALL STREET"

When members of the Five Civilized Tribes were forced from the southeastern parts of the United States many relocated to Indian Territory. The first African Americans arrived in Oklahoma as slaves of the tribe members. Most of them arrived between 1831 and 1839. By the year 1900 the African American population made up approximately five percent of Tulsa. By 1905 the blacks began to form their own community. Most groups built and located along Archer and Greenwood streets which is part of north Tulsa. Greenwood functioned as a separate city; self-sufficient, it was a neighborhood that served almost all of the needs of its African American residents. In the early 20th century, Greenwood was known as one of the most successful and wealthiest African American communities in the United States. This popular affluent community became known as America's "Black Wall Street." In 1906 a wealthy African American by the name of O.W. Gurley moved to Tulsa. Gurley was a young entrepreneur who had recently resigned from his presidential appointment under president Grover Cleveland. Gurley purchased forty acres of land which were "only to be sold to colored." Gurley built businesses and rooming houses in addition to other two–story buildings and residences. The importance of Greenwood Avenue was relevant in that it ran north for over a mile from the Frisco Railroad yards. It was one of the few streets that did not cross into the white neighborhoods of Tulsa. The thirty-five square block area boasted a variety of thriving businesses. Although racial segregation laws prevented them from shopping anywhere else, the community took pride in the fact that they had something all to themselves and were not forced to share it with the white community. Greenwood was centered on a street known as Greenwood Avenue. It was home to approximately 10,000 African American men, women, and children. Greenwood was home to many prominent black businessmen, many of them multimillionaires. Almost all of Tulsa's black attorneys, realtors, physicians, and other professionals were located here. There were fifteen well-known black doctors, one who was considered the "most able Negro surgeon in America" by one of the Mayo brothers. The area was plentiful with grocery stores, clothing stores, barber shops, beauty stores, hotels, cafes, nightclubs, movie theaters, shoeshine shops, and more.

GREENWOOD'S SUCCESS A THREAT TO SOME

Reportedly, some white residents of Tulsa felt threatened by the success of the African American community and worried about its growth. Some referred to the Greenwood area with derogatory names such as "Little Africa." The Ku Klux Klan (KKK) made its first major appearance in Oklahoma in the 1920s. It was estimated that there were 3,200 Klan members in the Tulsa area.

THE BEGINNING OF THE END OF GREENWOOD'S SUCCESS

On May 20, 1921, 19 year-old African American shoeshiner Dick Rowland entered the Drexel building downtown to use the segregated restroom. Dick tripped while approaching the elevator which had stopped unevenly with the floor. He unintentionally fell on 17 year-old white female Sarah Page. She hit Dick with her purse and he tried to stop the assault by grabbing her. Sarah screamed and Dick ran from the elevator and the building. Sarah told police that Dick had attempted to criminally assault her. She later changed her story by saying he grabbed her. Dick was arrested and spent the night in the county jail. Sarah refused to press charges.

"NAB NEGRO FOR ATTACKING GIRL IN ELEVATOR"

The *Tulsa Tribune* ran a story about the incident on the following day. Its headline was "Nab Negro For Attacking Girl In Elevator." The editor also called for a lynching. Approximately 400 whites gathered around the jail that evening with rumors that a lynching was about to occur. The African American community became aware of the threat to Dick Rowland's life. Approximately 25 African Americans armed themselves and headed to the jail. Upon arrival, they found the story had been exaggerated and, after talking to the deputy sheriff, he assured them that no harm would come to Dick Rowland. The African Americans went home.

ABOUT DICK ROWLAND

Jimmie Jones was born in 1902. By 1908 he was orphaned and taken in by Damie Ford, an African American woman in Vinita, Oklahoma. Damie took Jimmie to Tulsa, Oklahoma to live with her family, the Rowlands. Jimmie eventually took the last name Rowland as his own and selected his favorite first name, Dick. Dick Rowland attended Booker T. Washington High School but dropped out to take a shoe shining job in a white-owned and white-patronized shoe shine parlor. At the age of 19, Dick was accused of assaulting a white woman, Sarah Page. This accusation led to the infamous Tulsa Race Riot. Dick was arrested in May of 1921. At the end of September, 1921, the case was dismissed. Sarah Page stated that she did not want to prosecute the case. Exonerated, Dick reportedly moved to Kansas City.

THE NIGHT BLACK WALL STREET DIED

The African Americans who had been to the jail earlier left and returned with 75 others. As they left, a white man attempted to disarm one of them and shots were fired. Gunfire broke out on both sides. Two African Americans and ten whites died. Hours of violence began outside Dick Rowland's jail. This began the Tulsa race riot, one of the worst acts of racial violence in United States history. Three days of arson and violence against blacks by whites left many dead, hundreds injured. Over one thousand homes and hundreds of businesses were destroyed. African Americans were murdered, robbed, and raped. There are reports of

TULSA RACE RIOT

whites using machine guns and airplanes that dropped nitroglycerin and dynamite on the African American section of town. Mobs of whites drove the streets of Greenwood shooting any African American person they saw. A group of 10,000–15,000 whites gathered and marched, setting fire to every building standing. An estimated 10,000 people were left homeless. Over 800 people were admitted to local hospitals with injuries. It has been reported that thirty-nine people were killed, of whom ten were white. It is not clear as to the correct number of deaths, as conflicting reports have surfaced. Some go as high as 300 or more. Thirty city blocks, holding 1,256 residences, were destroyed. Over 600 successful businesses were lost. Among them were 30 grocery stores, two movie theatres, 21 churches, 21 restaurants, a hospital, post office, bank, schools, libraries, law offices, private airplanes, and a bus system.

The governor sent the Oklahoma National Guard and soldiers from Fort Sill to help control the riot situation. Authorities went door-to-door rounding up African Americans and their families. These families were taken to makeshift camps for protection. This effort resulted in more than 6,000 African Americans at the camps. For two months, African Americans were forbidden to leave the camps; the only exception was to attend work. Some African Americans chose to leave the city, buying one-way tickets to other cities. Within a week of the riot, African Americans were made to carry "green cards." Those working in a permanent job wore "green cards" signed by their employer as identification. Blacks that were found in the streets without "green cards" would be subject to arrest and taken to the fairgrounds. About 7,500 "green cards" were issued. A grand jury investigated the riot and indicted about 20 African American men, but no whites. No one went to jail. The community slowly rebuilt part of the Greenwood area within the next five years. Much of the area was leveled in the early 1970's. Several blocks of the old neighborhood were saved from demolition and have been restored, forming part of the Greenwood Historical District.

TULSA RACE RIOT COMMISSION

In 1997 the Tulsa Race Riot commission was created to study and develop a "historical account" of the riot. The report recommended the following: direct payment of reparations to survivors of the 1921 Tulsa race riot, cash payments of up to $150,000 as reparations to survivors and the descendants, scholarship fund available to north Tulsa students affected by the Tulsa race riot, a memorial honoring riot victims, and establishment of economic development enterprise zone in the historic area of the Greenwood District. In June of 2001, the Oklahoma legislature passed the "1921 Tulsa Race Riot Reconciliation Act." This legislation provided for more than 300 college scholarships for descendants of Greenwood residents and created a memorial to those who died in the riot.

The following was also submitted but was later rejected by the commission: funding to be given to north Tulsa schools; a historical archive to be created at Langston University; an interactive exhibit to be displayed at the Tulsa Greenwood Cultural Center; funding to construct an African American art and history wing at the Oklahoma Historical Society museum.

The Library of Congress reported that reparations and financial assistance had been promised to the pioneers of the Greenwood community. The community basically rebuilt on their own. An expressway was built through the two remaining blocks and today numerous colleges, universities, and cultural centers remain. After the 75th anniversary commemoration ceremonies, Representative Don Ross filed a bill with the Oklahoma Legislature requesting reparation for the victims of the riot. Today a nominal amount of claims have been paid.

PHOENIX RISING

The Greenwood Educational and Cultural Center made a vision a reality in the community. Capital funding was raised from the City of Tulsa and the state of Oklahoma, in addition to private contributions. The board of directors formed three organizations: The North Tulsa Heritage Foundation, The Business and Industrial Development Corporation, and the Oklahoma Jazz Hall of Fame. The Greenwood Center's last expansion was in 1995. It is dedicated to promote cultural programs for all races, creeds, religions and ethnic heritages. The Center offers classes and programs on African Dance, Ballet, Hip-Hop Dance, Tae Kwon Do, and African Hand Drumming. There is a multipurpose room that can accommodate 800 in a banquet setting and 1200 in a theatre setting. The Center also has 10 classes and meeting rooms in addition to four art galleries and a gift shop. It is also home to the Goodwin-Chappelle Gallery. The Cultural Center features a "Sunday Dinner" every Sunday which features a variety of adult and children's meals from 11:00 until 4:00 PM beginning in April. The Urban Kids Food & Fine Arts Summer Program is offered at the Cultural Center for children ages 5-11. The summer program accepts a limited number of children who enjoy dance, animation, vocal music, arts and crafts, creative writing, health, nutrition, physical fitness, and agricultural experiences.

The Mabel B. Little Heritage House is the only house that still stands of the original homes of 1920s residential area. It is listed on the National Register of Historic Places. The museum structure is the former home of Sam and Lucy Mackey. The Mackeys made a living doing domestic and yard work for wealthy Tulsans. The Mabel Little Home holds art, photos, authentic furniture, and memorabilia from the community.

The Greenwood Chamber of Commerce was founded in 1938 by several North Tulsa businessmen. It is part of the economic development program. Its purpose is to provide a medium for civic, business, and social organizations. It is an avenue that businesses have available to help locate office space and provide certain management and technical assistance. It is funded in part through a grant with the United States Small Business Administration.

GREENWOOD CENTRE

Deep Greenwood is the heart of Tulsa's black community. It earned the reputation as "Black Wall Street." The area is comprised of two and three story brick buildings lined up along the avenue. The building houses a variety of establishments including stores, theatres, groceries, restaurants, dry goods stores, and billiard halls. The building fronts date back to the late 1920s and 1930s and were a favorite place for black lawyers, doctors, and other professionals to house their businesses.

Answer the true - false questions below. Write f or t on the line for each sentence.

1. _____ Cash payments up to $150,000 were recommended as reparations to the survivors and descendants of the Tulsa Race Riot.

2. _____ The Greenwood District consisted of 100 square blocks of thriving businesses.

3. _____ Fifteen well-known black doctors lived in the Tulsa area in the early 20th century.

4. _____ Tulsa did not have any black multimillionaires living in the area at this time.

5. _____ O.W. Gurley worked under President Grover Cleveland prior to moving to Tulsa.

6. _____ The Tulsa Race Riot is one of the worst acts of racial violence in the nation's history.

7. _____ Blacks found without green cards were taken to hotels.

8. _____ After the riot, Dick Rowland was exonerated, left Tulsa, and moved to Chicago.

9. _____ Blacks were only allowed to leave camp during the riots to check on their homes.

10. _____ The Race Riot Commission was formed to develop a historical account of the riot.

11. _____ Sarah Page accused Rick Rowland of assault but later refused to file charges.

12. _____ O.W. Gurley purchased 30 acres of land to be sold to colored people only.

13. _____ There were 2,000 arrests made in Tulsa due to the riot.

14. _____ Dick Rowland's real name was Jimmie Hendrix.

15. _____ The Oklahoma legislature passed the "1921" Tulsa Race Riot Reconcilliaiton Act" in 1999.

1. Green cards were given to African Americans to carry with them during the weeks following the riot. The number of Green cards distributed was
a. 20,000
b. 7,500
c. 100
d. 100,000

2. The governor sent this group to the riot area to help control the situation.
a. The United States Army
b. The Oklahoma National Guard
c. The Bomb Squad
d. The Oklahoma City Police Department

3. Dick Rowland attended this high school.
a. Douglass High School
b. Tulsa High School
c. Booker T. Washington High School
d. Wewoka High School

4. Dick Rowland was accused of assaulting Sarah Page on this date.
a. June 29, 1902
b. September 9, 1921
c. August 31, 1908
d. May 20, 1921

5. In the earlier part of the 20th century, the Greenwood neighborhood in Tulsa, Oklahoma was known as the _____ in the United States.
a. most dangerous
b. most unhealthy
c. most successful and wealthy
d. most unkept

6. A grand jury investigated the Tulsa riot and indicted 20 African American men and _____ whites.
a. 200
b. 0
c. 500
d. 25

7. When the African American community became aware of the threat for Dick Rowland's life, they ___.
a. held a prayer vigil at the local church
b. started the riot
c. armed themselves and went to the jail
d. went to the elevator to find Sarah Page

8. There were reports that whites used this tactic to help destroy the African American section of town.
a. airplanes to drop nitroglycerin and dynamite
b. poison sent by U.S. mail
c. waiting until Sunday, during church service and fire bomb the homes
d. waiting until the school children were on the bus and throwing pipe bombs

9. Jimmie Jones was orphaned as a young boy. He lived in this town
a. Weleetka, Oklahoma
b. Vinita, Oklahoma
c. Oklahoma City, Oklahoma
d. Ada, Oklahoma

10. When Dick Rowland fell on Sarah Page, she began hitting him with
a. a stick
b. her shoe
c. her purse
d. a chair

BIOGRAPHICAL PROFILE

Clara Mae Shepard was born the daughter of Ezell and Isabell Shepard May 3, 1923 in Okfuskee County, Oklahoma. She was one of five children of dirt-poor sharecroppers. Her parents worked hard. Her father drove buses, moved houses, chopped cotton, and did farmwork. Clara attended high school in the all-black town of Grayson, then graduated from Langston University in 1944 with a degree in mathematics and history. She later became the first African American admitted to the graduate history program at the University of Oklahoma (OU), attaining her master's degree in 1951. Clara married Bert Luper. This marriage ended in divorce. She later married Charles P. Wilson in 1977. She had three children: Calvin, Marilyn and Chelle. Clara taught many students about history and civil rights during her over 40 years as an educator. Clara served many years as a civic leader and a leader in the Civil Rights Movement. Clara died in Oklahoma City on June 8, 2011, at the age of 88.

BLOODY SUNDAY

Clara grew up with parents who had different approaches dealing with injustices and segregation. "My dear mother believed in loving people, no matter what their color. She was always a bit afraid of the power of White people. She had actually seen a Black man hung by a White mob in Texas. So she was never eager to step out and challenge the status quo." Clara's father served in the United States Army during a time when segregation and injustices were high. He was more open to challenging the system believing that some day things would change. In 1963, Clara was among about 100 other people who rode a bus to Washington D.C. for the historical presentation of Dr. Martin Luther King Jr.'s speech. On August 28, 1963, Clara, along with 250,000 others, crowded to hear the influential speakers, including Dr. King's "I Have a Dream" speech. In 1965 Clara and two van loads of other protestors drove to Selma, Alabama from Oklahoma City to march against segregation. She refers to the atmosphere there as warlike. Civil Rights protestors were at one end of town and the police were on the other. She recalls even highway patrolmen pointing their guns at them as they drove into town. Over 600 civil rights marchers were attacked by local authorities. The men used tear gas and billy clubs. One of the "posse men" hit Clara in the leg which resulted in a deep cut. This visit to Selma was one of the many times Clara was arrested while demonstrating for justice. March 7, 1965 became known as "Bloody Sunday."

Copyright, The Oklahoman Publishing Company

FREEDOM CENTER

The NAACP would regularly meet at Clara Luper's home. Needing a larger place to meet, the group made a decision to purchase an old Mobile gas station. It was later converted to the Freedom Center. The Freedom Center is located at 2609 N. Martin Luther King Avenue in Oklahoma City. It is often used for NAACP and Youth Council meetings and activities. The site has survived vandalism due to a torch or bomb, but it was later rebuilt. By the year 2011, mounting debts, past due monthly bills and insurance payments in addition to the crumbling center put this historical haven at risk of being shut down. It is a building with a lot of historical memories, and is said to be the only civil rights building in the state of Oklahoma. NAACP chapters in the state are doing what they can, and it is hoped the community will come together again to save the center.

KNOWN AS THE MOTHER OF THE CIVIL RIGHTS MOVEMENT

In 1957, Clara took on the challenge of reorganizing and became advisor for the Oklahoma City National Association for the Advancement's (NAACP) Youth Council. Its membership consists of hundreds of state and county-wide participants. "The mission of the NAACP Youth and College Division shall be to inform youth of the problems affecting African Americans and other racial and ethnic minorities; to advance the economic, education, social and political status of African Americans and other racial and ethnic minorities and their harmonious cooperation with other peoples; to stimulate an appreciation of the African Diaspora and other people of color's contribution to civilization; and to develop an intelligent, militant effective youth leadership." The youth, who are normally teens, volunteer on a local, national, and sometimes international level. The youth group participate in the NAACP's annual conference each year. Admiring Martin Luther King, Jr and his success with the Montgomery Bus Boycott, Clara wrote a play about King and his nonviolent approach to problems. The play is entitled *Brother President*. Clara was invited to bring her Oklahoma City Youth Council to perform her play *Brother President* for the New York City NAACP in 1958. Due to segregated conditions, when blacks traveled they were forced to buy cold snacks at stores, carry lunches, or find all black restaurants. On their return trip back to Oklahoma, the youth voted to begin a campaign to end segregation in Oklahoma City by using the same non-violent approach that Martin Luther King, Jr. practiced. Clara and other participants studied how to be non-violent. Non-violence was a belief of Gandhi and Dr. Martin Luther King Jr. Participants were met with violent attacks. They were hit, pushed, kicked, dragged and spit on. They even received threatening phone calls. All of these unjust actions were met with non-violence and positive changes began. Clara was arrested twenty-six times working for equality and civil rights for all.

CLARA LUPER CORRIDOR

This freedom fighter was honored by the Oklahoma House of Representatives with the passage of House Bill 2715. This bill gives a portion of NE 23rd Street in Oklahoma City the name of "Clara Luper Corridor."

CLARA'S FIGHT FOR POLITICAL OFFICE

On November 16, 1971, Clara announced that she had made the decision to run for the United States Senate. Her opponents were Mike Turpen and Dewey Bartlett. One news reporter asked Clara as a black woman if she felt she would be able to represent white people. Her response was "Of course, I can represent white people, black people, red people, yellow people, brown people, and polka dot people. You see, I have lived long enough to know that people are people." Although she was defeated by Dewey Bartlett, she felt the experience was enjoyable and educational.

THE SUCCESS OF SIT-INS

The idea for sit-ins in Oklahoma came during a trip to New York. Clara and the youth council were enroute back to Oklahoma City and encountered segregation. During the long ride many "WHITE ONLY" signs were seen. The hungry youth decided to take a stand once returning home. Clara's daughter Marilyn suggested going into Oklahoma City's Katz Drug Store and ordering a Coke. Blacks were allowed to shop freely in Katz but they were only allowed to order sandwiches and drinks to be placed in paper sacks and eaten on the streets. The youth felt this tactic was unacceptable and wished to eat at the lunch counter just as white patrons were allowed to. On August 20, 1958, the first and longest sit-in protest of the civil rights movement began. Clara and three other adults led the youth. She stayed with them constantly. At the first sit-in at Katz Drug Store, one youth, Barbara Posey, approached the counter and said "We'd like thirteen Cokes please." The youth were refused service, tensions brewed, racial slurs were shouted, food, grease and other objects was thrown at them, but they refused to leave. The media and police were called to assist, but the group returned the next day. On their third day, Katz owners announced that its thirty-eight locations – which consisted of stores in Oklahoma, Kansas, Iowa and Missouri – would serve all races of people.

The thirteen youth were: Marilyn Luper Hildreth, Calvin Luper, Richard Brown, Dr. Barbara Posey Brown, Alma Posey Washington, Esq., Betty Germany, Lana Pogue, Linda Pogue (Ayanna Najuma), Portwood Williams Jr., Areda Carol Tolliver, Elmer Edwards, Gwendolyn Fuller Mukes, and Lynzetta Jones Carter. For over three years, the youth held sit-ins all over Oklahoma City. Hundreds of black Americans and white supporters, too, continued the sit-ins until 1964. The Oklahoma sit-in movement desegregated over 100 establishments.

BROADCASTING THE FIGHT

Clara used her own radio show to spread the word about boycotts, demonstrations and other tactics used to end segregation from 1960-1980.

The sit-in at Katz Drug, Aug 26, 1958
Copyright, The Oklahoma Publishing Company

CLARA'S MANY HONORS

Clara has received over 500 honors. She has been inducted into the Oklahoma Hall of Fame, the Oklahoma Afro-American Hall of Fame and the Oklahoma Women's Hall of Fame, in addition to many others. She personally spearheaded and assisted hundreds of campaigns to stomp out segregation. These efforts included cafes, restaurants, hotels, churches, theaters, equal banking, equal employment opportunities, equal housing, and voting rights.

CLARA LUPER SCHOLARSHIP

The Devon Energy Corporation in conjunction with Oklahoma Gas & Electric Company established a Clara Luper Scholarship program at Oklahoma City University. It was designed to honor Ms. Luper's generosity, contributions, and hard work towards the Civil Rights movements throughout the nation. The scholarship was set up to assist minority student with lower incomes who graduated from underserved high schools. This full scholarship has been awarded to over 60 students.

BEHOLD THE WALLS

Clara wrote a book in 1979 titled *Behold The Walls*. It gives first-hand detailed accounts of the civil rights struggle in Oklahoma in the 1960's. She writes about her tasks of knocking down the walls of the many faces of segregation. In her book, Clara's autobiography chronicled the segregated conditions and schools, writing, "The books . . . had been mainly discarded from the white elementary overabundance of promises for better books, equipment, and supplies that never came. We were Separate and Unequal." Clara attended a segregated high school in Grayson, Oklahoma five miles from her home. The school presented students with outdated encyclopedias and dictionaries, microscopes with no lenses, and handed-down history books with missing pages.

Views from the Freedom Center
Black History Monument and Wall

CLARA LUPER

Find the following terms related to Clara Luper in the word search below and circle each one

CIVIL RIGHTS	**FREEDOM CENTER**	**CLARA**
LUPER	**GRAYSON**	**SIT-IN**
PROTEST	**KATZ DRUG**	**NONVIOLENT**
NAACP	**DESEGREGATION**	**SENATE**
CORRIDOR	**YOUTH**	**COUNCIL**

```
F D C T P X S F E R J C A U R P D R G L
D Z L C T B E F B T I Y O C L R P R R I
H N A T N E L O I V N O N R N O E E A H
A A R P Y Y I L I C N U O C H T U O Y R
N I A Z E R C L K S A T B C N E S R S O
E E R O D I R R O C P T H E P S S I O O
E M E Z R I Z J S X X G C A H T T L N Y
E T K A G D B A R D G M R G T I A R Z M
P F A H M S G E P G O E C W N C R L Q S
E J T N V D E E R D R F A E E C I Q N E
Q S Z P E H A D E S E G R E G A T I O N
C T D E L S D E M N S R K N B S C T A E
S F R A S C R I N C V K S R L O S B Q S
H E U L R F U E T A L R S F E H E S S B
R E G K E S R B P G I U T A T R O R Q Y
R P N X W I F E S U C F E R C P S S B F
L A U T D A J Y T R L N P S Q R E O P C
T C Y L S N X C A R H T A S I N Q C G S
Z A H I L M O T F T A D P F I B N I H E
R S T Z I O S D J T I S G S E B Y D I R
```

CLARA LUPER
Fill in the blanks to answer the questions below.

1. Clara Luper is known as the _____ of the Civil Rights Movement.

2. The Katz Drug Store Sit-In was the _____ publicized sit-in in the nation.

3. Clara was one of _____ children born to Ezell and Isabell Shepard.

4. Clara was arrested _____ times marching and demonstrating the equal rights and desegregation.

5. Clara participated in the march in Selma, Alabama held on March 7, 1965, it became known as _____ _____.

6. This retired schoolteacher taught for _____ years.

7. The NAACP Youth Council consists of mostly _____.

8. The Freedom Center is the only _____ _____ building in the state of Oklahoma.

9. _____ members of the NAACP Youth Council accompanied Clara to the Katz Drug Store sit-in.

10. Oklahoma House Bill 2715 created the _____ _____ _____.

11. The Clara Luper Scholarship is sponsored by these two companies, _____ and _____.

12. Clara has received over _____ honors for her participation and leadership in the civil rights struggles.

13. The name of the book Clara Luper wrote is _____ _____ _____.

14. Clara was the first African American admitted to the graduate history program at the _____ _____ _____.

15. Clara has three children, their names are _____ _____ _____.

16. In Clara's book she states "We were separate and _____".

17. Clara attended a segregated school where students were given microscopes without _____.

18. At the first Oklahoma City sit-in, Clara accompanied the NAACP Youth Council. They ordered thirteen _____.

19. Two of Clara's children, _____ and _____, participated in the first sit-in.

20. Clara Luper died in Oklahoma City on _____.

AMUSEMENT PARKS

SPRINGLAKE AMUSEMENT PARK Owner Roy Staton opened Springlake Amusement Park in 1922. This historic park remained opened for more than 60 years. The park featured two ballrooms, a penny arcade, and the legendary "Big Dipper" roller coaster. By the mid-fifties, black families had moved into the immediate vicinity of Springlake park. They were not welcome to enjoy Springlake. With the passage of the Civil Rights Act of 1964, blacks began to enjoy the same accommodations that white patrons had enjoyed for many years. There remained areas of the park where blacks were still not welcome. Their attendance was allowed only on certain days of the week. Mr. Staton opened a swimming pool at the park. Many white patrons were willing to share the park's midway with blacks, but not the pool. Legally, Mr. Staton could not deny blacks access to the pool, but if blacks were allowed in, he risked losing many white patrons. Mr. Staton ultimately decided to close the pool to avoid a clash among the whites and blacks. The pool, once reserved for humans, became a Sea-Aquarium where dolphins would entertain the parks guests. On Easter Sunday, April 11, 1971, trouble began when a rumor spread through the racially-mixed crowd that a white teen had been pushed off the Big Dipper roller coaster by a black teen. This rumor triggered one of the worst civil disturbances in Oklahoma City's history. More than 100 law enforcement officers were called to the scene. No whites, but 29 blacks were arrested that day. The rumor proved to be completely false. Although state newspapers reported the incident as a "riot" or "melee," Mr. Staton insisted the incident had been overblown and the park remained completely safe. The public remained apprehensive. Mr. Staton began to develop health problems and spent the last few years of his life in a nursing home. The park had survived World War II and the Great Depression but could not survive the damage done from the 1971 Easter Sunday. Mr. Staton made the difficult decision to sell the park. In 1977, the park was sold to Dale Thomas. In June of 1981, an employee caused over $250,000 worth of damage due to arson. Poor maintenance, a change of ownership and other problems led to the sale of Springlake to Oklahoma City Vo-Tech Board. Springlake Amusement Park was closed for good. On June 28, 1982, Vo-Tech District #22 purchased the 95-acre park for a sum of $1.1 million. Demolition began on May 11, 1983. Metro Tech continues to honor the legacy of Springlake Amusement Park through its web page content. The web page is titled "The Thrills of Yesterday, The Skills for Tomorrow." Within the walls of the technology center, remains a vintage Big Dipper car from the roller coaster, merry-go-round horses and wall photographs. Many of the rooms in the facility have been given names reflecting the park, such as Carousel and Big Dipper, etc. All of the original light poles were saved.

Springlake's Bubble Bounce ride

Getting ready for the Easter egg hunt at Springlake

DOE DOE AMUSEMENT PARK Ben Hutchins, Sr. opened Doe Doe Amusement Park in Lawton in 1945. It had a large pool, skating arena, kiddie rides, train rides, and animal exhibits. Ft. Sill Military Base is located in Lawton. Although the black and white soldiers consistently fought together to defend democracy all over the world, they could not swim together at Doe Doe Park. The leaders and officers of the United States Army fell silent about the discrimination tactics used in Lawton against the black soldiers. A group of over a hundred blacks protested the park and were told by the owner, Ben Hutchins, "Get off my property. I don't want you on my property! Officer, arrest these people for trespassing on my property!" The group eventually left but returned a week later. They were met with Ben and his attorney. They were told to leave. But the group one-by-one politely requested entrance into the pool. They wanted to swim. Ben told the group, "This is your last chance. If you don't leave, we'll have to take you to jail." The group of blacks did not leave. They were all arrested. Even the children as young as five years old were taken to the juvenile ward. They were later released by paying a $20.00 fine. The Lawton City Council later passed an ordinance making it illegal for more than four people to congregate around a public building. In addition, they passed a public accommodations ordinance which stated that privately-owned pools and amusement parks were excluded from integration. Another march led by Clara Luper and E. Melvin Porter was organized. The group pledged to walk from Oklahoma City to Lawton, Oklahoma, a one-hundred-mile march, on June 16–18, 1966. Over one hundred marchers gathered at the Oklahoma state capitol. The marchers were followed by a volunteer in an old pick-up truck filled with food, pop, water, and fruit which had been donated by supporters. The group made plans to stop in Chickasha as their halfway point. There they were met by volunteers who fed the group. The marchers were fed well; their were tables filled with ham, roast beef, chicken, barbecue, fruit, salads, hot rolls, cakes and cookies with all types of drinks and water. On reaching Lawton, the marchers were exhausted as they had endured rain with tired, swollen and bloody feet. Blacks and other supporters arrived from Oklahoma City, Ardmore, Boley, Tatums, Holdenville and Okmulgee. The owner of the park, Ben Hutchins, indicated he was ready to negotiate. Lawton's mayor, Wayne Gilley, came forth with a pledge that the city council had created human relations commission and an ordinance had been proposed to end discrimination in all public places. The pool was segregated, but when the owners were forced to integrate the pool they chose to close the pool instead. The pool remained closed for many years. It later reopened allowing everyone to come in. The owners of the park raised the prices of park events and concessions which meant most could not afford to attend. Doe Doe Park closed permanently in 1985.

Clara Luper led protesters in a march on Lawton's Doe Doe Park, 1966
Copyright, The Oklahoma Publishing Company

WEDGEWOOD Maurice Woods owned Wedgewood Village Amusement Park. The park opened in 1958 on Northwest Highway in Oklahoma City. In June of 1963 Woods announced a "one day per week" integration policy. The park offered this option on Thursday of each week. Other days of the week, the park was opened "only to non-negro customers." Over fifty black and white demonstrators arrived at the park. Park management stopped the marchers as they attempted to enter the park saying, "I told you this morning that you would not be admitted. We can't force the people of Oklahoma City into something they can't accept." Woods stated that he had $2 million dollars invested into the park and could not risk integration. The next day Woods announced that he had made the decision to integrate the park and for nearly a month this practice continued without incident. The last week of July of 1963, Woods announced a "one day per week" integration policy. The park offered this option on Thursday of each week. Other days of the week the park was opened "only to non-negro customers." The park closed in 1969.

THE FIGHT TO INTEGRATE WEDGEWOOD VILLAGE AMUSEMENT PARK JUNE 1963.

Copyright, The Oklahoman Publishing Company

SEGREGATED PARKS

The only park available for blacks in the Oklahoma City area was Riverside Park. This continued for many years. Roscoe Dunjee describes the park as "an underdeveloped, unlighted, unsupervised tramp redezvous in a red light district where no decent black man would want to send his children or go himself." In the 1920's, giving in to pressure the city finally built a park for the black community, it was named Booker T. Washington Park. After the discovery of an active oil field on the land, the city took back the park. Many promises came to build another one but years went by before a "segregation ordinance" was set aside and provided three parks for "Negroes Only." The parks: Washington, Hassman and Riverside, were never improved to the level of similar white parks.

SEGREGATED ZOOS

Blacks were banned from visiting Lincoln Park. The black community argued that black taxpayers and their children were denied the educational value of the zoo's presence. People in black communities paid taxes which helped to support these institutions and contributed to their upkeep and other expenses. In May of 1930, the Negro Businessmen's League informed the Oklahoma City Council that they want arrangement made to be able to enjoy Lincoln Park but would prefer a special zoo in Booker Washington Park.

LESLIE B. BROWN, SR

Leslie B. Brown, Sr., was born July 1, 1912 to Albert and Ida Brown in Broken Bow, Oklahoma. Leslie's family moved to Arkansas due to the many problems from the race riot. When Leslie was fourteen years old he decided to leave Arkansas and return to Oklahoma. He worked long hours shining shoes, washing dishes, and working other odd jobs. Leslie married Martha Watts on October 28, 1944. Five children were born to this union: Leslie Jr., Glendale, Albert, Karla and Rochelle. He died May 20, 1996 in Oklahoma City.

COMMUNITY ORGANIZATIONS

Leslie joined the National Association for the Advancement of Colored People (NAACP) in 1933. He was a member of this organization for more than 55 years, serving in many capacities including president. He was also a long-time member of the Urban League of Oklahoma City in addition to being the founder of the Oklahoma County Chapter of the A. Philip Randolph Institute, even serving as President for a short time. He worked as an employee at the Equal Employment Opportunity Office before retiring in 1992.

CIVIL RIGHTS DEEDS

Leslie's work and achievement for the civil rights movement knew no boundaries – black, white, young old. Leslie dedicated more than sixty years of his life to helping others. His deeds often went unnoticed.

THE ONE MAN PICKET

In the early 1960's Leslie took a job as a parking lot attendant at the Biltmore Hotel in downtown Oklahoma City. Leslie, along with other African American bellhops, doormen, maids and waiters, did not receive any pay from the hotel. Their only form of compensation was relied on tips. White employees regardless of their work ethic, education or ability received hourly wages and better positions. Leslie knew this was wrong. He confronted management about it and accomplished nothing but a termination. He began picketing outside the Biltmore – a one-man picket line. For 18 long months, Leslie endured the blistering heat and frigid Oklahoma weather. He was subjected to racial and anti-union insults. With the help of Oklahoma City attorney George McCaffrey, Leslie won a lawsuit against the hotel, winning his job and back pay. From this experience came the formation of Local Union 246, a branch of the International Union of Hotel and Restaurant Workers. This local branch received a union contract which included hourly wages and improved working conditions for parking lot attendants, maids, bellhops, and doormen. He later became the first black elected to serve on the board of directors of the AFL-CIO in Oklahoma.

THE SIT-INS
Leslie was very involved in the civil rights struggle and worked quietly behind the scenes giving assistance. He and others formed a committee to solicit funds and support for the sit-in participants and marchers. Funding was needed for food, water, gasoline, and other supplies during these demonstrations.

Leslie Brown, Sr.'s son, Glendale Brown, remembered the civil rights movement. He was also a participant of the sit-ins and demonstrations. Glendale was born on February 8, 1945, in Walnut Grove, a black community in Oklahoma City. Glendale remembers being a member of the NAACP Youth Council and being tutored in math by Clara Luper. All of the youth were required to undergo training prior to going to actual sit-ins or protests. Clara was their mentor. Responding with violence to the racism, taunts and other forms of hatred was not tolerated. Glendale and Clara visited the all-white First Baptist Church which is still located in downtown Oklahoma City, in 1959. The minister, Reverend Hobbs, and other members of the congregation greeted them with respect and kindness. The two visited the church twice in an effort to integrate. Once the congregation found that Glendale was interested in joining the church, deacons of the church visited the Brown household. The media also came. Clara, the deacons of First Baptist Church, and Mr. and Mrs. Brown sat at the Brown's kitchen table to discuss the situation. The deacons of the church made it clear they would not vote for young Glendale to become a member. Soon after, the family began receiving threats. Glendale never became a member of this church.

Students occupy the lobby of the Skirvin Hotel in Oklahoma City to protest segregated dining there in June 1961.

Copyright, The Oklahoman Publishing Company

PORTWOOD WILLIAMS, SR

Portwood Williams, Sr., was born in the Sand Town community of Oklahoma City on July 27, 1915. He was one of three children born to Clara and John Williams. Portwood had two sisters. The family was very poor. They grew up on 121 E California. He was always a hard worker and can remember working since he was nine years old. Portwood would help his mother by gathering fruit and vegetables which they would sell. She would give him part of his earnings and he would sometimes catch a show at the Aldridge Theater for ten cents.

TREATMENT OF BLACKS

All the blacks he knew growing up were afraid of whites. The blacks endured terrible treatment. "Nobody was treated like black people. I can't remember nobody being treated like we were treated." He remembers seeing the Ku Klux Klan around 1924 in the downtown area at the Rock Island train station when he was only nine years old. He talked about how scared he was running all the way home. He remembers blacks had to sit in areas designated for "COLOREDS" when riding on trains and buses. Portwood talks about how he once moved the sign up a few benches because there wasn't enough seats for the blacks. One of the white passengers told him to "Put that sign back there, n-----." He was later drafted to the United States Army. Portwood talks about how the white citizens treated him after serving the country. He even wore his uniform on some occasions but still experienced disrespect and racism. He looked at it as "being kicked down – just not with your feet." Portwood married Lucille Echols. They raised four children: Shirley, Clayportice, Portwood, Jr., and Donda. Mr. and Mrs. Williams were married for seventy-two years prior to her passing in 2009. His father-in-law, Clarence Echols, drove a cab for the black-owned cab company which was located on second street. Portwood was a shoeshine guy. Shoeshines were five cents then but he made good money doing it. He remembered hearing n----- jokes and derogatory stories about n----- women as he shined shoes. "If you wanted a tip sometimes you would grin even though it wasn't funny." Portwood sent his first child to college by shining shoes in the Capitol Hill area of Oklahoma City. During that time Portwood says there was a sign on SW 25 and Robinson that said "N----- don't let the sun go down on you."

HELPING WITH THE SIT-INS

He remembers staying on the Park Street with Clara Luper. She approached him and asked him if he was tired of eating in the back. She asked for his help and he was happy to do it. He said "Yes, I'm ready to go." Clara taught the children about the non-violent approach. They were trained and were always well-behaved. Portwood took his children, Donda (who was only five years old at the time), and Port, to the sit-ins. He said people often asked him if he realized the danger he was putting his children in by allowing them to participate in the protests. He said he'd rather see them dead than to go through what he went through. "Man, that's a h--- of a life; being looked down all your life like you ain't nothing. Going through that – like you're nothing – going through the back doors – that's not living. Pretty soon, you lose that fear." There were only two or three cars, called the Freedom Cars, taking the volunteers to the sit-ins. But most blacks were afraid to help. Portwood's car led the way to the first sit-in at Katz Drug Store. They were instructed to take the sit-in participants to the locations and wait for them.

NINETY FIVE AND GOING STRONG

In 2011 Mr. Williams was ninety-five years old. He remains active in the community. He accepts many speaking engagements at schools, colleges, and other institutions of education. He says, "I've used that, every time I speak, any place, man, I want them to know. And I use "n-----," and I tell them what a bad word it was." I also tell them, "don't you fear nothing." He still enjoys visiting others, going to church and working in his yard planting flowers and tending his garden. He is also retired from operating his upholstery business and Portwood's Jewelry Shop which was located on N. Martin Luther King Blvd. in Oklahoma City.

THE FOUR STRATEGIC STEPS IN NON-VIOLENCE

These rules of non-violence were taught and reviewed over and over with the demonstrators in order to get peaceful results:

The **first** was INVESTIGATION: Get the facts. Make sure that an Injustice had been done. A non-violent approach will fail if it is based on false or shaky assumptions.

The **second** was NEGOTIATION: Go to your opponent and put the case directly to him. It could be that a solution could be worked out and that there could be a grievance that we didn't know about. Let the opponent know that you are going to stand firm in order that you'll be ready to negotiate anywhere and anytime.

The **third** was EDUCATION: Make sure that the group is well informed on the issues and that men have always hated change, yet change must come.

The **fourth** was DEMONSTRATION: This is the final step only to be taken when all others have failed. Non-violent demonstration call for discipline that is firm. Every provocation must be answered with continued good will. You must be ready for self-sacrifice that will leave no doubt as to your integrity, your dignity and your self-respect. Suffering is a part of the non-violent approach. It is to be endured, never inflicted. This approach will give you the moral victory upon which the eternal struggle for Freedom, Justice, and Equality can be won.

Taken from Clara Luper's book *Behold the Walls*.

SEGREGATED PUBLIC ACCOMODATIONS

Find the following terms related to Clara Luper in the word search below and circle each one

DOE DOE
PORTWOOD WILLIAMS SR.
STRATEGIC NON-VIOLENCE
SIT-INS
EDUCATION

ONE MAN PICKET LINE
BEHOLD THE WALLS
WEDGEWOOD
PROTESTERS
DEMONSTRATION

CLARA LUPER
SPRINGLAKE
LAWTON
NEGOTIATION
INVESTIGATION

```
L G S N F L A P L S O H G I P P M T A T
E I N O I T A C U D E T A E S O I R G L
H E W S H G I O S H O I T L X R F E H B
M D E G S E T Y N E G O T I A T I O N E
J P O A A W L D C A E O W E Y W S G E H
L R D E A A L W M D A E A E T O E K Q O
C O P T D D O X O O F V N H G O O M Y L
O T R R K O D L M N F E M Q Y D F R Y D
B E M F Z E E C O E E A V H T W E I H T
E S F N O I T A G I T S E V N I O W F H
S T R A T E G I C N O N V I O L E N C E
I E E O N E M A N P I C K E T L I N E W
T R T N E A A U R G T E X E K I J U R A
Q S S S P N P R R E P U L A R A L C N L
T H M N A N O I T A R T S N O M E D L L
W A E I O O E K A L G N I R P S F E E S
I N E T D G O S V G I E T R G S O P E K
M O W I G S E A R J O O H O H R F E S D
N A F S I C R D D D E D W N S E Y E N G
L O J P H M I S G Z I V P E E E D E O N
```

BIOGRAPHICAL PROFILE

Hannah Diggs was born in Winston-Salem, North Carolina on November 1, 1923, the fifth of six children. Hannah came from a family of teachers and ministers. Her parents were "college people" and were adamant about their children earning degrees. Hannah grew up reading, reading, reading — she was surrounded by books. Hannah received a degree in education from St. Augustine College in 1943. While there she met Charles Nathaniel Atkins. They married May 24, 1943. To this union three children were born: Edmund Earl, Charles Nathaniel, and Valerie Ann. Her husband Charles went to medical school at Meharry Medical College in Tennessee. Hannah went on to attend the University of Chicago. In 1949, she received a second degree in library science. Hannah and her family moved to Oklahoma City in 1951. She later attained her Master of Public Administration degree from the University of Oklahoma and a doctoral degree in education. Hannah passed on June 17, 2010, at the age of 86. She was known as a trailblazer who led the way for other black women. In 2011, State Representative Mike Shelton filed legislation to honor Hannah's memory by naming a section of Interstate 35 in her name.

A SPECIAL WELCOME

In 1968, Hannah became the first African American woman Representative elected to the Oklahoma legislature. She was surprised when one of the legislators presented a picture of men dressed in the white hoods of the Ku Klux Klan (KKK), pointed to one hooded man, and said, "That's me." It was shocking to know that any person elected to office would be affiliated with the KKK. During her tenure, she authored many important bills to improve areas in mental health, adult protective services, school age children immunization requirements, tax reform, child welfare, and open meeting laws. Hannah served in this position from 1968-1980. President Jimmy Carter named Hannah to the General Assembly of the United Nations in 1980. Governor Henry Bellmon appointed Hannah in 1987 to the position of Oklahoma Secretary of State, the highest state government post ever held by a black woman in the state of Oklahoma.

On August 19, 1969 Hannah marched on City Hall in the Oklahoma City sanitation workers strike. Clara Luper was the spokesperson for the strikers. They fought for pay hikes, a shorter work week, and new grievances rules. She said she "handcuffed herself to a truck to be dragged along. Fortunately, they didn't drag us." She was arrested and taken to jail where she spent a few hours behind bars before Oklahoma County Commissioner Ralph Adair helped to get her released. The strike ended on November 7, 1969.

THE UNITED NATIONS

The United Nations consists of six organs, the General Assembly was established under its charter. The first session of the assembly was held on January 10, 1946 in London and 51 countries are represented. It is made up of 192 members and plays an important part in international peace and security. They meet in regular session from September to December each year, where they discuss and make recommendations to maintain friendly relations among nations. The General Assembly is the only body where every member of the organization is represented and allowed to vote. Many nonmembers, such as organizations, states and other entities (e.g., Intl Committee of Red Cross, the Vatican, etc.) maintain observer status which allow them to participate in the work of the General Assembly.

HANNAH DIGGS ATKINS

Rewrite the sentences to make them into true statements

1. Hannah became the first African American woman elected to the Oklahoma state legislature in 1988.

2. Hannah died in 1999.

3 Hannah loved to cook; she cooked whenever she had time.

4. President Barack Obama named Hannah to the General Assembly of the United Nations.

5. She participated in a strike to help improve the working conditions for the Oklahoma City firefighters.

6. Hannah's husband Charles was a physician. They met at the University of Oklahoma.

7. Hannah died at the age of 97 on June 17, 2010.

8. Hannah was appointed to the highest state government post ever held by a black woman in the state of Oklahoma. It was the position of Superintendent of Education.

9. The United Nations has fifty-one organs. The General Assembly falls under its charter.

10. Nonmembers of the General Assembly can participate in the work of the Assembly and cast votes about important issues.

ADA L. SIPUEL FISHER

BIOGRAPHICAL PROFILE

Bishop Travis B. and Martha Sipuel lost their home, church, and possessions in the 1921 Tulsa Race Riot. Bishop Travis Sipuel was the son of former slaves. The Sipuels escaped the violence from the Tulsa Race Riot and moved to Chickasha, Oklahoma. Ada Lois Sipuel was born in Chickasha, Oklahoma on February 8, 1924. Ada was the youngest of four children. Other siblings are Lemuel and Helen. Ada sang in the choir and played basketball and the trumpet in school. She graduated as class valedictorian in 1941 from Lincoln High School in Chickasha. Ada enrolled in Arkansas A&M College in Pine Bluff, Arkansas and transferred to Langston University in 1942, majoring in English. She married Warren Fisher on March 3, 1944. They had a daughter, Charlene, and a son, Bruce. Ada passed on October 18, 1995.

SHE WAS UP FOR THE CHALLENGE

Ada graduated from Langston University with honors on May 21, 1945. She never stopped dreaming of being a lawyer, but Langston University did not have a law school and Oklahoma state statutes did not allow blacks to attend white state universities. There was a provision that allowed funding for "Negroes" to attend out-of-state law and graduate schools that accepted blacks. Ada's brother Lemuel was originally chosen by the National Association for the Advancement of Colored People (NAACP) leaders to challenge the segregation laws in Oklahoma and apply to the law school at the University of Oklahoma. Not wanting to delay his law career, Lemuel decided that he would enroll in Howard University. Ada was selected due to her strong grades and cool demeanor. On January 14, 1946, accompanied by Roscoe Dunjee, the state president of the NAACP, Ada applied for admission to the University of Oklahoma College of Law. Her application was denied based on the law that would not allow white and black students to attend classes together. Dr. George Lynn Cross, president of the University of Oklahoma, explained that instructors breaking this law could be charged with a misdemeanor and white students who attended mixed-race classes could also be fined.

THE LEGAL BATTLE

On April 6, 1946, Ada with the help of a young attorney, Thurgood Marshall, and resident attorney Amos T. Hall, filed a lawsuit which prompted a three-year legal battle with the state of Oklahoma. Ada's case was lost in the district court and an appeal was made to the Oklahoma Supreme Court. The Oklahoma Supreme Court ruled that the state's policy of segregation in education did not violate the federal constitution. Ada then filed an appeal with the U.S. Supreme Court and on January 12, 1948, the highest court in the nation ruled in *Sipuel v. Board of Regents of the University of Oklahoma*. The U.S. Supreme Court ruled that the state of Oklahoma must provide Ada with equal educational opportunities which are equivalent to other citizens in the state. The Oklahoma legislature decided that instead of admitting Ada to the Oklahoma University law school, they would create a separate law school just for her to attend. The new school was thrown together in five days and named the Langston University School of Law. The school would be held in the State Capitol's

Senate rooms. Refusing to attend the Langston University School of Law, Ada filed a motion on March 15, 1948 that Langston's law school was not equal to OU's law school, where white students attended. On June 18, 1949, Ada again applied to the University of Oklahoma College of Law.

The university's president, Dr George Lynn Cross, reviewed Ada's credentials and found no academic reason to deny her application for admission. Oklahoma, along with sixteen other states, prohibited whites and blacks from attending classes together. Although Dr. Cross could have been fined up to $50.00 per day and white students who attended class with Ada were subject to a fine of $20.00 per day, George Cross instructed the admissions office to enroll her. Ada said the students made her feel welcome, but she was still separated. There was a sign placed in the classroom that said "Colored" and she was forced to sit at the back of the room. During lunch Ada sat behind a chained area and ate alone. She was even watched by a gun-toting guard. Ada was the first African American woman to be admitted to an all-white law school in the South. Twelve days later, Langston University's law school closed. In 1991, Ada was awarded an honorary doctorate of humane letters from OU. On April 22, 1992, Oklahoma Governor David Walters appointed Ada as a member of OU's governing board, the Board of Regents of Oklahoma University. The university subsequently dedicated the Ada Lois Sipuel Fisher Garden in her honor. It is located on the Norman campus. The garden displays a bronze plaque commemorating her dedication and contributions to the state of Oklahoma. It reads, "In Psalm 118, the psalmist speaks of how the stone that the builders once rejected becomes the cornerstone."

BLACKS WERE KEPT SEPARATE

Although Ada was admitted to the University of Oklahoma, all black students were provided separate eating facilities and restrooms, separate reading sections in the library, and were forced to sit in the back of the room behind a row of empty seats with a wooden railing and a sign reading "colored." Ada was given a chair marked "colored." These conditions were endured through 1950. The United States Supreme Court ruled that segregated seating in the library, classroom, and cafeteria unfairly limited a student's ability to learn. Segregation of races in education was abolished. On August 6, 1951, Ada graduated from the University of Oklahoma College of Law and later earned a master's degree in history.

ADA'S LOVE OF HELPING OTHERS

Ada began practicing law in 1952. She later worked at Langston University and her tenure there lasted a total of 30 years. After her retirement, Ada continued her work in civil rights and other educational and community contributions. In 1992, Governor David Walters appointed Ada to serve on the Board of Regents for the University of Oklahoma. She wrote a book about her life, *A Matter of Black and White*, which was released in November of 1995. There are two pictures of her hanging in the Oklahoma State Capitol. One was unveiled in 2007, making Ada's the first portrait of an African American woman to be hung in the state capitol.

The Ada Lois Sipuel Fisher Garden and Fountain on the campus of the University of Oklahoma

George Lynn Cross and Ada reunite after fifty years

ADA LOIS SIPUEL FISHER
Choose the correct letter below to answer the multiple choice questions.

1. Ada Lois Sipuel was one of four of Bishop Travis and Martha Sipuel's children. She was born in
a. Norman, Oklahoma
b. Tulsa, Oklahoma
c. Chickasha, Oklahoma

2. Ada wrote a book about her life. It was not released until after her death. The name of the book is
a. *My Life at the University of Oklahoma*
b. *A Matter of Black and White*
c. *Ada Lois Sipuel Fisher's Garden*

3. Oklahoma and _____ other states had laws that prohibited blacks from attending schools with whites.
a. 30
b. 10
c. 16

4. When Ada applied for admission to the University of Oklahoma College of Law, what NAACP president accompanied her?
a. Roscoe Dunjee
b. Thurgood Marshall
c. Lemuel Sipuel

5. Prior to Ada's birth, her parents lost their church, home, and possessions due to this
a. tornado
b. Tulsa Race Riot
c. flood

6. In addition to singing in the choir and playing basketball, Ada played this instrument in school.
a. violin
b. tuba
c. trumpet

7. In 2007, Ada's became the first African American female to have her portrait hung here
a. library at the University of Oklahoma
b. Oklahoma State Capitol
c. Chickasha High School

8. Ada married Warren Fisher in 1944. They had two children. Their names are
a. Helen and Warren, Jr.
b. Charlene and Bruce
c. Thurgood and David

9. Instead of allowing blacks to enroll at the University of Oklahoma's College of Law, a decision was made to create a makeshift law school named
a. Langston University School of Law
b. Ada, Oklahoma College of Law
c. Norman, Oklahoma School for Lawyers

10. The Ada Lois Sipuel Fisher Garden displays a bronze plaque recognizing her for her contributions and dedication to Oklahoma. The plaque reads:
a. In dedication to Ada for her endurance
b. In Psalm 118, the psalmist speaks of how the stone that the builders once rejected becomes the cornerstone
c. A special welcome to our newest member of the Board of Regents

BIOGRAPHICAL PROFILE

Charles Lawrence Owens was born on April 13, 1930 in Tulsa. He graduated from then segregated Booker T. Washington High School in Tulsa, Oklahoma. Charles began his working career early in life, operating his own paper route in junior high school and later working as a baggage handler at the Tulsa Airport. Charles attended Lincoln University in Jefferson City, Missouri, graduating with a bachelor of science degree in business in 1952. He was the first in his family to graduate from college. In December of 1952, Charles joined the United States Army, later being assigned to Europe. He was honorably discharged two years later. Charles and his wife Edythe, have two children, Charles Jr. and Melanie. Charles Jr. followed in his father's footsteps and chose a career in law enforcement.

FIRST BLACK DISTRICT COURT JUDGE

After spending time in the military, Charles returned to Tulsa seeking employment as an accountant. Due to his race he was unable to find employment. As a last resort, Charles joined the city's police department. His interest in law began in college. He said, "I was always fascinated with law and the ability of law to change things." Charles worked the graveyard shift as a Tulsa police officer and took classes for the next four years at The University of Tulsa Law School, receiving his law degree in 1960. He was admitted to the Oklahoma Bar Association in August of 1960 and became partners with Edward L. Goodwin in the law firm of Goodwin and Owens. In 1963 Charles was appointed to work as assistant attorney general and headed the criminal division. On November 20, 1968, Oklahoma Governor Dewey Bartlett appointed Charles Oklahoma District Court judge. These appointments made 38 year old Charles the first African American to hold such posiitions. Judge Owens presided over several high-profile cases, including *State v. Roger Dale Stafford*. It was the first and only case to be televised in Oklahoma. Stafford was convicted of murdering nine people. Six were employees of a Sirloin Stockade Restaurant in Oklahoma City during a robbery. Judge Owens was the winner of the 2002 Lifetime Achievement in Law Award.

SERVING THE DISABLED

Charles' only daughter, Melanie was born blind. He says, "I'm very proud of her and all of her accomplishments." Charles has served as president of the board for the Oklahoma Council of the Blind. The foundation provides licensed adult care choices for individuals 18 and over who have mental and physical disabilities. He has also served as Board Treasurer and currently serves as Vice-President of the Oklahoma Foundation of the Disabled. This foundation is a 50 year old not for profit organization that provides services for adults with developmental disabilities in the central Oklahoma area. They work with clients to attain basic life and socialization skills and encourage recreational activities and exercises. They also provide respite to caregivers, allowing them time away from their loved ones. Clients enjoy meals, movies, dancing, field trips, computer keyboarding, music, and numerous other activities. The organization gets funding from private contributions in addition to several other charitable campaigns and agencies.

CHARLES L. OWENS
Answer the multiple choice questions by circling the correct answer.

1. Charles worked the graveyard shift as a police officer while taking classes at this university.
a. The University of Oklahoma College of Law
b. University of Tulsa Law School
c. Langston University Law School

2. This Oklahoma Governor appointed Charles to serve as an Oklahoma District Court Judge.
a. Governor Dewey Bartlett
b. Governor David Hall
c. Governor Mary Fallin

3. Charles and Edythe's only daughter, Melanie, was born with this disability.
a. deafness
b. blindness
c. epilepsy

4. Charles Jr. followed in his father's footsteps by becoming a
a. attorney
b. judge
c. police officer

5. The Oklahoma Foundation for the Disabled gives support for individuals who are
a. minorities in elementary school
b. 18 and over who have mental and physical disabilities
c. low income babies and are unable to walk

6. Charles graduated from this high school in Tulsa, Oklahoma.
a. Booker T. Washington High School
b. Edison Prepatory School
c. Bishop Kelley High School

7. Charles presided over many high profile cases. Which was the first trial in Oklahoma to be televised?
a. Oklahoma v. Terry Nichols
b. Oklahoma v. Roger Dale Stafford
c. Oklahoma v. Ersland

8. Charles was the first in his family to do this
a. join a law enforcement agency
b. graduate from college
c. graduate from high school

9. Charles volunteers for the Oklahoma Foundation for the Disabled. He has served in this capacity
a. Vice-President
b. instructor
c. accountant

10. The Oklahoma Foundation for the disabled has served communities for over _____ years.
a. 10
b. 100
c. 50

BIOGRAPHICAL PROFILE

Edward Melvin Porter (E. Melvin) was born May 22, 1930 in Okmulgee, Oklahoma. He knew very early in life that he would be active in the civil rights movement. E. Melvin joined the army upon completion of high school to earn money to go to college. After his stint in the service, he enrolled in Tennessee State University where he served as president of the student body his senior year. He was one of the first African American's to attend Vanderbilt law school in 1956. E. Melvin experienced racism and tension from some of the whites there. He was not included in study groups, fraternities or other organizations and was initially told that he would not be allowed to eat on campus. E. Melvin received his law degree in 1959 from Vanderbilt. In the 1960's, E. Melvin began practicing law in Oklahoma City and later began his political career. In 1964, he became the first black man to be elected to the Oklahoma State Senate. He served for two terms. Senator Porter was then reelected in 1966 and in 1970, when he served four year terms.

CIVIL RIGHTS BATTLES

E. Melvin worked tirelessly in the civil rights movement. He was elected president of the Oklahoma City National Association for the Advancement of Colored People (NAACP) in 1961. He served two terms and during his tenure he and other NAACP members participated in boycotts, sit-ins, protests and marches. E. Melvin was arrested on several occasions during his fight for civil rights. By 1962, the Oklahoma City chapter had opened doors for African Americans to over 170 restaurants and vowed to continue its fight until all establishments were open to everyone. E. Melvin introduced Oklahoma's Anti-Discrimination Act which makes it illegal for an employer or labor organization to discriminate against someone because of their sex, race, color, national origin, age, or disability.

THE NAACP

The National Association for the Advancement of Colored People was founded February 12, 1909. It is an organization that promotes the rights of minorities. It is one of the oldest and most influential civil rights organizations in the United States. The organization was founded by a diverse group: WEB Dubois (African American), Ida Well-Barnett (African American), William English Walling (Caucasian), Henry Moscowitz (Jewish), Oswald Garrison Villard (German-born Caucasian), Mary White Ovington (Caucasian), among others. The group came together to discuss racial injustice on behalf of the rights of colored people including Jews, Native Americans, and African Americans. The NAACP consists of different departments that are concerned with numerous aspects of minority rights, such as legal education and employment.

OKLAHOMA COUNTY ASSESSOR

In 1993, E. Melvin was appointed Oklahoma County Assessor. What does a county assessor do? He/she is responsible for listing and maintaining records on taxable real property (land and buildings), and personal property in Oklahoma County. What is done with the property tax money? It is given to local schools, vocational and technical education, city and county government and libraries.

Senator E. Melvin Porter introduced Oklahoma's Anti-Discrimination Act. It was enacted during the Thirty-First Legislature Second Session – 1968. It states:

Be it enacted by the People of the State of Oklahoma:
Chapter 1. Declaration of Purposes; Construction
    Sect. 101. Purposes – Construction
(a) The general purposes of this Act are to provide for execution within the State
Of the policies embodied in the Federal Civil Rights Act of 1964 and to make uniform the law of those states which enact this Act.
(b) This Act shall be construed according to the fair import of its terms and shall be liberally construed to further the general purposes stated in this Section and the special purposes of the particular provision involved.
Sect. 102. Effective date
This Act takes effect one year after enactment. . .
Chapter 4. Discrimination in Public Accommodations
    Sect. 401. Definitions
    As used in this Act unless the context requires otherwise:
(1) "place of public accommodation" includes any place, store, or other establishment, either licensed or unlicensed, which supplies goods or services to the general public or which solicits or accepts the patronage or trade of the general public or which is supported directly or indirectly by government funds: except that
(1) a private club is not a place of public accommodation if its policies are determined by its members and its facilities or services are available only to its members and their bona fide guests;
(2) "place of public accommodation" does not include barber shops or beauty shops or privately-owned resort or amusement establishments or an establishment located within a building which contains not more than five rooms for rent or hire and which is actually occupied by the proprietor of the establishment as his residence.
Sec. 402. Discriminatory practice
It is a discriminatory practice for a person to deny an individual the full and equal enjoyment of the goods, services, facilities, privileges, advantages, and accommodations of a "place of public accommodation" because of race, color, religion, or national origin.

Fill in the blanks with the correct answer.

1. E. Melvin Porter was born May 22, 1930 in _____, _____.

2. Porter was one of the first African Americans to attend _____ Law School.

3. He was elected president of the Oklahoma City _____ _____ for the _____ of _____ _____.

4. Property tax money is given to local schools, city and county government and _____.

5. In 1964, Porter became the first black man to be elected to the _____ _____ _____.

MAXINE HORNER

BIOGRAPHICAL PROFILE

Maxine Edwyna Cissel was born in 1933 in Tulsa, Oklahoma. Maxine graduated from Booker T. Washington High School. She received a scholarship to attend Wiley College in Marshall, Texas and graduated with an associate's degree. Due to finances, her education had to be put on hold. She returned home and worked to allow her siblings the opportunity to attend college as well. She vowed to return to college one day and obtain her degree. Although she was in her fifties when she returned, Maxine graduated from Langston University with a degree in personnel management. Maxine is married to the late Donald M. Horner and has two children Shari Tisdale and Donald M. Horner, Jr.

LEGISLATIVE TERMS

Maxine was elected to represent her North Tulsa district as a State Senator in 1987. She and Vicki Miles LaGrange shared the title of being the first African American women to serve in the Oklahoma State Senate. This elected position also made Maxine the first African American female from Tulsa to serve in the state senate. Maxine is known for her commitment to education and arts. During her time as a legislator, Maxine was instrumental in passing several key items of legislation. In 1992, the Oklahoma Higher Learning Access Program (OHLAP) was passed. This bill secured scholarship funding for students who maintained a minimum grade point average of 2.5 and completed the program's high school requirements. In addition the student's family yearly income must be $50,000 or less. The scholarship money must be used to attend a college or university in the state of Oklahoma. Maxine also sponsored legislation to create the Juneteenth statewide holiday which is celebrated on the third Saturday of June each year. Due to term limits, Maxine retired from the Senate. She served her district from 1987-2005.

Maxine came from a family of music lovers. In 1988 she sponsored legislation to create the Oklahoma Jazz Hall of Fame, also known as "The Jazz Depot," in downtown Tulsa. Its mission is to improve the quality of life and inspire creativity for Oklahomans through education, preservation and performances of jazz, blues and gospel. Maxine was able to secure $1.5 million in bonds for its improvements. In 2007 the Hall of Fame moved to its 28,000 square foot new home in Tulsa's old train depot. Part of the Hall of Fame's mission is to identify, document, and honor Oklahoma musicians.

SENATOR HORNER SPONSORS JUNETEENTH LEGISLATION

On September 22, 1862, President Abraham Lincoln issued the Emancipation Proclamation, which ended slavery on January 1, 1863. On June 19, 1865, Union soldiers arrived in Texas with news that the Civil War had ended and that two and a half years prior, President Lincoln had freed the slaves in the South.

General Order Number 3 freed the last 250,000 slaves from bondage. Senator Horner sponsored a bill making Juneteenth a statewide holiday in Oklahoma celebrated on the third Saturday of every June. Also known as Freedom Day, it is the oldest celebration of ending slavery in America. It is now recognized as a statewide holiday in 39 states. Some states celebrate a day, a week, or a month. Some areas have resisted the celebration barring the use of public property for the celebration. Some employers were reluctant to grant leave for celebration.

MAXINE HORNER

Use the words from the word bank to complete the sentences.

slavery	improvements	blues	2005	third
grade point average	senator	Wiley College	term limits	
General Order Number 3	Oklahoma Higher Learning Access Program			

1. OHLAP stands for _____.

2. President Abraham Lincoln issued the Emancipation Proclamation on September 22, 1862. This ended _____.

3. After high school Maxine received a scholarship to _____ College.

4. Maxine retired from the Oklahoma legislature due to _____. She retired as an Oklahoma Senator in _____.

5. Maxine was the first African American female _____ from Tulsa, OK.

6. To qualify for the Oklahoma Higher Learning Access Program, the student must maintain a minimum _____ of 2.5.

7. The Jazz Hall of Fame seeks to preserve jazz, gospel and _____ music.

8. _____ freed the last 250,000 slaves from bondage.

9. The Oklahoma Jazz Hall of Fame received $1.5 million for making _____.

10. Juneteenth is a statewide holiday in Oklahoma. Its yearly celebration is held the _____ Saturday each June.

HUBERT AUSBIE

BIOGRAPHICAL PROFILE

Hubert "Geese" Ausbie was born on April 25, 1938 in Crescent, Oklahoma. He was the youngest son of eight children born to Bishop and Nancy Ausbie. Hubert played and excelled in tennis, track, baseball and basketball. Hubert once scored seventy points in a basketball game at Crescent's Douglas High School and assisted the team to win four straight Oklahoma Basketball State Championships. Hubert graduated from high school in 1956 and was offered more than 200 athletic scholarships from major colleges. He accepted a basketball scholarship from Philander Smith College in Little Rock, Arkansas due to its religious affiliation and the fact that his brother Attaway was already attending college there. While attending Philander Smith, Ausbie met and married Awilda Lee. They had four children. After graduating from Philander Smith in 1960, Ausbie turned down a professional baseball offer with the Chicago Cubs and chose to try out for the Harlem Globetrotters basketball team. In 1961, Hubert was chosen over more than 500 players from around the country and was offered a job with the Harlem Globetrotters.

HARLEM GLOBETROTTERS

Hubert had been called "Goose" since his childhood years, but his nickname was changed to "Geese" when he joined the Globetrotters because another veteran player, Reece "Goose" Tatum, already used the name. Because of his natural flair for visual humor, dazzling and irrepressible pranks in addition to his basketball skills, Hubert was known as the "Clown Prince of Basketball" for his entire career with the Globetrotters until his retirement as a player in 1985. Ausbie received a Globetrotters Legends ring. This honor is only given to a few elite former players. During his 24 years of charming crowds, Hubert traveled to over 100 countries on six continents and performed for more than 100 million fans. In 1995 Hubert returned to the Globetrotters as head coach and manager of operations.

AUSBIE'S TV DEBUT

The Harlem Globetrotters expanded into television entertainment. They had their own Saturday morning cartoon show and frequently appeared on ABC's *Wide World of Sports*. This NBC Hanna-Barbera cartoon named *Harlem Globetrotters* aired from September 1970 until May 1973. The cartoon was such a success, in 1979 Hanna-Barbera created a new series, *The Super-Globetrotters*. The basketball stars portrayed undercover superheroes with the ability to fly. When entering magical lockers, they would emerge as heroic Super-Globetrotters. In this series Hubert had cloning powers and carried a shield. His character was known as Multiman. Hubert starred in a children's show called *The Harlem Globetrotters Popcorn Machine* and co-starred in *The Harlem Globetrotters on Gilligan's Island*.

HUBERT AUSBIE

Answer the true - false questions by placing F or T next to each sentence.

1. _____ Hubert was born in Crescent, Oklahoma.

2. _____ Hubert was known as the "Admirable Prince of Basketball."

3. _____ Hubert was offered over 200 athletic scholarships from major colleges once he completed high school.

4. _____ Hubert has been nicknamed Geese since he was a child.

5. _____ In 1961 the Harlem Globetrotters picked Hubert out of a group of over 900 players from around the country.

6. _____ Hubert's cartoon name on the Super Globetrotters was Liquid Man.

7. _____ The Super Globetrotters cartoon ran on television from September 1970 until May 1973.

8. _____ Hubert turned down a contract with the Oklahoma City Redhawks baseball team to allow him to play with the Harlem Globetrotters.

9. _____ Hubert was the oldest of eight children born to Bishop and Nancy Ausbie.

10. _____ Hubert attended the University of Oklahoma after graduating from high school.

11. _____ During his employment with the Harlem Globetrotters, Hubert traveled to over six continents and 100 countries.

12. _____ During the twenty-four years of working with the Harlem Globetrotters, Hubert performed for more than 100 million fans.

13. _____ After joining the Harlem Globetrotters, Hubert used the nickname Geese, because one of the other players already used the nickname Goose.

14. _____ Hubert retired from the Harlem Globetrotters in 1995.

15. _____ Hubert married Awilda. They have eight children.

BIOGRAPHICAL PROFILE

Willa Johnson was born in Longview, Texas on February 26, 1939. Her parents Pearline and Orelious (O.T.) Thompson moved their family to Oklahoma City in 1942, when Willa was three years old. Willa lived in northeast Oklahoma City, growing up in the Edwards addition. Willa attended Edwards Elementary School and graduated from Douglass High School in Oklahoma City. She later attended Rose State College, Central State University, Oklahoma State University and the University of Oklahoma. Willa has three children; Steven, Nikki and Warren. She was employed at Tinker Air Force Base in Midwest City, Oklahoma, for over twenty years. After retirement, Willa began her career in politics. Throughout her campaigning and political career, she coined the phrase "Where there's a Willa, there's a way!"

WILLA SERVES COMMUNITY

In 1993, Willa was elected to the Oklahoma City Council. This made her the first African American councilwoman in Oklahoma. She served Ward 7 for fourteen years. Willa worked on many economic development projects which helped several major businesses locate in her ward. In 2007, Willa was elected to serve as Oklahoma County Commissioner for District One. Her main responsibility was to repair and maintain roads and bridges. District One has over 241 miles of road and has 56 bridges. She is responsible for approximately 41% of the total road miles in Oklahoma County but only receives 1/3 of the available funding. As a result, Willa's office actively pursues grant money and also receives funding from a variety of other sources to include county, state, and federal dollars. Her district ranges from far northeastern Oklahoma County to west of Downtown Oklahoma City.

THE FIRST TEE

Willa is founder of the First Tee Program in Oklahoma City. The program builds character, instills life-enhancing values, and promotes healthy choices for young people through golf. The learning center opened in 2011 at the Douglass Center Park in Oklahoma City. The program consists of a plan called the "Ladder of Achievement," a series of seven levels. Participants meet weekly for eight weeks for classes of 1-2 hours. Upon completion of a level, a test of golf and life skills is given. Participants with passing grades move to the next level. The program provides youth of all backgrounds the opportunity to develop life-enhancing values, perseverance, judgment, and confidence. Membership fees are charged for each session, but scholarships are available.

Douglass Center Park located at 600 N. Martin Luther King in Oklahoma City

WILLA JOHNSON

LEADERSHIP OKLAHOMA CITY (LOKC)

Willa is founder of this nonprofit organization designed to enable people to become effective forces of positive change in their community. The group educates individuals about community needs, resources and opportunities and connects citizens from diverse backgrounds who want to improve their community. Leadership Oklahoma City offers programs for adults, young adults and youth. The Youth Leadership Exchange (YLX) program is for high school sophomores, juniors, and seniors. The Leadership Skills Program does not include high school seniors. It teaches up to 45 class members about personal leadership skills and community service. The Youth in Action program class sessions focus on sophomores, juniors and seniors. It teaches meeting management, fund raising and group dynamics. The Youth Council of Oklahoma City (YCOKC) is for high school juniors and seniors and the group's leaders educate about city government. Eighteen high school students are chosen annually with two representatives from each of the eight wards working with the mayor, city personnel, attorneys, law enforcement, physicians, educators, journalists, and non-profit executives. Applications are mailed to all Oklahoma City high schools or to any individual upon request. Applicant requirements include an overall GPA of at least 2.75, residency in Oklahoma City, and high school junior or senior rank at the time of application.

WILLA JOHNSON
Answer the true false questions below

1. _____ Willa used this slogan during her political campaigns: "Where There's A Willa, There's A Way."

2. _____ The First Tee Program is located on Martin Luther King Avenue in Oklahoma City. The program consists of seven levels known as the "Ladder of Achievement."

3. _____ Willa represented Ward 2 during her term as City Councilwoman.

4. _____ As County Commissioner for District One, Willa is responsible for the maintenance and repair of over 56 bridges.

5. _____ Membership fees are charged for participation in the First Tee program. If children can't afford to pay the fee, they are not allowed to participate.

6. _____ LOKC is a program founded by Willa Johnson. It stands for Leading Oklahoma Kids to College.

7. _____ In order for a person to participate in the YCOKC program, he/she must have an overall grade point average of at least 3.00.

8. _____ Willa graduated from Douglass High School in Wewoka, Oklahoma.

9. _____ Participants in the YCOKC program, must be between the ages of 50 and 75 years old.

10. _____ The First Tee Program has a mission to use golf to promote healthy choices and instill life long values in young people.

RUSSELL M. PERRY

BIOGRAPHICAL PROFILE

Russell M. Perry was born in 1939. He graduated from Oklahoma City's Douglass High School in 1957. Russell attended Maryland State University. He later married Ranola Chappelle and three children were born from this union: Kevin, Velvet and Shannon. Russell M. Perry Ave. in Oklahoma City's Deep Deuce section was named for in honor.

PERRY FILLS A VOID

Perry Publishing and Broadcasting Company (PPBC) is Oklahoma's largest African American owned media company. It consists of *The Black Chronicle*, 12 radio stations, the O'City Source store, and a cable television program (*The Urban Outlet*). Oklahoma City had gone for more than fifteen years without an urban-formatted radio station. In 1993 Russell purchased KVSP 1140 AM. He now owns stations in Oklahoma City, Tulsa, Lawton, Anadarko, and Duncan, Oklahoma. In 2004, Perry Publishing and Broadcasting installed the tallest radio and television tower in Oklahoma. It measures 2,000 feet. In 2007, PPBC purchased radio stations outside the state of Oklahoma. Five radio stations were purchased in Augusta, Georgia, creating the Perry Broadcasting of Augusta division.

THE *BLACK CHRONICLE*

On April 22, 1979, Russell started the Perry Publishing Company. The *Black Chronicle* is a weekly newspaper. His goal was to focus on issues and interests that affect the African American community. The publication serves the entire state of Oklahoma and covers topics of education, health, entertainment, business, politics, sports and religion. It is Oklahoma City's longest running black newspaper.

OKLAHOMA FOOTBALL INTEGRATES

Russell attended high school at Douglass in Oklahoma City. Douglass coach Moses "Pie-Eye" Miller and Capitol Hill coach C.B. Speegle agreed to match the two best football teams in the city. On November 3, 1955, the first integrated football game in the state was held with 6 foot, 175 pound Russell Perry quarterbacking for Douglass and Dick Soergel quarterbacking for Capitol Hill. Douglass' football team was on a 46 game winning streak that dated back to 1952. The crowd of over 10,000 fans packed into the Southside Stadium. The Trojans lost to Capitol Hill that night, 13 - 6. The same year, Douglass High School won the Class AA state championship. Douglass, along with many other all black schools, joined the Oklahoma Secondary School Activities Association (OSSAA) in 1956. The Douglass-Capitol Hill game made history; this game was so significant that each schools' stadium was named after the coaches of the teams; Moses F. Miller Stadium and C.B. Speegle Stadium.

Perry owns many businesses like these on NE 23 in Oklahoma City

RUSSELL M. PERRY
Circle the correct letter to answer the multiple choice questions below.

1. Russell Perry attended this high school.
a. Millwood High School in Oklahoma City
b. Douglass High School in Oklahoma City
c. Booker T. Washington High School in Tulsa, Oklahoma

2. Russell played in the first integrated football game in Oklahoma. They played against this school
a. Capitol Hill High School
b. Northeast High School
c. Lawton Ike High School

3. *The Black Chronicle* newspaper was started in what year
a. 1952
b. 1979
c. 1993

4. Douglass High School joined the OSSAA in 1956. OSSAA stands for this
a. Oklahoma Stadiums Section for Aquatic Athletes
b. Oklahoma Secondary Sports for African Americans
c. Oklahoma Secondary School Activities Association

5. Russell attended this University
a. Maryland State University
b. Langston University
c. The University of Oklahoma

6. Perry Publishing and Broadcasting installed the tallest radio and television tower in Oklahoma in
a. 1993
b. 2004
c. 1955

7. Russell M. Perry Avenue is located in this section of Oklahoma City
a. Capitol Hill
b. Carverdale
c. Deep Deuce

8. Russell's high school football coach was Moses "Pie-Eye" Miller. This was named after him at Douglass
a. Baseball Stadium
b. Football Stadium
c. Cafeteria

9. In 2007, Russell Perry purchased radio stations outside the state of Oklahoma. The name of the state is
a. Texas
b. Kansas
c. Georgia

10. This many fans attended Oklahoma's first integrated football game at Capitol Hill's Southside Stadium
a. 10,000
b. 500
c. 100,000

BIOGRAPHICAL PROFILE

Horace Stevenson was born in Elmore City, Oklahoma in 1939. Elmore City is 63 miles south of Oklahoma City. His family later relocated to Oklahoma City. Horace grew up in the old fairground area and graduated from Douglass High School in 1957. He attended Oklahoma City University and pursued a degree in Business Administration. Horace began his career in food service at Jack Sussy's Restaurant, later becoming head waiter at Oklahoma City's Sportman's Country Club in 1958. Horace married Jean in 1959. They have been married for 52 years and have four children.

FIRST AFRICAN AMERICAN McDONALD'S FRANCHISEE IN OKLAHOMA

Horace's dream to become a business owner goes back to when he was only in the sixth grade. In 1953, he was a member of the Douglass High School character building club, Jr. Sr., HI-Y. In 1968, he opened Horace's Grill. The restaurant was located in the predominately black community in Oklahoma City. He then purchased and operated Cherry's Cafeteria in 1969 and from there went on to manage the OCCE Cafeteria on the University of Oklahoma's campus in Norman, Oklahoma. He remained there 1974 – 1977. His relationship with McDonald's began on August 7, 1977. He joined the McDonald's Management Program. There, Horace focused on two goals: to become an owner/operator within ten years and to retire in twenty years. During the next ten years Horace worked his way into mid-management and reached one of his goals in 1987, purchasing his first McDonald's franchise. Horace moved to Tulsa, Oklahoma in 1990 and opened three McDonald's restaurants but moved back to Oklahoma City in 1999 to enjoy his retirement. The life of his retirement was short, as he purchased three restaurants within weeks. In 2010, Horace purchased four more stores, all of his franchises are located in the Oklahoma City area. In 2011, he sold one of his McDonald's stores to one of his daughters. He now is owner/operator to six McDonald's, with a goal of owning ten. Owner of H&J Management, Horace's secret to success is hard work, setting goals, and not giving up until you reach them.

HORACE'S RECOGNITIONS

Horace is a man of few words but his actions are many. He is a giver and serves on numerous boards and charities. Horace participates in the Ronald McDonald House Children's Charities and the First Tee golf program. He serves on the board of the American State Bank, YMCA, National Black McDonald's Operators Association and McDonald's Co-Op. He has been Businessman of the Year three times, Retailer of the Year, and Minority Employer of the Year. He and Jean are lifetime members of the Oklahoma City Urban League.

HORACE STEVENSON

HORACE STEVENSON

Find the words below in the word search puzzle below.

MCDONALDS	MANAGEMENT	GOALS
RONALD MCDONALD HOUSE	HARD WORK	ELMORE CITY
BUSINESS DEGREE	TEN RESTAURANTS	H J MANAGEMENT
HORACE	STEVENSON	CAFETERIA
DREAM	FRANCHISE	FIRST TEE

```
I M C E I O E T N S E S O E E A P E T Z
I C A E R T O K G P O X M Q U H S H N W
E C K M S T Z C D S Y I I E J E F L G O
D N H N X P E P E I N A L N G A Z P E N
P C A Y S L A O G M S P A S N N W O S X
P Z R V G S Q T L G A E O A L X T W E C
S S D L A N O D C M A N N W M M S E L E
S T W J A E D S Q E X Q A E I I T E M H
I N O T N T C E G E E D O G E N J S O Q
O A R E H A Z A R N T E E Y E D D I R C
Z R K U A L E R R A Q S T M N M A H E Q
E U J S O I O M O O O S E T I G E C C L
C A Y F P I R S G T H G T G S R I N I G
R T O W T L E E B D A E W E V R S A T X
H S T G S E L T T N M I X T V C I R Y E
T E W F R R G G A E E A A S N E O F T Q
T R I J J S E M J L F U E S O X N E G P
F N A G E P J C S U H A R R T S Z S Q N
E E S U O H D L A N O D C M D L A N O R
T T B J B U S I N E S S D E G R E E M N
```

AL DOWNING

BIOGRAPHICAL PROFILE

Al Downing was born on January 9, 1940 in Centralia, Oklahoma. Big Al was one of 14 children. He had 11 brothers and two sisters. His family worked farms; they were sharecroppers and very poor. They would sometimes look for herbs used to make medicines and sell them at the market. Al recalls being hungry many times and having to share one pair of shoes with several siblings. They would take turns and if it wasn't their day they had to go barefooted. His early years were spent tending to horses and cattle.

A JUNKYARD PIANO

Al's first love for country music came while listening to trucker's music as he and his family were loading hay. He spent his early years listening to country music and felt that a black guy could achieve success as a country musician. One day Al and his brother stopped by the junkyard. There was an old piano there but several keys were missing. Only 40 of them worked. Al took the piano home and by the time he was 10 years old, he was teaching himself to play it. Al decided to put his radio on top of the piano. When his family listened to the radio, he would listen and pick out the music on the keys of the piano. Four years later he was performing at community and high school functions. Al's first musical experience came when his father and brothers started a gospel quartet. He mastered being a musician, songwriter and entertainer. Big Al said, "I grew up in Oklahoma hauling hay, riding horses and doing all the things country folk do. So how can anyone say Country music is white?" He had great success in not only country music, but also R&B, rock-n-roll, rockabilly, and disco. In addition to his love of music, Big Al enjoyed gardening, fishing and woodwork.

MAKING HIS MARK ON THE WORLD

Big Al's early influence was Fats Domino. His parents arranged for him to take piano lessons from an elderly lady. Once she heard Al play, he was told to "get up and get out." She said, "Look, that's a gift that God gave you what you're doing, and I'm not going to touch it." He entered a local radio contest and his Fats Domino impression of Blueberry Hill won him first prize. After the contest, a local singer, Bobby Poe, asked Big Al to join his band. He gave up a basketball scholarship offer to attend Kansas State University. Al was the only black in Poe's band. Since they played in white establishments, Al couldn't leave the stage to use the "whites only" restrooms. In order to sneak Al into "white only" motels, one of the band members would distract the desk clerk so that Al could go in unnoticed. During the beginning of his career, Big Al made $2 to $5 a night. At seventeen, he became a professional entertainer and scheduled tours all over the world. He toured places such as Sweden, Libya, North Africa, Italy, England, Spain, Holland, Hong Kong, Hawaii, and Guam. These performances earned him lots of awards and recognition. He was admitted to the Rockabilly Hall of Fame. Big Al had lots of big hits. His songs were recorded by Bobby Blue Bland, Fats Domino, Tom Jones, and Webb Wilder. Big Al died of leukemia on July 4, 2005 in Nashville, TN at the age of 65.

BIG AL DOWNING

Name ways in which Al's poverty was described. _____

_____

_____

_____

_____

Describe Al's experience(s) with learning to play the piano. _____

_____

_____

_____

Describe Al's segregation challenges. _____

_____

_____

_____

Write about Al's musical career. Where did he perform, and what were his accomplishments?

_____

_____

_____

_____

BIOGRAPHICAL PROFILE

Don R. Ross was born on March 11, 1941, in Tulsa, Oklahoma. He is the son of Israel Ross and Pearline Vann (Evette) Ross. Don came from a poor family. He remembered not having his own bedroom and having to sleep in the living room. He once visited a friend who had his own bedroom. Then Don went to camp for two weeks, where he had his own room and regular meals. He saw these two experiences as "turning points in his life." He knew he could get these things if he succeeded in life. Don graduated in 1959 from Booker T. Washington High School in Tulsa, Oklahoma. He served in the United States Air Force for four years. In 1963, Don began working at a bakery in Tulsa and became the state's first black union baker in Oklahoma. Don attended the University of Central Oklahoma and earned Bachelor's of Science and master's degrees. He later attended the University of Tulsa College of Law, Rutgers University and Columbia University. Don has five children: James, Reginald, Ronald, Edward and Donna.

OKLAHOMA LEGISLATURE

In 1982, Don was elected to the Oklahoma State Legislature. During his over 18 years of service, his main focus has been affirmative action, education, the arts, economic development, and labor relations. He has authored Oklahoma's first affirmative action law which establishes preferences for minority vendors. He also helped to establish a state holiday for the birthday of Dr. Martin Luther King, Jr. Don has been named "legislator of the year" 13 times.

UNCOVERING TRUTH ABOUT RIOT

Don was one of the first journalists to write about the Tulsa Race Riot. He was known for uncovering the truth about one of the most violent race riots in American history. For more than fifty years, the riot was hushed up. Some criticized Don for "opening old wounds." In 1997, he drafted a bill that created the Tulsa Riot Commission to investigate the riot. During the 75th anniversary ceremony, a ten-foot granite monument was dedicated. "The Black Wall Street Memorial" has the names of over 200 black-owned businesses inscribed upon it. The memorial represents businesses destroyed as a result of the riot. In memory of the riot, Don wrote, "To escape white violence, many of Tulsa's African Americans had been chased from everywhere. Their bravery was an obligation of pride. In black history, Greenwood's last stand is as symbolic as the Alamo is to American history. They may have been overpowered and imprisoned in concentration camps, but they never surrendered their hearts, minds and tenacious resilience." In 2003 Don wrote a book about the Tulsa race riot titled *A Century of African American Experience – Greenwood: From Ruins to Renaissance.*

Don R. Ross poses with George Curry beside the memorial he helped create.

DON R. ROSS
Answer the multiple choice questions below by circling the correct letter.

1. Don attended this college in Tulsa, Oklahoma
a. University of Tulsa College of Law
b. Langston University College of Law - Tulsa Campus
c. Tulsa Lawyer's University of Greenwood

2. The Tulsa riot was hushed up for more than _____ years. Some Tulsa history books omitted the riot altogether.
a. 100
b. 10
c. 50

3. Don was one of the first _____ to write about the Tulsa race riot.
a. attorney's
b. journalists
c. Senators

4. Don wrote a book about the Tulsa race riot titled *A Century of African American Experience – Greenwood: From Ruins to Renaissance*
a. 1921
b. 2003
c. 1959

5. Don was one of the key organizers for the 75th anniversary of the 1921 Tulsa riot. During the ceremony this was revealed.
a. Don's new family home
b. a picture of the University of Oklahoma
c. The Black Wall Street Memorial - a ten foot granite monument

6. In 1959, Don graduated from this Oklahoma high school.
a. Booker T. Washington
b. Union High School
c. Sapulpa High School

7. Don became Oklahoma's first black union baker in
a. 1961
b. 1963
c. 1982

8. In 1997, Don wrote a bill that created the Tulsa Riot Commission. The purpose of the commission was to
a. find the names of the individuals responsible for the riot
b. investigate the riot of 1921 and find out what happened
c. organize a celebration for the survivors

9. Don was named this 13 times during his legislative service
a. journalist of the year
b. father of the year
c. legislator of the year

10. Some criticized Don during his efforts to find out the truth about the riot saying he was
a. opening old wounds
b. not qualified to head an investigation
c. not old enough

LELIA K. FOLEY DAVIS

BIOGRAPHICAL PROFILE

Lelia Kasenia Smith was born on November 7, 1942 and raised in Taft, Oklahoma. She was the youngest of 10 children born to Willie and Canzaty Smith. Willie was a sharecropper and Canzaty was a midwife. The large family was very poor but displayed generosity to others, once taking in a homeless family. Canzaty would often accept food in place of her $15 midwife fee for delivering babies. Lelia graduated from Moton High School in 1960. She was a divorced mother of five when she ran for a position on the Taft school board. She lost the election but soon after reading a book about A.J. Cooper, mayor of Pritchard, Alabama, she was inspired to run for mayor of Taft. On April 16, 1973, she was elected to the office of mayor to the all-black town of Taft, Oklahoma. She became the nation's first elected African American woman to serve as mayor. Taft's local highway signage proclaims the town "Lelia Foley Davis Home Place."

LELIA'S SPECIAL MISSION

Lelia's upbrining impressed on her the importance of caring. There are two areas in Taft, Oklahoma that have unclaimed/unmarked graves. The small grassy area surrounded by a chain link fence formerly known as the Institute for Colored Deaf, Blind and Orphans (DB&O), now known as the Eddie Warrior Correctional Center. When the institute was created by the Oklahoma state legislature in 1907 it was an orphans' home. A 1937 publication states the home had 344 black children up to age 16. Foley Davis states that many of the children that lived there were not really orphans, but rather their parents simply could not care for or provide for them and left them at the home. The children are buried in the fenced-in area with no names and no markers. Down the road there is another chain-link fenced area with unmarked children's graves. This area was for residents of a mental institution for blacks that is now the home of the Jess Dunn Corrections Center. There are efforts being made to raise funds to put memorial markers for both areas. Requests to state officials are being made seeking permission to put markers there.

A MAYOR'S JOB

The mayor can't hold another public office. They enforce regulations, laws, policies and procedures. They assign employees and work to individuals, negotiate and execute contracts, review accounts and funds, and appoint persons to serve on boards and commissions.

LELIA K. FOLEY DAVIS
Write a paragraph about the DB&O Institute.

_____

_____

_____

_____

_____

_____

Answer the multiple choice questions by circling the correct letter.

1. Lelia was born in Taft, Oklahoma. She was the youngest of 10 children. Her father made a living as a
a. truck driver
b. dairy worker
c. sharecropper

2. Lelia K. Smith graduated from this high school
a. Taft High School
b. Moton High School
c. Eddie Warrior High School

3. The sign on the local highway into Taft, Oklahoma reads
a. Welcome to Taft, Oklahoma
b. Looking for a mayor
c. Lelia Foley Davis Home Place

4. Lelia's mother Canzaty was a midwife. She sometimes accepted this as payment instead of her usual $15.00 fee.
a. medical supplies
b. food
c. farm equipment

5. A.J. Cooper's book inspired Lelia to do this
a. run for town mayor
b. open a day care for orphans
c. raise funds to buy memorial markers for the graves

KENNETH C. WATSON

BIOGRAPHICAL PROFILE

Kenneth C. Watson is a native of Shawnee, Oklahoma. Kenneth is a third generation Oklahoman. Kenneth graduated from Shawnee High School. He later attended Langston University (LU) starting on the LU football team. Kenneth earned a bachelor's degree in history. In 1966, he relocated to Cleveland, Ohio. In 1975, he obtained his Juris Doctor Degree from Cleveland State University, Cleveland Marshall College of Law. Kenneth married Rita James. They have one daughter, Shanna, and one grandson.

WATSON'S LEGAL EXPERIENCE

After being admitted to the Ohio Bar Association in 1976, Kenneth served as a municipal prosecutor in Cleveland, Ohio for five years. He was admitted to the Oklahoma Bar Association (OBA) in 1981. Kenneth worked in Oklahoma County as a criminal trial litigator for 18 months. He then went in to private law in 1983 where he practiced in Oklahoma County for 23 years. He was very committed to providing his clients with the best possible legal representation. In 2006, Kenneth was elected to serve the community members of the Seventh Judicial District as Oklahoma County District Judge. In 2010 he was recognized by the Black Lawyer Association as their Champion of Justice recipient.

PROUD LANGSTON TIES

Kenneth is a very proud Langston Lion and is an avid supporter and life member of their Alumni Association and former president of the Langston University Booster Club. He helped to establish the Langston University Sports Hall of Fame. Both of Kenneth's parents are graduates of LU and are former professors. Kenneth also worked as an adjunct professor at Langston University School of Business for 10 years. In March of 2007, Kenneth was the keynote speaker at Langston's Founder Day Celebration. There he was presented with the LU Distinguished Alumni award.

JUDGE WATSON GIVES BACK

Judge Watson is a member of the national and state bar associations as well as the Oklahoma City Black Lawyers Association. He participates in their annual Law Day activities. In 1961 a Joint Resolution of Congress created Law Day as a "celebration by the American people in appreciation of their liberties and the reaffirmation of their loyalty to the United States" and as an occasion for "rededication to the ideals of equality and justice under laws." In 2011 the OBA offered many activities to benefit and educate the community, including the popular Ask a Lawyer Program where the public can receive free legal advice from volunteer attorneys. The Central Oklahoma Association of Legal Assistants sponsored 10 high school students on a tour of the Oklahoma County Courthouse. These students also attended the Law Day Luncheon. There were also Civic Speakers and a Moot Court Team at Douglass High School. Law Day activities and themes vary each year. Since becoming an Oklahoma County District Judge, Watson holds an annual court docket at local high schools. This practice gives area youth an opportunity to observe how the judicial system works. He is also an active supporter of the St. John Boot Camp, a summer military camp for youth which teaches discipline and respect. He also serves on the Board of the Ralph Ellison Friends of the Library.

KENNETH C. WATSON

Write paragraphs to answer the questions. Then answer the true – false questions.

1. Judge Watson participates in Law Day activities each year. Write about how Law Day Celebration began. _____

_____

_____

_____

2. Kenneth Watson is an avid supporter of Langston University in Oklahoma. Write about his ties to this University. _____

_____

_____

_____

3. Name some of the jobs Kenneth Watson has held that involve the legal field.

_____

_____

_____

4. When Kenneth was adjunct professor at Langston University for 10 years. He taught students about this subject. _____

5. Write about some of the Oklahoma Bar Association's Law Day activities for 2011.

_____

_____

_____

6. _____ Attorney Watson practiced law in Oklahoma County for 23 years.

7. _____ Kenneth Watson was admitted to the Oklahoma Bar Association in 1981.

8. _____ Kenneth Watson received his Juris Doctor Degree from Langston University in 1975.

9. _____ Kenneth Watson once worked at the Oklahoma Metropolitan Library System at the Ralph Ellison branch.

10. _____ The St. John Boot Camp is a summer military camp for young people.

BIOGRAPHICAL PROFILE

Judy Eason was born on May 21, 1945 in Tulsa, Oklahoma. She is the oldest of four children; Judy has two sisters and one brother. In 1963 she graduated from Booker T. Washington High School in Tulsa, Oklahoma. She recalls her years at the University of Oklahoma (OU). Judy remembers within the classroom and dorms being called the "N" word so many times she almost forgot her name. Her parents insisted on all of their children getting a college degree. Judy disliked the atmosphere at OU, she remembers calling home many times telling her dad the people were mean, seeking her dad's permission to withdraw from school and go home. Her dad did not give in, telling her she would have to finish school. Judy stayed and earned both Bachelor's and Master of Science Degrees in Social Work. While attending college, Judy married OU basketball player Howard Johnson. The marriage lasted 8 months. Her real interest and love for politics came when she met and married her second husband, Oklahoma State Representative and Senator, Bernard McIntyre, in 1971. This marriage ended after eleven years.

WORKING FOR THE BETTERMENT OF FAMILIES OF ALL COLORS

Judy's experience at OU filled her with anger and rage. She had been sheltered as a child and had never realized that people didn't like you because of the color of your skin. Judy began doing the same thing she accused others of – thinking all whites were the same just because some were unkind to her. After college, she got a job in 1967 at the Department of Human Services, Child Welfare Division. She told her supervisor "I will not work with any white families." Surprisingly, she wasn't forced to for a couple of years. Judy isolated herself from other employees, refusing to eat or socialize with them because of the hurt she had experienced earlier in life. It took her a while but she slowly began to understand Martin Luther King's statement, "You don't judge people by the color of their skin, but by the content of their character." Judy spent the next 31 years living by this creed, working for the Oklahoma Department of Human Services, Child Welfare Division. Although she never had children, Judy served for 16 years on the Tulsa Public School Board, acting as President for two of those years.

LEGISLATIVE DUTY

Judy was elected to the Oklahoma Senate District 11. She served in this position for two years. She began serving district 73 in the HouseBoth times she represented part of Osage and Tulsa counties. In 2011, Judy was selected to serve as Democratic Whip.

RESPONSIBILITIES OF A SENATOR

The State Senate is the upper house. They write and vote on laws and make changes to the Oklahoma Constitution. The 48 Senators are elected to four year terms and meet in regular session from February to May. The Governor may call special sessions if needed. Candidates must be at least 25 years old at the time of election, live in the county they wish to represent, and cannot be found guilty of a felony. No one can serve more than twelve years in the Oklahoma State Legislature. The Democratic Whip helps the Democratic leadership manage the party's legislative program on the House floor. They also keep track of legislation and ensure all party members are present for important votes.

MARTIN LUTHER KING, JR. HOLIDAY

President Ronald Reagan signed a new holiday bill declaring Dr. King's birthday a federal holiday. The bill was signed on August 27, 1985. The holiday isn't observed on the actual birthday of Dr. King but rather on the third Monday of January, his birthday month. Federal employees began observing the new holiday in 1986. Oklahoma Senator Bernard McIntyre, former husband of Judy Eason McIntyre, authored Senate Bill 133 which sought to eliminate Columbus Day and replace it with a holiday to honor Dr. King. Oklahoma Governor George Nigh later signed the bill making its observance a state holiday, saying to set aside a day honoring Dr. King is the highest honor a government can give. The first Oklahoma celebration for the event would have been Dr. King's 57th birthday.

KOMEN ADVOCACY DAY

In August of 2006, Judy was diagnosed with breast cancer after having a routine mammogram. She made the decision to have a double mastectomy to decrease the chances of the cancer returning. Chemotherapy or radiotherapy were not needed. While hospitalized, Judy received a visit from the Susan B. Komen for the Cure organization. Judy knew she was destined to raise the awareness of breast cancer. She and Oklahoma State Representative Lucky Lamons of Tulsa co-authored legislation to bring awareness to allow women greater access to breast cancer education, screening, treatment programs, and needed funding. Representative Lamons wife was also diagnosed with breast cancer and is now cancer free. Judy is also an officer with the group Soulful Survivors. The group incorporated in January of 2011. It is a group of seventeen African American females who are all breast cancer survivors. They meet monthly at the Rudisill Library in Tulsa, OK.

WHAT IS KOMEN FOR THE CURE ?

Nancy Brinker had promised her sister, Susan G. Komen, who was dying from breast cancer, that she would vigorously fight to end breast cancer forever. In 1982, a global breast cancer movement was launched. Komen for the Cure is the largest grassroots network, composed of breast cancer survivors and activists fighting to save lives, search for cures, and ensure quality care for those needing it.

A STATE GOSPEL SONG

In 2010, Judy introduced Senate Bill 73 to make "Swing Low, Sweet Chariot" the state's official gospel song. The song was written by Oklahoman Wallis Willis who was a Choctaw freedman who lived in Indian Territory before 1862. Judy even sang verses of the song to the other senators as she lobbied to get the bill passed. In 2011, Governor Mary Fallin signed the law making it official. Other state emblems include: Country and western song, "Faded Love" by John and Bob Wills; Song/anthem: "Oklahoma!"; Rock song: "Do You Realize?" by the Flaming Lips; Beverage, Milk; Insect, Honeybee; Tree, Redbud; Flower, Oklahoma rose; Bird, Scissor-tailed flycatcher; Fruit, Strawberry; Vegetable, Watermelon; Rock, Rose rock; and Floral emblem, Mistletoe.

Senator Judy Eason McIntyre in the state capitol rotunda with "Strength In Pink". Law makers officially declared April 21, 2009 as the first ever Breast Cancer Awareness day in Oklahoma.

SENATOR EASON McINTYRE WILL NOT SEEK 2012 RE-ELECTION

Senator Judy Eason McIntyre announced in January 2011 that she would not seek re-election of her Senate seat. She had served the state by completing two years in the Oklahoma House and eight years in the Oklahoma Senate. She shared that she was excited at the opportunity to do something different and stated she had "a bucket list of things she wants to do." Judy expressed an interest in travel, volunteer work and artwork.

JUDY EASON McINTYRE
Circle the number that corresponds with the true sentences.

1. Judy Eason McIntyre graduated from the University of Oklahoma.

2. The Governor of Oklahoma appointed Judy to the United States Senate.

3. Judy worked on the Tulsa Public School Board for 16 years.

4. Judy got a job at the Department of Human Services, Child Welfare Division in 1967.

5. Columbus Day and Martin Luther King Jr. Day are celebrated on the same day.

6. Former Oklahoma State Representative and Senator, Bernard McIntyre, married Judy in 1999.

7. A Democratic Whip is what was used on former slaves.

8. The official Oklahoma fruit is the pomegranate.

9. Susan G. Komen was a personal friend of Judy's

10. The first Oklahoma Breast Cancer Awareness day was April 21, 2009.

11. Senate Bill 133 was authored by Senator Bernard McIntyre. It is a bill to make Martin Luther King, Jr.'s birthday a state holiday.

12. Senator Judy Eason McIntyre will run for re-election in 2012 because she still has a lot of things she would like to do.

13. Senate Bill 73 was introduced to make the official state gospel song "Swing Low, Sweet Chariot."

14. Nancy Brinker is Susan G. Komen's mother.

15. To become an Oklahoma State Senator, you must be at least thirty years old.

JUDY EASON MCINTYRE

Fill in the blanks with the correct answer.

1. Judy plans to do these things once she retires from the legislature _____ _____.

2. The Oklahoma Constitution allows for this many senators in the state _____.

3. Judy served as Oklahoma state senator for _____ years.

4. Twelve years is the longest a person can serve in the Oklahoma State _____.

5. The governor can call these _____ _____.

6. Judy and representative _____ _____ co-authored breast cancer legislation.

7. Swing Low, Sweet _____ has been introduced in Senate Bill 73 to become the official Oklahoma gospel song.

8. In order to run for Oklahoma state senate, the person must live in the _____ they wish to represent.

9. The Oklahoma state senate's regular session begins in _____ and ends in _____ _____.

10. The member's of the Oklahoma senate are responsible for writing _____.

11. Judy has followed this statement spoken by Dr. Martin Luther King Jr., You don't _____ people by the color of their skin, but by the _____ of their _____.

12. Governor _____ signed legislation to make Martin Luther King Jr.'s birthday into a state holiday.

13. Judy was born on May 21, 1945, in _____ Oklahoma.

14. Representatives for District 73 represent Oklahoma state residents in these two counties, _____ and _____.

15. The Soulful Survivors are a group of African American women who have survived _____ cancer.

SUSAN WOODARD BRAGG

BIOGRAPHICAL PROFILE

Susan Woodard was born on April 21, 1949 in Wichita, Kansas to A. Price Woodard, Jr. and Bernice Jefferson Woodard. Bernice was a school librarian while Susan's father's and grandfather's chosen profession was law. In 1968 her father became the first black mayor of Wichita. In 1970 Susan received a degree from Wichita State University and spent two years teaching school. She met and married Leon Bragg and they had two children, Amber and Leon, Jr. The family moved to Oklahoma so Leon, Sr. could complete dental school. Susan decided to follow in her father's and grandfather's footsteps and become an attorney. In 1979 she earned her Juris Doctor from the University of Oklahoma. Susan was licensed in the courts of Oklahoma and the Western District of the United States District Court. Judge Susan L. Woodard Bragg passed on July 17, 2005 after a courageous battle with cancer. Dr. Leon D. Bragg, Sr. continues his career in dentistry. Both children chose the career paths of their mother and grandparents – Leon D. Bragg, Jr. is a practicing attorney and Amber is employed as an educator.

SUSAN'S SERVICE OF JUSTICE

Susan's legal career began as a staff attorney for an Oklahoma City law firm. She also taught at South Oklahoma City Junior College. Susan was selected in 1981 to join the Oklahoma County District Attorney's office working under the leadership of Oklahoma County District Attorney Bob Macy. During her tenure Susan served in the Juvenile, Civil, and Felony Divisions and also lead the Juvenile Division for two years. In 1988, due to her legal experience and excellent knowledge of the law, Susan was appointed Special Judge of the Oklahoma County District Court, serving until 1995. Judge Bragg heard misdemeanor juvenile and domestic cases. With the support of her husband Leon, and Judge Charles Owens, Judge Bragg made the decision to venture into politics. Judge Charles Owens announced his retirement and Judge Bragg fought and successfully won election to his office, making her Oklahoma's first black female district judge in the State of Oklahoma. On January 1, 1999, Judge Charles Owens, who was Oklahoma's first black male district judge, swore in Judge Bragg. She was later re-elected to serve a second term and continued serving this term until her death.

BRAGG STRIKES JURY PANEL

An African American woman had been charged with drug trafficking in 2000. The racial makeup of the jury consisted of 32 whites, 2 other minorities and 1 black. District Judge Bragg dismissed the pool of jurors saying that blacks were underrepresented 34 to 1. Oklahoma County District Attorney Bob Macy asked the appellate court to overturn the order but the court refused the case. Representative Opio Toure felt a built-in bias in the jury selection system allows prosecutors to exclude minorities from juries. Representative Toure, who is also a former public defender and attorney, began his focus of eliminating discrimination in the legal system in 1994. He attempted to file legislation in the 2001 session of the Oklahoma legislature to address discrimination in jury pool selection.

SERVING HER COMMUNITY

Susan was very active in the community. She was involved in and a member of the Oklahoma City Association of Black Lawyers in addition to the Oklahoma Bar Association. January 13th was proclaimed "Judge Susan Woodard Bragg Day" in Sedgwick County, Kansas. The *Ebony Tribune* newspaper chose her for the "Keeper of the Dream" award and the Oklahoma City Association of Black Lawyers honored her with the first Champion of Justice Award. Judge Bragg was also a member of the Advisory Committee of One Church One Child. The One Church One Child program has a goal of helping African American children become successfully moved from foster care into permanent adoptive homes in a timely manner. They strive to ensure permanency for African American children.

ANSWER THE TRUE–FALSE QUESTIONS BELOW

1. _____ Susan Woodard was born to A. Price Woodard Jr. and Bernice Jefferson Bragg.

2. _____ Judge Susan Bragg was the first female African American elected to become judge in the Oklahoma County District Court.

3. _____ The One Church One Child program has a goal to make sure each child has at least one sibling in the home.

4. _____ Susan was in dental school when she met her future husband, Leon Bragg.

5. _____ Susan's father was the first black mayor in Oklahoma City, Oklahoma.

6. _____ Susan was attending school to become a dentist, but later dropped out in order to join her husband in Oklahoma to raise their family.

7. _____ Former Oklahoma County District Attorney Wes Lane appointed Susan prosecutor in 1981.

8. _____ In 1981 Susan taught at Rose State College.

9. _____ Judge Susan Bragg, Oklahoma's first black female District Court Judge was sworn into her position by Charles Owens, Oklahoma's first black male District Court Judge in 1999.

10. _____ Susan Woodard Bragg earned her Juris Doctor from the University of Chicago in 1979.

11. _____ Judge Susan Bragg was once head of the Juvenile Courts Division in Oklahoma.

12. _____ Susan's mother was the first principal at her high school in Wichita, Kansas.

13. _____ When Susan was elected district judge she won the election against Judge Charles Owens.

14. _____ In 2000, Judge Bragg made the decision to dismiss the pool of jurors that were chosen for the trial against an alleged drug trafficker because all of the jurors were male.

15. _____ The appellate court overturned Judge Bragg's ruling concerning striking jurors due to blacks being underrepresented and summoned the original jurors back to court.

LEONA MITCHELL

BIOGRAPHICAL PROFILE

Leona Pearl Mitchell was born October 13, 1949 in Enid, Oklahoma. She is the tenth of 15 children born to Pearl Olive Leatherman and Bishop Reverend Dr. Hulon Mitchell. Leona grew up in a home exposed to every kind of musical instrument. All fifteen children either played musical instruments or sang in their father's church and traveled throughout Oklahoma making appearances on radio and television. They were known as "the Musical Mitchells". She received a music scholarship to attend Oklahoma City University. She received her bachelor's degree in music in 1971, later enrolling in graduate studies at the Juilliard School of Music in New York City. She has been award honorary doctorates in music from OCU and the University of Oklahoma. Leona's first marriage was in 1971. Two years later her husband was killed in a tragic car accident. While in Los Angeles, Leona met her current husband, Elmer Bush III. He was a public school teacher. They have and has one son, Elmer Bush IV.

KNOWN WORLDWIDE

Leona, an Ethnic Native American with African Ancestry (Chickasaw, Cherokee, Cheyenne/Arapahoe), is known as one of the greatest sopranos to ever perform in the most prestigious opera houses in the world. She remains in high demand for recitals, concerts and television appearances. Leona has appeared on the *CBS Morning Program*, *Merv Griffin Show*, and *Good Morning America*. She has sung in performances at major opera houses all over the world. Leona has sung for four Presidents of the United States: Bill Clinton, Ronald Reagan, Jimmy Carter, and Gerald Ford. In January of 2003 she sang for the new Governor of Oklahoma, Brad Henry. She was also featured during the dedication of the new Capital Dome of Oklahoma. In 2005 Leona participated in Macy's Thanksgiving Day Parade in New York City. Leona has been inducted into the Oklahoma Music Hall of Fame. She is a Grammy-award winner and has released two CDs. Every year Leona, along with the Leona Mitchell Southern Heights Heritage Center and Museum, hosts the Leona Mitchell Music Camp for one week in Enid for youth. The focus is on performing arts with Ms. Mitchell as Master Teacher. The highlight is is a special performance with Leona Mitchell.

MUSEUM TO HONOR LEONA

The Leona Mitchell Southern Heights Heritage Center and Museum in Enid, presents the story of the Ethnic Native Americans, Black Indians and Freedmen from pre-history to the present. Her sister, Barbara Finley, is the Executive Director. They serve as the official repository for the unique history, heritage and memorabilia of those groups. Special collections and exhibits include the Freedmen of the Five Civilized Tribes, Leona Mitchell, and Ethnic Native American Genealogical Research Collections.

LEONA P. MITCHELL
Fill in the blanks to answer the questions correctly.

1. Leona was born to Pearl Olive and Rev. Hulon Mitchell. She was the _____ of fifteen children in her family.

2. She is known all over the world and is one of the greatest African Americans to sing _____ at the opera houses.

3. The Leona Mitchell Southern Heights Heritage Center and Museum opened in October 2001. It is located in _____, Oklahoma.

4. Leona has sung for _____ United States presidents.

5. Leona completed graduate school at the _____ School of Music which is located in New York City.

6. In January of 2003 Leona sang at a special dedication for Oklahoma Governor _____ _____.

7. The Leona Mitchell Music Camp lasts for one _____ each year.

8. Leona attended _____ _____ _____ after completing high school.

9. In November of 2005 Leona participated in the _____ _____ Parade held annually in New York City.

10. Leona and her husband _____ _____ have one child.

11. Leona began _____ at an early age at her father's church in Enid.

12. Leona earned a _____ award for her great singing ability.

13. She received an honorary doctorate in music from these schools _____ and _____.

14. The Leona Mitchell Music Camp is held for youth ages 8 - _____.

15. The higlight of the annual camp is a special performance with _____ _____.

TOM COLBERT

BIOGRAPHICAL PROFILE

Tom Colbert was born December 30, 1949 in Oklahoma City, Oklahoma. He grew up in a poor family, one of five children raised in a single parent home. Tom is a graduate of Sapulpa High School, which is near Tulsa, Oklahoma. During his high school years, Tom's school counselor spoke to his class and advised them to come to her to discuss college options. Tom later went for his visit to the counselor. He was told that the advice was not meant for him, that he should probably enroll in a trade school. Recognizing his need to overcome obstacles and negativity, he enrolled in college. Tom received a bachelor's degree from Kentucky State University in 1973. While there, he was considered "a gifted track star," being named All-American in track and field. He later attended Eastern Kentucky University and earned a master's degree in 1976. He also taught in public schools for a while in Chicago, Illinois. Tom served in the United States Army and received an honorable discharge in 1975. In 1982, Tom attained his Juris Doctor degree from the University of Oklahoma.

GOVERNOR BRAD HENRY APPOINTS JUSTICE COLBERT

On October 7, 2004, Governor Brad Henry appointed Tom as Oklahoma's first African American Supreme Court Judge. While being sworn in, Justice Colbert stated, "There are so many people across this country of all races and nationality that never thought they would live to see this day." He had previously served as Chief Judge of the Oklahoma Court of Civil Appeals and was also the first African American to serve in this position. Before becoming a judge, he worked as general counsel for the Department of Human Services, assistant district attorney in Oklahoma County, and as assistant law school dean at Marquette University Law School in Milwaukee, Wisconsin.

GIVING BACK - BLEAK STATISTICS

Justice Colbert frequently accepts speaking engagements in the community. During one 2008 symposium which was held at the Langston University Tulsa campus, he discussed sobering information. The symposium was entitled, "African American Men at the Corner of Progress and Peril." Justice Colbert stated that black men will be an endangered species by the year 2020, and 4.5 million black males are expected to be in prison. He spoke about the negative impact society has on blacks and that 7 of 10 black babies are born out of wedlock, with only 50% of black high school freshmen expected to graduate. Justice Colbert encouraged the attendees to overcome statistics and persevere. The courage to believe in yourself is most important in order to be successful. Oklahoma Supreme Court Justice Tom Colbert overcame negativity and poverty and managed to succeed.

WHAT IS THE OKLAHOMA SUPREME COURT?

A Supreme Court is the highest court within a jurisdiction. Its decisions are not subject to appeal or reversal by another court unless it involves federal law. The U. S. Supreme Court has jurisdiction over all federal cases. An Oklahoma Supreme Court case that involves federal law, can be appealed to the U. S. Supreme Court.

TRACK AND FIELD MASTERS

Tom participates in the Track and Field Masters Level mentoring program. This program mentors young men in a summer reading program for school-aged children.

ANSWER THE TRUE - FALSE QUESTIONS BELOW

1. _____ Tom Colbert decided to become a high school counselor while in high school.

2. _____ Justice Colbert is the first African American appointed Supreme Court Judge in Oklahoma.

3. _____ Tom was a gifted baseball player in college. He was named All-American.

4. _____ A mentoring program called Track and Field Masters Level is something Justice Colbert enjoys. He mentors young men in reading.

5. _____ The Supreme Court is also known as the "court of last resort."

6. _____ The Oklahoma Department of Human Services once employed Tom as a social worker.

7. _____ Justice Colbert received his Juris Doctor degree from the United States Army.

8. _____ Justice Colbert regularly gives speeches and presentations to the community.

9. _____ Tom was one of five children.

10. _____ Justice Colbert encourages perseverance to overcome obstacles.

11. _____ The United States Supreme Court has jurisdiction over all federal law.

12. _____ During Tom's symposium presentation in 2008, he stated that black men will be an endangered species by 2020.

13. _____ Tom's former occupation was a Tulsa county detention officer.

14. _____ During his high school years, Tom was a hard worker and worked part time as a junior newspaper editor at the *Oklahoma Eagle*.

15. _____ Justice Colbert earned his Juris Doctor degree from the University of Texas.

16. _____ After attending college, Tom briefly taught for a public school in Chicago, Illinois.

17. _____ Justice Colbert was the first black to serve as chief judge of the Oklahoma Court of Civil Appeals.

18. _____ The Track and Field Masters Level program mentors young men and offers a summer reading program.

19. _____ During one of Justice Colbert's speaking engagements, he spoke of a statistic that says 7 out of 10 black babies are born our of wedlock.

20. _____ Tom's high school counselor tried to persuade him to go to trade school instead of college.

Top row: Cecil Dixon, E. K. Russell, Herb Ford, Algie Lawrence, M. O. Nelson, M. A. Franklyn
Bottom row: Willard Jenkins, Carl Holmes, Bob Summers, James Coffey, Charles Wright
Not Pictured: J. H. Young

OKLAHOMA FIRST TO MAKE CHANGE

In 1950, the city of Oklahoma City asked the black community to support an upcoming bond election. The community asked for something in return, diversity. They wanted to see African American men integrated into the Oklahoma City Fire Department. At the time, there were no black firefighters anywhere in the South Central Region; Arkansas, Kansas, Kentucky, Louisiana, Missouri, Oklahoma, Texas or West Virginia. The city's initial response was that "No, we can't do that, we can't do that." But in 1951 officials at the city finally agreed. This decision was before Rosa Parks refused to give up her seat in Montgomery, Alabama, before the Supreme Court ruled in *Brown v. Board of Education*, and before the Oklahoma City National Association for the Advancement of Colored People (NAACP). The community celebrated the integration of the Oklahoma City Fire Department. The Urban League, along with the several key civil rights leaders in the city, selected 12 men to join the firefighters' academy. Practically all of the men already had a college education, and they were all successful in passing the academy requirements. "The Original 12" were hired by the Oklahoma City Fire Department on November 22, 1951. The following men made up the group: James H. Young, Bob Summers, James B. Coffey, Charles Wright, Herbert Ford, Willard A. Jenkins, Marvin O. Nelson, Algie Lawrence, Cecil Dixon, Edward K. Russell, Carl Holmes, and Melvin A. Franklin. The change wasn't easy. Some white counterparts were supportive, but racism was always present. For instance, the communication system was taken out of their truck so they had no way of communicating once they left the station to fight a fire. By 1959 the black firefighters had integrated six fire stations in Oklahoma City.

TROOP AWARDED

The twelve men got statewide attention, even receiving trophies from the insurance commission for three consecutive years noting them as being the best troop in the city. The trophy was to be displayed in their firehouse but was picked up a couple of weeks after receiving it with an explanation that it would be taken to the headquarters. Chief Holmes says years later, when the training center was being cleared out to move to a new location, one worker came and told him about a discovery he had found on the top floor (hardly anyone ever went in there). After describing the find, Chief Holmes knew immediately what it was – the trophy he and his friends had worked so hard to get. It had been desecrated and discarded. It was ultimately restored with Willa Johnson's personal funds and lists the names of the 12 men. The trophy is now displayed at the Oklahoma Firefighters Museum in Oklahoma City.

WHAT IT TAKES TO BECOME A FIREFIGHTER

Being a firefighter is a very important job. You must be between the ages of 18 and 44 years old. You can't have any felony convictions in the last 10 years. You must have an Emergency Medical Technician license and possess a valid Oklahoma driver's license. You have to work as a team and be able to communicate and understand oral and written instructions. You must be willing to work irregular hours and perform a variety of duties. Physical strength and agility are required to perform tasks under adverse and strenuous conditions. Future firefighters must complete a written examination in addition to a physical ability test, successfully complete an oral interview, medical evaluation, and background investigation.

A LOOK AT SOME OF THE WORKING CONDITIONS

Firefighters are subjected to being exposed to the elements for an extended period of time in extreme fluctuation of temperatures. The job is physically demanding and sometimes requires working in 400 degrees plus temperatures. Some calls require working from heights, walking or crawling along dark uneven surfaces, climbing ladders, and operating in close proximity to electrical power lines. They are required to work in unpredictable emergency situations for long periods of time without meals, hydration, medications or rest periods. It is sometimes necessary to make life or death decisions during emergency situations. They are exposed to trauma and burn victims which sometimes lead to exposure of undesirable sights and smells. Firefighters are the first line of defense when flames and other emergencies are threatening lives. They are nicknamed "Oklahoma's Bravest."

DR. CARL HOLMES

Carl Holmes was raised in Oklahoma City's West Town. This was a predominately black community whose boundaries were from Western to McKinley and Reno to Main. Carl remembers groups of kids from his neighborhood swimming in the North Canadian River under the railroad trestle near Western Avenue. His father was instrumental in getting the area's first park installed for the children. He and his wife Marvella have one daughter. Carl Holmes was one of the first 12 African American men to join the Oklahoma City Fire Department in 1951. Carl rose through the ranks and at age 44, he was named deputy chief, assistant to the fire chief. This made Carl second in command to over 1200 personnel in this organization, and the third black in the southwestern United States to ever hold this position. During his tenure, he developed a method to hydraulically remove burn victims from crashes and has lectured at the University of Kansas and other departments all over the nation on this topic. He also redesigned the employment process which has been duplicated by many department's across the nation. Carl was an adjunct professor at the University of Oklahoma and an instructor at Oklahoma State University in Stillwater. Carl has also served as an advisor to many small Oklahoma cities helping to supervise formation of firefighting operations, conducting drills and inspections, and teaching classes. These include Langston, Boley, and Coyle, Oklahoma. Carl's career as a firefighter lasted 30 years. He retired as assistant chief. He received many offers including San Francisco, Los Angeles, and Chicago, but he turned them all down. At the time of his retirement, there were nearly 100 black firefighters in the department. Carl has received numerous prestigious awards and recognitions for his tireless efforts and contributions to our country.

TEACHING OTHERS

In 1991, Carl organized the Carl Holmes Executive Development Institute (EDI). Based at Dillard University in New Orleans, EDI teaches firefighters from all over the world in a five-year program. Over 2,000 have attended the institute. Their mission is "Preparing Tomorrows Leaders in the Fire/EMS Service" with a motto of "All I am...I owe... I live eternally in the red!" Many of EDI's attendees now hold Administrative and Fire Chief positions. Five of the 12 female fire chiefs in the United States have attended EDI.

Above: The new Fire Station #6 opened in Bricktown in 2011 with a display honoring the "Original 12."

Left: Carl Holmes at the original Station #6

THE ORIGINAL 12

Fill in the blanks to answer the questions below

1. Name two sources that submitted the names for the original twelve hirees. _____ _____.

2. Oklahoma was the first state in the _____ to hire black firefighters.

3. The Original 12 were employed with the Oklahoma City Fire Department on this date _____.

4. The city of Oklahoma City solicited support of an upcoming _____ in exchange of integrating the fire department.

5. Six fire stations had been integrated in Oklahoma City by the year _____.

6. The troop gained statewide recognition for their efficiency, then won rights to a _____ for three consecutive years.

7. The new Bricktown Fire Station will have a _____ to honor the Original Twelve.

8. In order to become a firefighter, you have to possess a valid Oklahoma _____.

9. Future firefighters must pass an oral _____, a physical _____ test, medical evaluation and a _____ investigation.

10. Firefighters are the _____ line of defense when flames are threatening lives.

11. The Original 12's trophy is now displayed at the _____.

12. Carl Holmes was one of the first 12 African American firefighters for Oklahoma City. He rose through the ranks and prior to retirement, he realized the position of _____ _____.

13. Oklahoma's firefighter's are nicknamed _____.

14. Carl Holmes organized the Executive Development Institute (EDI). It is an instructional program for firefighters. The institute is now located in _____.

15. The job of a firefighter requires working in temperatures that sometimes reach _____ degrees.

BIOGRAPHICAL PROFILE

Kevin C. Cox was born in 1950. He is a graduate of Bishop McGuinness High School. He later attended Universities in Florida and Georgia and has a Creole heritage. He later married Carlise Ann Washington and they have one son Kenny. Kevin is involved in the community and sometimes serves as referee for local youth sports activities. Kevin Cox's political career began in 1980, when he was elected by the members of District 97 to represent them. Kevin served twelve consecutive two-term sessions, but in 1990 the people of Oklahoma passed a vote to limit legislative terms to 12 years. Due to term limitations, he was not allowed to run again. He is the longest serving African American legislator in the Oklahoma House of Representatives and ranked third in seniority. He also holds the record as the longest serving standing committee chair in the Oklahoma House of Representatives. He has served 24 years in the House of Representatives with 21 of those years as chair of the House Insurance Committee. In November 2004, he concluded his service as an Oklahoma legislator. In 2005, he was awarded an Honorary Doctorate of Humane Letters from Langston University.

BILL NEVER LOST ON HOUSE FLOOR

During his tenure, Rep. Cox never lost a bill he authored on the House Floor. When he ran for the House of Representatives, Cox said, "I promised that I would only serve for the good of our district." During his term he authored hundreds of bills that became law. Many of these bills addressed senior citizens care and rights, human rights, education, economic development, protection of children and prevention of drug abuse in addition to regulating insurance coverage. He credits his success to writing bills which are people-oriented. The Parental Responsibility Act and School Dress Code Bill give local school leaders more authority to control student dress codes in an effort to help end violence. His legislation placed tougher consequences on minor juvenile crimes by holding parents responsible for their children's actions. He supported legislation which prohibited students from carrying beepers/pages into the schools and classrooms. He authored the Bully Prevention Act to curtail bullying in school. Kevin supported giving teachers a $3000 per year raise in an effort to retain the brightest and best teachers. Another law gave Oklahomans a right to sue HMOs that refuse or fail to provide proper medical care to their patients. The Elderly Housing Act made it a felony to inform nursing homes of upcoming state inspections and required nursing homes to increase their staffing levels and properly train staff members. Representative Cox hopes that House Bill 2134, which was signed into law in 1994, will "Put some teeth into existing law in the area of penalty," when it comes to hate crime activities. Hate crime bills were designed to discourage hate groups from expanding in Oklahoma. "All law enforcement agencies shall report to the Oklahoma State Bureau of Investigation (OSBI), incidents of crime, which are apparently directed against members of racial, ethnic or religious groups, and further provide information on the disposition of the reported incident." The law enforcement agency has 72 hours to report any violations to the OSBI. A person found guilty the first time would be charged with a fine of $1000, 1 year of jail time plus 100–300 hours of community service. A subsequent act would create a fine up to $10,000, up to 10 years not subject to probation, and suspended or deferred sentences.

LOWERING THE CONFEDERATE FLAG

Oklahoma State Representative Kevin Cox led the effort to prevent any version of the Confederate flag from flying on the Capitol grounds. A 1988 resolution mandated that the 14 flags that have flown over Oklahoma be displayed at the Capitol, including the Confederate States of America flag. After many protests, the flag was removed. Fifteen years later a bill to restore the display of the 14 historical flags included a specific version of the Confederate flag carried by Cherokee Indians in 1862. This flag was not the one associated with white supremacy groups. Rep. Cox, claimed that "anything dealing with the Confederacy means hatred" and is inappropriate and offensive. He suggested the 14 flags be flown in another location. A compromise placed the 14 flags at the Oklahoma Historical Society's History Center. The amended bill also stated that only flags of the United States and the state of Oklahoma flag be displayed at the Capitol. Cox stated, "The newly-amended bill preserves the state's history and ensures that we will never have the Confederacy flag flown again at our state Capitol."

THE "KEVIN COX – A WORK HORSE AND NOT A SHOW HORSE" AWARD

The Metropolitan Better Living Center created a special award in honor of former Oklahoma Representative Kevin Cox. The award was to recognize his tireless community leadership and his efforts to improve health and wellness for senior citizens in the community. The Metropolitan Better Living Center was created in 1992 with the commitment to improve lives by providing adult day health and social services. Kevin says he feels ". . . humbled and extremely appreciative of this recognition. In all my years of service, I have never been honored in this manner." The first award was given in 2009.

ANSWER THE TRUE FALSE QUESTIONS BELOW

1. _____ Kevin Cox was a graduate of Booker T. Washington High School in Tulsa, Oklahoma.

2. _____ Representative Kevin Cox left the legislature because of term limitations.

3. _____ Representative Cox holds a record as the longest serving black in the Oklahoma House of Representatives.

4. _____ Representative Cox voted for laws allowing for Oklahoma students to carry beepers and pagers to class.

5. _____ Kevin Cox is known for authoring hundreds of bills that later became law.

6. _____ House Bill 2134 gives Oklahomans the right to sue HMO's if they refuse or fail to provide proper medical care to patients.

7. _____ Kevin and his wife have five children.

8. _____ Representative Cox served his district in the Oklahoma House of Representatives for 30 years.

9. _____ Kevin Cox serves in his community and is sometimes the referee for NBA teams.

10. _____ The first "Kevin Cox – A Work Horse and Not a Show Horse" award was given in 2011.

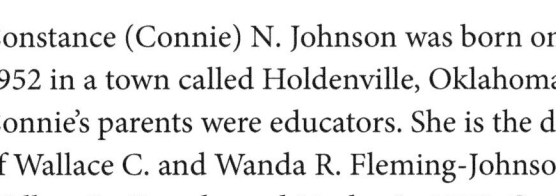

BIOGRAPHICAL PROFILE

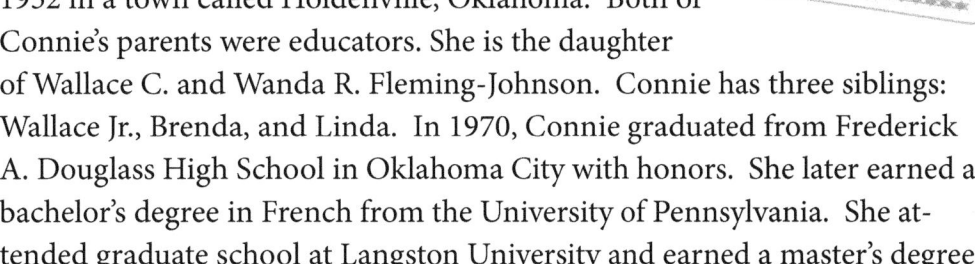

Constance (Connie) N. Johnson was born on May 11, 1952 in a town called Holdenville, Oklahoma. Both of Connie's parents were educators. She is the daughter of Wallace C. and Wanda R. Fleming-Johnson. Connie has three siblings: Wallace Jr., Brenda, and Linda. In 1970, Connie graduated from Frederick A. Douglass High School in Oklahoma City with honors. She later earned a bachelor's degree in French from the University of Pennsylvania. She attended graduate school at Langston University and earned a master's degree in Vocational Rehabilitation Counseling in 2009. Connie has three children.

ELECTED TO SENATE

Constance worked as a senior legislative analyst for the Oklahoma State Senate from 1981-2005. She won the Senate seat to represent District 48 in September of 2005 when the position was vacated by Senator Angela Monson. Constance was re-elected in 2006 and 2010. She feels her 24 years of experience aided her victory. She serves on the following legislative committees: Health and Human Services Appropriations Subcommittee and standing committee, Public Safety, Transportation, Veteran and Military Affairs standing committees. In 2010, the Oklahoma Chapter of the National Association of Social Workers named Senator Johnson Public Official of the Year.

CENTENNIAL PLAZA

In 2006, Senator Johnson and Representative Jabar Shumate co-authored Senate Bill 1919. This bill proposed a monument to the contributions of African Americans to Oklahoma history. As Oklahoma celebrated its first 100 years in 2007, Governor Brad Henry signed the bill into law. The African American Centennial Plaza will be built in the median of Lincoln Boulevard north of the capitol. The plaza will include 21 pieces of art depicting scenes and characters from Oklahoma's African American history. Included will be 51 black towns, Langston University, Tulsa's Black Wall Street, African American military history, and Deep Deuce. Bruce Fisher, son of the late Ada Sipuel Fisher, who represents the Oklahoma Historical Society on the planning committee says, "Oklahoma is going to be on the cutting edge. We are going to be only the second state in the United States to have this type of representation of African Americans on the capitol grounds. It is something that we are going to be absolutely proud of. It will be something that other states will emulate." To date the legislature has rescinded on the donation of the land for the plaza. However, Senator Johnson continues to actively work for the plaza's construction and she feels challenges to its construction will be overcome.

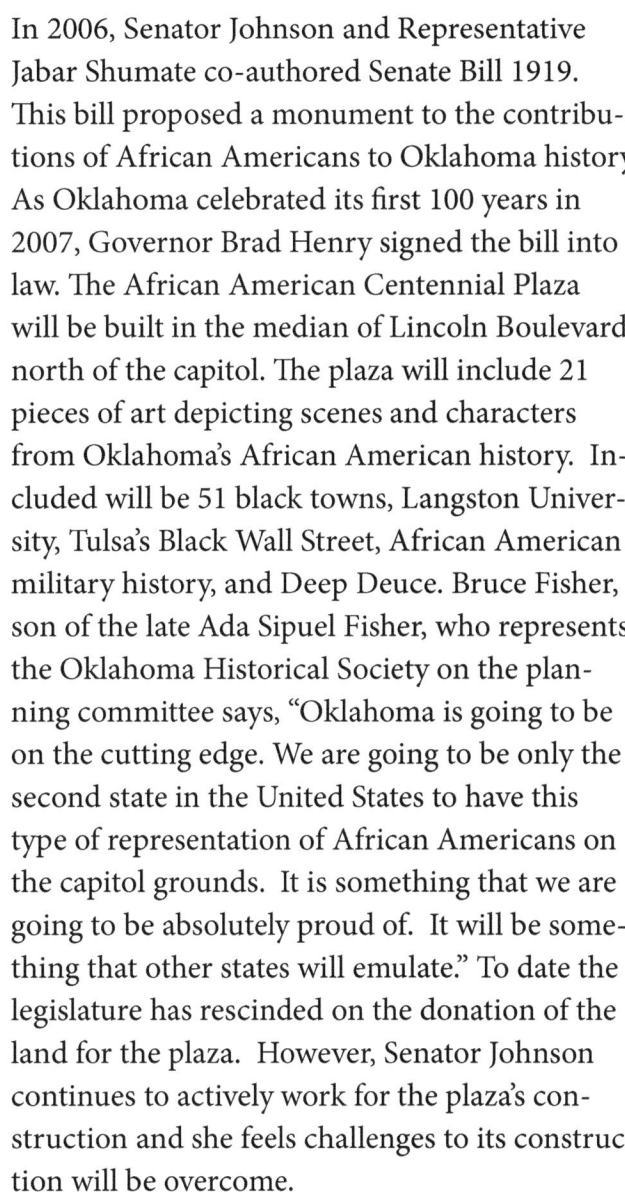

Detail of the African American Centennial Plaza
Copyright Daub Firmin Hendrickson Sculpture Group

CONSTANCE JOHNSON

CONSTANCE N. JOHNSON
Use the words below to fill in the blanks.

veteran & military affairs	Angela Monson	Holdenville	opposition
legislative analyst	public official of the year	Ada Sipuel-Fisher	Oklahoma City
Langston	second	French	Brenda
Clara Luper	Jabar Shumate	Douglass	

1. Connie was born in _____, Oklahoma.

2. Senator Constance Johnson and State Representative _____ wrote legislation for Senate Bill 1919.

3. The African American Centennial Plaza is hoped to be constructed on NE 18th St and Lincoln Boulevard in this city. _____

4. _____ spearheaded private fundraising efforts.

5. In 2005 Constance replaced a vacated seat by this Senator_____.

6. Constance received her master's degree in Vocational Rehabilitation Counseling from this University. _____

7. Constance continues to fight for the creation of the African American Centennial Plaza despite its challenges and _____ .

8. Oklahoma Historical Society's Bruce Fisher is the son of _____.

9. Senator Constance Johnson is a member of these legislative committees: transportation, public safety, health and human services in addition to _____.

10. The organization of The Oklahoma Chapter of the National Association of Social Workers presented Constance with this award. _____.

11. Constance graduated from high school at _____ in Oklahoma City.

12. Constance earned her bachelor's degree from the University of Pennsylvania. It was in _____.

13. Connie has three siblings. Their names are Wallace Jr, Linda, and _____.

14. Connie worked as a _____ for the Oklahoma State Senate from 1981 - 2005.

15. By constructing the African Amerian Centennial Plaza, Oklahoma will be the _____ state in the nation to build something of this nature on the grounds of the Capitol.

The Selmon Brothers

Sharecroppers Lucious and Jessie Selmon had nine children. The Selmon children were raised in a Christian home in Eufaula, Oklahoma where great values were instilled. Three of the Selmon boys attended the University of Oklahoma, where the fearsome trio played defensive linebackers. They are still regarded as the most famous set of brothers in OU history. All three brothers went on to play in the National Football League. The town of Eufaula has changed a local street to "Selmon Drive" and has placed signs throughout town reading "Home of the Selmons."

Dewey Selmon was born in Eufaula in 1953. He was named All-State football player at his high school. In addition to his farm chores, Dewey also cleaned the school, worked as a crossing guard, and still kept up with homework and football practice. Dewey had never eaten in a restaurant until recruiters came to visit during his senior year. In 1976, after playing for OU, Dewey signed with the Tampa Bay Buccaneers. In Dewey's six year NFL career he also played for the San Diego Chargers. After retirement from the NFL, Dewey worked as an oil and gas consultant and later opened a construction company, Selmon Enterprises, Inc. in Norman, Oklahoma. The company became very successful, with over $7 million in annual contracts. Dewey and his wife Kathryn have four children.

Lucious Selmon, Jr. was born in Eufaula. Being the oldest of the trio, he introduced football to his other two brothers. The trio played on the defensive line at the University of Oklahoma in the 1970's. Lucious earned a degree in special education in 1974. He was drafted into the NFL in 1974 by the New England Patriots. He played two years for the Memphis Southmen in the World Football League before returning to OU in 1976 as a defensive line coach. He remained there until 1994. Lucious married Clarice Lawson and they have three children. The recipe for Selmon Brothers barbecue sauce was developed by Clarice, Lucious' wife. The barbecue sauce is manufactured in Oklahoma City and can be found in grocery stores, restaurants, convenience stores and other institutions.

The youngest Selmon, Lee Roy, was born in Eufaula in 1954. He played track, basketball, and football and graduated from Eufaula High School in 1971 as a member of the National Honor Society. He joined his brothers Lucious, Jr. and Dewey on the OU football team. He was the first pick in the NFL draft in 1976. He joined Dewey on the Buccaneers. Lee Roy went to six Pro Bowls and was once Most Valuable Player. In 1984, Lee Roy retired due to a back injury. He was inducted into the Pro Football Hall of Fame and the College Football Hall of Fame. After retirement, Lee Roy was a bank executive and an athletic director in Georgia and Florida. In 2000, Lee Roy opened a soul food restaurant, in Florida with the motto "Cheer Hard, Eat Well." Lee Roy passed away Sept. 4, 2011 at the age of 56.

THE SELMON BROTHERS
Use the words below to fill in the blanks.

OIL GAS	COACH	PROFESSIONAL	DEFENSIVE LINEBACKERS
BACK	DEWEY	EUFAULA	LEE ROY
FLORIDA	CLARICE	CHRISTIAN	HOME OF THE SELMONS
$7 MILLION	SHARECROPPERS	SPECIAL EDUCATION	

1. The Selmon trio were all born in _____, Oklahoma.

2. In 1984, Lee Roy retired from the Tampa Bay Buccaneers because of a _____ injury.

3. This Selmon brother graduated from Eufaula High School in 1971 and was a member of the National Honor Society. _____

4. When college recruiters came to visit, _____ had the experience of eating in a restaurant.

5. Dewey opened Selmon Enterprises, which is located in Norman, Oklahoma. The company has an annual amount of _____ in contracts.

6. The Selmon children were raised in a _____ home.

7. After leaving the World Football League, Lucious returned to the University of Oklahoma to _____ football.

8. Lucious' wife _____, created the recipe for Selmon Brothers barbecue sauce. It is manufactured in Oklahoma City.

9. Lee Roy opened a soul food restaurant named "Lee Roy Selmon's." It is located in _____.

10. After graduating from the University of Oklahoma, all three Selmon brothers played _____ football.

11. In 1984, Dewey worked for an _____ and _____ consultant.

12. The town of Eufaula, Oklahoma is fondly known as _____.

13. The Selmon trio played this position in football at OU. _____

14. Lucious Sr and Jessie Selmon were the parents of nine children, Lucious Sr made his living as a _____.

15. In 1974 Lucious earned his college degree in _____.

VICKI MILES LAGRANGE

BIOGRAPHICAL PROFILE

Vicki Lynn Miles was born on September 30, 1953 in Oklahoma City, Oklahoma. She was born to Charles C. and Mary Greenard Miles who were both educators. She graduated from Douglass High School in Oklahoma City. She later attended Vassar College graduating cum laude in 1974. Vicki received her Juris Doctor degree in 1977 from Howard University in Washington, D.C.. Vicki has one daughter, Johnna.

VICKI'S LOVE OF LAW

Vicki owned a private law firm, Miles LaGrange & Colbert, and practiced law during her term in the Oklahoma Legislature 1986-1993. She prosecuted sex crimes as an assistant district attorney in Oklahoma County. In 1986, Vicki became the first African American female to be elected to the Oklahoma State Senate. She served as chairwoman of the Oklahoma Black Legislative Caucus. She worked as a criminal trial attorney for the United States Department of Justice in Washington, D.C. and was assigned to prosecute Nazi war criminals. President Clinton appointed Vicki to serve as United States Attorney for the Western District of Oklahoma. She was the first African American woman to hold that position, and one of the first female U.S. attorneys in the nation. Vicki now serves as Chief Judge Vicki Miles LaGrange. On November 28, 1994, she was the first African American to be appointed to the federal bench in Oklahoma. President Bill Clinton selected her to serve as Federal judge in the 10th Circuit Court of Appeals. The 10th Circuit Court includes six states: Oklahoma, Kansas, New Mexico, Colorado, Wyoming and Utah.

COURAGEOUS LAWYER AWARD

United States Magistrate Judge K. Couch nominated Judge Miles LaGrange to receive the Fern Holland Courageous Lawyer Award. Judge Miles LaGrange has used her legal expertise to assist Rwanda, Ghana and Liberia. She spent two and ½ years working to restore peace and justice in Rwanda, working 18 – 19 hour days. Nearly one million people were in genocide in Rwanda, 1994. Judge Miles LaGrange and her team had a goal of establishing a court system which was represented by impartial judges who ruled by a code of judicial ethics and conduct. The group led to establish new laws needed to bring Rwanda forward and away from the outdated laws and inadequately funded system. Her nominator states, "Judge Miles LaGrange has worked diligently, far from safety and her home, to make the freedom and opportunities we have here a reality for others…Her work unites her a powerful way with people all over the globe struggling to create and hold faithful to the rule of law."

CO-AUTHOR OF BOOK

Vicki Miles LaGrange is co-author of the book: *A Passion For Equality: The Life of Jimmy Stewart*. The book chronicles the life of Jimmy Stewart. It discusses his struggle to combat racism and poverty and Mr. Stewart's journey from janitor to vice president of one of Oklahoma's most powerful utility companies. The book also tells about others who were instrumental in fighting racism and segregation in the state of Oklahoma. There are numerous photographs included that will help you visualize the era of the civil rights movement.

LAW DAY SPEECH

In a speech for Law Day, Vicki used one of her favorite hobbies–gardening–to inspire the audience. She challenged the audience to "reach out (not just on Law Day) but consistently (and with commitment) to nurture, feed, water, prune, weed, love, encourage, touch, transplant and teach the ropes to just one person" - even if that youngster is "not our own." Vicki's cause is infant and prenatal care. She feels teen-age pregnancy, at-risk African American males, poverty, drug abuse and low levels of education are all linked to African Americans falling behind economically.

VICKI MILES LAGRANGE

Word Search – Find the words in the puzzle.

HOWARD UNIVERSITY **FEDERAL BENCH** **JOHNNA**
JURIS DOCTOR **PROSECUTOR** **CHIEF JUDGE**
LAW DAY **OKLAHOMA COUNTY**
JIMMY STEWART **GARDENING**

```
L I N I O S Z F C R N D M K T U X S O Z
E A R N S K W G H N S I D A I O J H U I
N U W G Y T N U O C A M O H A L K O X I
H T G D L B I H D P T C G P H I D W Q C
I L G C A I S S O I P H S O L T E A T Q
X R B S D Y N O A E Q G M Y E I A R R A
P C E G J F M G D J N A T U U R O D P A
S R F T P E T A R O T C O D S I R U J P
J G R D N D W E T I I X A I S Y K N J H
E D N I F E W F C O H I R T O D S I I A
D V W A D R M G A P F T H N G G S V I C
N Y H A O A R V A X S O E A S I F E M L
L I H P N L E M I R D Y N M O D S R N O
Z A A M Q B S Y L E D E J E E L M S U P
H E E L K E A T R A W E T S Y M M I J E
R T E Z A N R E J B N S N G M T E T O R
C R O T U C E S O R P S K I I L C Y H S
T W T J C H I E F J U D G E N T N T N K
C A C D O N O R R I O E W P E G H R N O
O E J L V L L M H N S P E E C H I V A A
```

OPIO TOURE

BIOGRAPHICAL PROFILE

Opio Toure was born Ezellmo A. Stephens, but later changed his name. Opio was born on March 31, 1954 in Muskogee, Oklahoma. He was the oldest of five children born to Delores J. Carter Stephens. Opio married Linda Ware in 1977 and two sons, Jelani and Jabari were born. Opio received a degree in 1976 from Langston University. Opio went on to earn a Juris Doctor degree from the University of Oklahoma School of Law in 1979. In 2001, Opio received a master of divinity from Phillips Theological Seminary. He served as associate pastor of the St. Paul Baptist Church in Meridian, Oklahoma. Opio died at the age of 53 on February 4, 2008 while waiting for a lung transplant.

ACTIVE IN OKLAHOMA LEGISLATURE

Opio served the Oklahoma Democratic Party from 1994 until 2006. He is former president of Oklahoma City Association of Black Lawyers. Opio served as State Representative for district 99. He was also House Judiciary Committee chair. His legislative career includes writing legislation in 2003 giving those who had been wrongfully convicted and imprisoned the right to claim up to $175,000 in compensation. Opio was a staunchly against the death penalty and authored House Bill 2635 to stop the execution of mentally disabled offenders with an intelligence quotient (IQ) of 70 or below. Later, the United States Supreme Court ruled that executing the mentally disabled was cruel and unusual punishment. This legislation earned Opio the Angie Debo Award from the American Civil Liberties Union in 2002. Debo wrote histories of Native Americans and Oklahoma.

DEDICATION TO LANGSTON

Opio received a bachelor of arts degree from Langston University in 1976. He was a dedicated and proud alumnus, being the recipient of Langston University's Distinguished Alumnus Award. For over 30 years he advocated for the advancement of Langston. He had taken the position of assistant professor at Langston in 2007. He worked hard at developing a Pre-Law Initiative at the University. The program was geared towards interesting more African American students into pursuing law degrees.

MEMORIAL SCHOLARSHIP

The family of Opio Toure created the Opio Toure Memorial Scholarship in his honor. Opio was active in the black community. He left behind his legacy as a church pastor, an attorney, an Oklahoma state representative, husband, father, grandfather, community leader and friend. He valued education, believing all children deserve an opportunity to enhance their lives. The applicant must be a resident of or attend Oklahoma City Public School in District 99. They must be a high school senior with a minimum 3.0 GPA and attend a 4 year university in the state of Oklahoma.

The Opio Toure Memorial Highway, a portion of Interstate 35 in Oklahoma City, was dedicated in October of 2010.

OPIO TOURE
Answer the multiple choice questions below by circling the correct letter.

1. The Opio Toure Memorial Scholarship requires that the applicant
a. has a minimum 3.0 grade point average
b. knows the United State Bill of Rights
c. wants to become an attorney

2. Opio received his bachelor's of arts degree from this university
a. University of Oklahoma
b. St. Paul University
c. Langston University

3. Angie Debo was acclaimed as Oklahoma's "greatest historian." She wrote the history of
a. African Americans
b. Native Americans
c. Hispanics

4. Who created the Opio Toure Memorial Scholarship?
a. Langston University
b. his family
c. the University of Oklahoma

5. Opio was an associate pastor at St. Paul Baptist Church. It is located in
a. Muskogee, Oklahoma
b. Norman, Oklahoma
c. Meridian, Oklahoma

6. Opio authored House Bill 2635. The bill made it illegal to execute people who
a. are African American
b. are mentally disabled
c. choose to go to college

7. Opio's Pre-Law Initiative at Langston University was geared towards
a. African Americans working towards a law degree
b. Native Americans
c. former Oklahoma City University students

8. He formerly served as president of this organization
a. American Civil Liberties
b. Langston University
c. Oklahoma City Association of Black Lawyers

9. Opio earned his Juris Doctor degree from the University of Oklahoma School of Law in
a. 1979
b. 2002
c. 1976

10. Opio was the oldest of _____ children born to Delores J. Carter Stephens.
a. ten
b. four
c. five

ANGELA Z. MONSON

BIOGRAPHICAL PROFILE

Angela Zoe Monson was born in Oklahoma City in 1955. She is the daughter of Herman Sr. and Epron Provo-Monson. Angela has two sisters, LaVonne and Denise, and two brothers, Herman Jr. and Artemus. She attended Oklahoma City Public Schools from kindergarten to 12th grade, graduating from Douglass High School. Angela earned a bachelor's degree in Corrections from Oklahoma City University in 1977, then a master's degree in Public Administration from the University of Oklahoma. After the death of her sister Denise in 1997, Angela took on the responsibility of raising her niece and nephew, Donovan and Danielle Gaddis.

SENATOR MONSON INTRODUCES MENTAL HEALTH BILL

Angela helped pass state laws improving health benefits for people with mental illness. Angela's legislation required insurance companies to provide mentally challenged individuals with equal benefits. Insurance companies would be required to cover treatment and medication for schizophrenia, major depression, panic disorder, substance abuse, schizoaffective disorder and obsessive-compulsive disorder. There were already federal mandates in place to require employers to provide similar coverage.

POLITICS USED TO HELP THE PUBLIC

Angela began her political career in 1990 as a State Representative in Oklahoma. In 1993, she was elected into the Oklahoma State Senate representing District 48. Through her legislative efforts, Angela worked on healthcare reform. She was instrumental in making laws to allow for absentee voting to be held on the Saturday before elections. She also helped to write legislation to put a cap on ATM fees in our state. Senator Monson left the legislature in November 2005 due to term limits.

FIRSTS

Angela is the first woman *and* first African American assistant majority floor leader of the Oklahoma Senate. She is also the first African American woman president of the National Conference of State Legislatures, where state lawmakers meet, discuss and research ideas and issues. In 2009, Angela was elected the first woman and first African American chair of Oklahoma City Public Schools.

SCHOOL BOARD CHAIR

2009 marks the year Angela Z. Monson defeated former Oklahoma City mayor, Kirk Humphries. During her bid for chair, she stated, "We can improve the academic success of our children; we can reduce our drop out rate; we can reduce the rate of suspensions and expulsions; we can hold teachers, administrators and board members accountable for their actions; we can make sure our children understand school is for learning and that they have a responsibility to be the best students they can be. We can be the change we seek - YES WE CAN!" Angela won the election.

ANGELA Z. MONSON

Write T or F on the line next to the statements below.

1. _____ Angela Monson first entered into politics in 2005.

2. _____ Angela graduated from Douglass High School in Oklahoma City.

3. _____ Angela has four children that attend Oklahoma City schools.

4. _____ She was the first African American to become employed at the Oklahoma University Health Sciences Center.

5. _____ Senator Monson represented District 1285 while serving in the legislature.

6. _____ Angela received her master's degree from Oklahoma City Public Schools.

7. _____ Angela represented District 48 while serving as state senator.

8. _____ Angela left the legislature in 2005 because she lost to Oklahoma City Mayor Kirk Humphries.

9. _____ In 2011 Angela was elected to become the first woman and the first African American to chair the Oklahoma City Public Schools.

10. _____ In 1990 Angela became a Oklahoma State Representative.

11. _____ As part of Angela's campaign for school board chair, she said "we can be the change we seek."

12. _____ Angela serves as president of the PTSA at the University Health Sciences Center.

13. _____ She was instrumental in writing legislative language to allow individuals to vote on the Saturday before an election.

14. _____ Angela wrote legislation requiring insurance companies to pay for medical treatment of mental illnesses.

15. _____ Angela was the first woman and first black to have an ATM card.

DAVID B. LEWIS

BIOGRAPHICAL PROFILE

David Blaine Lewis was born 1958 in Ardmore, Oklahoma. He and his wife, Dr. Sharon Lewis, have two children. She is a professor of chemistry at Langston University. He graduated from the University of Oklahoma with a Business Economics degree. In May 1983, Judge Lewis obtained his Juris Doctor degree from the University of Oklahoma College of Law. Upon graduation from law school, Judge Lewis moved to Lawton, Oklahoma to begin his private practice. He continued his practice until 1987. He served as Assistant District Attorney in Lawton for nearly four years. Judge Lewis was appointed to Special Judge in 1991, before his appointment to District Judge by Governor Frank Keating in 1999.

GOVERNOR HENRY MAKES HISTORY

On August 5, 2005, David B. Lewis was appointed as the first African American to serve on Oklahoma's Court of Criminal Appeals. Governor Henry called it an "historic day for Oklahoma." Judge Lewis was sworn in by Supreme Court Justice Tom Colbert, the first African American appointed to the Oklahoma Supreme Court, also by Governor Henry. The Court of Criminal Appeals Presiding Judge, Charles Chapel, stated "if our citizens are to have trust and confidence in the works of the courts, they should see people who look like themselves when they come in contact with the judicial system."

JUDGE LEWIS' HONORS

Judge Lewis has received numerous awards for his dedication to state organizations and other law communities. Some of these include serving as president of the Oklahoma Judicial Conference in 2004, the Oklahoma Access To Justice Commission, the Oklahoma Bar Association Professionalism Committee and the OBA National Mock Trial Task Force. He was selected as a member of the Class of 2008 Henry Toll Fellowship Program of the Council of State Governments. He currently serves on the OBA Bench and Bar Committee and as Board Chairman of the Reach Out and Read Oklahoma Program.

QUALIFICATIONS AND DUTIES OF CRIMINAL APPEALS JUDGE

A candidate for the Oklahoma Court of Criminal Appeals must be at least 30 years of age. They have to be a registered voter in the district they would like to represent for at least a year before accepting the position. The candidate must be a licensed, practicing attorney or judge for at least five years before an appointment. During this time, they must remain certified as an attorney or judge.

DUTIES

The Oklahoma Criminal Appeals sifts through approximately 1,800 cases each year. The cases they hear involve the death sentence and all other cases involving criminal matters. Their jurisdiction comes from the Oklahoma state constitution, which was adopted on September 17, 1907. The court is held in the Oklahoma Capitol Building in Oklahoma City, Oklahoma.

REACH OUT AND READ PROGRAM

The Reach Out and Read (ROR) program was founded in 1989. They partner with doctors, nurses and other medical professionals helping to prepare America's youngest children to succeed in school. Reach Out and Read Oklahoma serves children at 37 locations statewide and reaches over 18,000 infants, toddlers and preschoolers, distributing more than 25,000 new books each year. Oklahoma medical facilities which participate in the ROR create literacy-rich waiting rooms with child-sized furniture and bookcases. Volunteers model reading with the children while families wait for their appointments and parents leave with understanding the importance of reading. Carefully selected, new, and age-appropriate books are given to children to take home after each medical visit. ROR children have the potential to own a home library of up to 10 books by the start of kindergarten.

DAVID B. LEWIS

Describe the Reach Out and Read Program and its goal. _____

_____

_____

_____

Write about David B. Lewis' education. _____

_____

_____

_____

What are the duties of the Oklahoma Criminal Appeals Court?_____

_____

_____

_____

What are the qualifications to become a Criminal Appeals judge? _____

_____

_____

_____

BIOGRAPHICAL PROFILE

Currie Ballard was born on May 25, 1958 in Los Angeles, California. Currie grew up in the South-Central Watts area. Both of his parents were incarcerated and he and his four siblings – three brothers and one sister –were raised by his grandparents. All of his brothers have been incarcerated at some point in their lives. After serving time, they have all become productive members of society. Even though Currie was raised in a rough neighborhood he has persevered and lived a comfortable, productive, and successful life. His love of history came from his family ancestors, some of which were slaves of the Choctaw Indians in Oklahoma. Two of his ancestors, Wallace and Minerva Willis, were slaves who composed the official state gospel song, "Swing Low, Sweet Chariot." Currie earned his history degree from Langston University and currently lives in Langston. He is also a former employee of the Oklahoma City General Motors plant where he supervised inspections.

PRESERVING HISTORY

Currie has collected black artifacts and documents for over 30 years. His collection boasts 12,000 items, one of the largest African American history collections by one single individual. The collection includes well over 3,000 books, and hundreds of magazines and documents, maps of Africa from the 1600's, 140 year-old letters from runaway slaves, sheet music, autographs, and photographs of famous African Americans. He believes that black history should be celebrated year round. Currie worked at Langston University as Historian-In-Residence from 1993 until 2006. In 1997 he won a Regional Emmy award for his historical documentary "The Ebony Chronicles." Currie produces, writes and provides the voice for this award winning monthly segment. The show aired on Oklahoma educational television and features the history of black Americans. On April 30, 2010 he was inducted into the Oklahoma Historians Hall of Fame.

THE JOB OF A HISTORIAN

A historian studies the past. They gather information, images and documents from the past, analyze and study them to authenticate them, and share their findings with the world. A historian requires attributes of neatness and organization.

CURRIE'S APPOINTMENTS

In 1992 Currie was named Curator of Black History Exhibits by the Oklahoma Historical Society. His job as Curator included developing new exhibits using artifacts, manuscripts, and photos. He was responsible for documenting items in the museum in addition to cataloging and indexing historical items. In 2002, President George W. Bush appointed Currie to a presidential commission responsible for an African American history Museum in Washington, D.C. In 2005, the Speaker of the U.S. House of Representatives appointed Currie to a special taskforce that would study the history of the contributions slaves made to the construction of the United States Capitol. Currie says "I thank Jesus. He brought me a mighty long ways from Watts to the White House." He was appointed in 2009 to serve as Assistant Secretary of the Oklahoma State Senate. In 2011, Currie resigned from his Assistant Secretary of State position to accept an appointment to the Oklahoma Pardon and Parole Board, which makes parole recommendations to the governor. Oklahoma's first female governor, Mary Fallin appointed Currie to this position, the second time Currie has served on the board.

CURRIE BALLARD

Answer the multiple choice questions below by circling the correct letter.

1. Currie says his love of researching history comes from
a. The many Oklahomans he has grew to love
b. His family ancestors
c. President George W. Bush

2. His job of Curator of Black History Exhibits at the Oklahoma Hisorical Society called for him to
a. Develop new exhibits using photos, artifacts and other material
b. Clean and sanitize historically black items to be put on display
c. Create signage, posters and pamphlets for upcoming events

3. Members of the Oklahoma Pardon and Parole Board are appointed by the state governor, Currie served on this board _____ times.
a. six
b. two
c. thirteen

4. When Currie was appointed to a special taskforce in 2005 to study the history of slaves who helped to build the White House, Currie said Jesus "brought me a mighty long ways from _____ to the White House.
a. poverty
b. Oklahoma
c. Watts

5. Currie's African American collection is one of the largest in history. It has over _____ items.
a. 3,000
b. 12,000
c. 140

6. A historian studies the past and collects information and documents and shares the information with the _____.
a. world
b. organizations
c. media

7. Currie received his degree from this University.
a. University of Oklahoma
b. University of Tulsa
c. Langston University

8. In 2011, Currie resigned from his position as Assistant Secretary of the Oklahoma State Senate. What was his reason?
a. ill health
b. he was called to go to Washington D.C.
c. He was appointed to serve on the Oklahoma Pardon and Parole Board

9. When felons are going through the Oklahoma pardon and parole process, who has the final say?
a. the state governor
b. the president of the united states
c. Currie Ballard

10. Currie believes this should be celebrated all year long.
a. black history
b. historians
c. building of the United States Capitol

JOSEPH C. CARTER

BIOGRAPHICAL PROFILE

Joseph (Joe) Christopher Carter was born on March 7, 1960 in Oklahoma City, Oklahoma. He is the eighth of eleven children born to Joseph Sr. and Athelene Carter. Their mother, Athlene, played basketball at Booker T. Washington in El Reno, Oklahoma. Their father played baseball, tennis, basketball and football. All of the Carter children proved to be athletically inclined, using the family backyard for sports practice. At the age of nine, Joe worked at his father's Conoco station in Oklahoma City. He would help with working the cash register, keeping books, and learning about values. He even had his own little green uniform with "Joe" stitched onto the front. Joe graduated from Millwood High School in Oklahoma City where he played basketball, football, and baseball. Although Joe favored basketball more than the other sports, he later attended Wichita State University on a football scholarship. Joe completed three years of college before making the decision to play professional baseball. He and his wife, Diana, have three children: Kia, Ebony and Jordan.

JOE'S BIG HOME RUN

Joe was drafted by the Chicago Cubs in the 1st round (2nd pick) of the 1981 amateur draft. His major league debut was July 30, 1983. Joe has played for the Chicago Cubs, Cleveland Indians, San Diego Padres, Toronto Blue Jays, Baltimore Orioles, and the San Francisco Giants. During his career, Joe hit 396 home runs and drove in 1445 runs. He was the first player ever to record 100 RBI for three different teams in three consecutive seasons. His career was highlighted by a home run hit in the 1993 World Series. Joe played for the San Francisco Giants for his final game on September 28, 1998. Since his retirement, he has served as announcer and play-by-play man. Joe contracts bookings to speak at events about being a Christian athlete, sports announcer and other inspirational sports topics.

JOE CARTER AVENUE

Joe Carter Avenue was named after the famous major league baseball player. It is located on the side of the AT&T Bricktown ballpark located in Oklahoma City.

JOSEPH C. CARTER
Answer the True - False Questions below. Write T or F

1. _____ Joe Carter Avenue is located in El Reno, Oklahoma.

2. _____ At the age of 16, Joe learned to be a bookkeeper at his father's Conoco station.

3. _____ Joe attended three years of college at Wichita State University.

4. _____ Since his retirement, Joe coaches former sports players to become announcers.

5. _____ In 1981, Joe was drafted by the Chicago Cubs baseball team.

6. _____ Joe and his wife, Diana, have eight children.

7. _____ Joe's mother, Athlene, played tennis at Booker T. Washington high school in Tulsa, Oklahoma.

8. _____ When Joe was nine years old, he wore a green uniform with his name stitched onto it.

9. _____ Joe graduated from Millwood High School, which is located in Oklahoma City, Oklahoma.

10. _____ While in high school, Joe preferred to play basketball more than any other sport.

11. _____ The AT&T Bricktown ballpark is located in Wichita, Kansas.

12. _____ During his career, Joe hit 396 home runs.

13. _____ Joe's last baseball game was on September 28, 1998. He played for the Toronto Blue Jays at this time.

14. _____ Since his retirement, Joe accepts speaking engagements to talk about things of inspiration.

15. _____ Joe's major league baseball career began on July 30, 1983.

BIOGRAPHICAL PROFILE

Wayman Lawrence Tisdale was born June 9, 1964 in Fort Worth, Texas. He was raised in Tulsa. He was born to Reverend Louis L. and Deborah Tisdale. He graduated from Booker T. Washington High School in Tulsa. Wayman excelled at basketball and was recruited by nearly 200 colleges. Wayman chose to attend the University of Oklahoma where three times he was named All-American in Division I. Wayman averaged 25.6 points and 10.1 rebounds per game. Wayman was a member of the gold medal winning U.S. Olympic team in 1984. Wayman was drafted by the Indiana Pacers, the 2nd overall draft pick in the 1985 National Basketball Association (NBA). He later played for the Sacramento Kings and Phoenix Suns. On November 16, 1993 Wayman became a member of the NBA 10,000 club. In 1997, Wayman retired from the NBA to focus on his musical career. Wayman married his wife Regina in April of 1987. Their children are Tiffany, Gabrielle, Danielle and Wayman Jr.

TRAGEDY STRIKES

In 2007 Wayman fell down a flight of stairs in his Los Angeles home and broke his leg. It was discovered that he had bone cancer. He had a partial leg amputation hoping to rid his body of cancer. Though he fought bravely, Wayman died on May 15, 2009 in Tulsa. He was 44 years old. The Wayman Tisdale Foundation was created to help amputees and people with cancer by providing support and resources. The foundation raises funds to help amputees with the prosthetic process. The University of Oklahoma-Tulsa dedicated a new specialty health clinic in Wayman's honor.

A LOVE FOR MUSIC

Wayman fell in love with the bass guitar while watching the guitar players at his father's church. He thought they were really cool. One day his father bought Mickey Mouse guitars for Wayman and his two brothers. He began teaching himself how to play. Wayman, the left-handed bassist, worked with many musical greats like Dave Koz and Bob James. Wayman was inducted into the Oklahoma Jazz Hall of Fame in 2002 and nominated in 2004 for the NAACP "Outstanding Jazz Artist." Wayman recorded 8 albums.

WAYMAN'S LIGHTNING

The Christian Basketball Youth Association (CBYA) and Access Sports have formed Wayman's Lightning Youth Basketball League. This program teaches techniques and fundamentals of basketball to kids in grades kindergarten through sixth grade. The program builds character and sportsmanship in a Christlike manner. Their mission is to build a positive environment for coaches, players, parents, and fans.

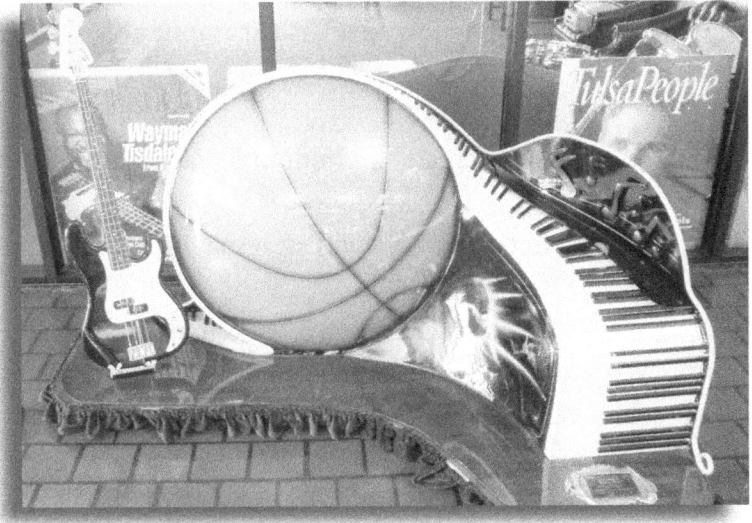

Memorial to Wayman Tisdale at the Oklahoma Jazz Hall of Fame

Wayman is still very popular in Tulsa. Local artist Paul Yeakey created this mural as a tribute.

WAYMAN TISDALE

Answer the True - False statements below.

1. _____ Waymon was recruited by nearly 200 colleges.

2. _____ Wayman's parents are Rev. Louis L. and Deborah Tisdale.

3. _____ In 1985 Wayman was drafted to play in the NBA, where he played for the Miami Heat team.

4. _____ Wayman died on May 15, 2009, at the age of 44. He had bone cancer.

5. _____ Wayman's Lightning Youth Basketball League was developed for children kindergarten through sixth grade. Its purpose is to teach kids the fundamentals of basketball.

6. _____ Wayman broke his arm after falling down a flight of stairs in his home.

7. _____ Wayman's first guitar was a Donald Duck guitar given to him by his father.

8. _____ Wayman was inducted into the Oklahoma Jazz Hall of Fame.

9. _____ Wayman left the NBA to give more attention to his musical career.

10. _____ Wayman agreed to have his leg amputated due to bone cancer. He was later fitted with a prosthesis.

11. _____ A memorial created in honor of Wayman can be found at the University of Nebraska.

12. _____ Wayman married his wife, Regina, in 2010.

13. _____ Wayman played Division 1 basketball at the University of California.

14. _____ The Wayman Tisdale Foundation helps families whose lives are affected by cancer.

15. _____ Wayman preferred the bass guitar and played it with his left hand.

BIOGRAPHICAL PROFILE

Tammy Bass was born in Mineral Wells, Texas in 1967. She was raised by her grandparents. Tammy worked hard, sometimes working two or three jobs to get through school. She received a degree in political science from the University of Oklahoma (OU). After she graduated, her grandfather expected her to go to work full time but Tammy was determined to go to law school. In 1992, she graduated from the OU College of Law. She married Karlos LeSure and they have seven children: Tristan, Karlos II, Davion, Brandon, Justice, and adopted foster kids, Jazln and Jakobi Booker. Tammy is active in her community where she lectures college students and gives motivational speeches.

HISTORICAL APPOINTMENT

After law school Tammy joined the Oklahoma County Public Defender's Office. There she served the underprivileged and poor for many years. She joined the law firm of Watson & Clayborne in 1995. In 1998 Tammy was elected District Court Judge in Oklahoma County, taking the bench at age 32 and making history by becoming one of the first African American females to be elected to this position in the state. She strongly believes in education. She went into the legal profession to make a difference in lives. She strives to make sure defendants, victims, and the public know she cares about them. She implemented a rule that she would not accept a plea agreement if the defendant did not have a high school diploma or General Equivalency Diploma (GED), or have a plan to obtain either of them. Judge Bass-LeSure says, "That is just how strongly I believe in people getting an education. I have had defendants tell me that no one ever cared whether they graduated or not, but I told them I do. I have attended many of their GED graduations and even those who went back to college and earned their degrees. I try and encourage them that one mistake should not deter you from becoming whatever you want, that you can change for the better and do something different with your life. Being a judge is a hard job, but I love it!"

JUDGES HOLD MOCK COURT

Oklahoma District Court Judges Tammy Bass-LeSure and Kenneth Watson use a different angle to reach the youth in nearby high schools. The Court in the Classroom program allows Oklahoma County inmates to go to area high schools to be tried in a mock courtroom filled with teens. Students learn the importance of staying in school, off of drugs, and out of trouble. Judge Watson told students, ". . .we don't want to see you downtown. . .This is what happens when you make bad decisions." He'd rather see them walking across the stage at graduation than into his courtroom. Judge Bass-LeSure told how a criminal record limits your career choices. Felons cannot hold occupations that require a professional license. "It scars you for the rest of your life," she says.

DISTRICT COURT JUDGE DUTIES

They can rule on any type of case in the county. A person unhappy with the ruling of a district court judge may appeal the decision in the Court of Criminal Appeals or the Court of Civil Appeals. These are considered the court of last resort. Elected judges must be registered voters and a resident of the appropriate county for at least six months before the first day of the application filing period. They must have a law license and able to practice law in Oklahoma.

TAMMY BASS-LESURE
Answer the multiple choice questions below by circling the correct letter.

1. Tammy received a political science degree from
   a. The University of Oklahoma
   b. Oklahoma State University
   c. Mineral Wells Community College

2. In 1998 Tammy became the first African American female district court judge in Oklahoma County at age
   a. 35
   b. 45
   c. 32

3. A District Court Judge in Oklahoma County can hear these types of cases in their county
   a. murder cases
   b. any type of case
   c. civil cases

4. If a person is not happy with the ruling of a District Court Judge they can
   a. file a complaint with their immediate supervisor
   b. have the attorney file an appeal with the same judge again
   c. file an appeal in the Court of Criminal Appeals

5. Through Class in the Courtroom, judges Bass-LeSure and Watson hope to steer young people to
   a. stay in school and out of trouble
   b. work in the court house
   c. become teachers

6. Tammy is active in her community and works with college students. She also gives
   a. motivational speeches
   b. money to the homeless
   c. her time to the prisoners in her county

7. Tammy requires a person entering a plea to have a high school diploma or a GED. GED stands for
   a. Going to school Every Day
   b. General Equivalency Diploma
   c. Good for Everyone Diploma

8. After she graduated from college, Tammy's grandfather expected her to do this
   a. get married
   b. become a minister
   c. work full time

9. Tammy strongly believes in this
   a. education
   b. singing
   c. exercising

10. How does Tammy feel about serving as a judge?
    a. She loves it
    b. She says it takes a lot from her children
    c. She wishes she would have studied to be something else

BIOGRAPHICAL PROFILE

Anastasia Pittman was born in Miami, Florida on July 19, 1970. Her parents are C. Anthony Pittman and Maye B. Pittman. Anastasia attended the University of Oklahoma, and in 1999 she received a bachelor's degree in Journalism/Public Relations. She continued her education and received a master's degree in Urban Education & Behavioral Science from Langston University in 2002. Anastasia has one daughter, Ayshia, and one foster son.

STATE REPRESENTATIVE

In 2006, Anastasia was elected to represent District 99 as their State Representative. Prior to being elected, she wore many hats at the Oklahoma State Capitol. For seven years she worked as a research, legislative, media and administrative assistant for the Oklahoma Senate. She also chaired the House District 99 Precinct in addition to the publicity committee for the Metro Federation of Democratic Women. Anastasia is a champion for children and supports literacy, the arts and culture. She shares the dream of Dr. Martin Luther King Jr and is involved in the yearly King birthday celebrations. She is also involved with community service, serving the state of Oklahoma for the past 30 years. This commitment has earned her the Outstanding Community Service Recognition award from past President Bill Clinton.

JOB OF A STATE REPRESENTATIVE

The House of Representatives is the lower of two houses of the Oklahoma Legislature. The state is divided into 101 House districts each representing about 35,000 residents. A Representative serves a two-year term. They meet from February to May to discuss problems in the state and make laws. The Governor may call special sessions. A candidate must be at least twenty-one years old at the time of the election and not have a felony record. The candidate must live in the county they wish to represent. Officers of the United States or State government are ineligible. No one can serve more than twelve years in the legislature.

PITTMAN ADDRESSES SICKLE CELL DISEASE

Representative Pittman authored House Bill 1980, legislation that would direct the Oklahoma State Health Department to provide information and resources about the sickle-cell disease. As of early March of 2011, the bill was awaiting consideration of the House. "Sickle cell disease affects an estimated 70,000 to 100,000 Americans, according to the Centers for Disease Control and Prevention. There is a vaccine that protects against invasive pnemococcal disease and has nearly halved the number of sickle cell-related deaths among children less than four years of age. . . " Pittman feels it is important that Oklahomans are knowledgeable about ways to fight this health problem. Passage of the bill will increase Oklahoma's chances of receiving federal grant money for sickle cell research. In 2006, The Sickle Cell Cure Foundation, a nonprofit organization in the state of Oklahoma was incorporated. In 2010, the foundation received a grant for $600,000 from the Bill Gates foundation in support of Sickle Cell Research.

HOUSE BILL 1976 - SCHOOL BULLYING AND CYBERBULLYING

Representative Pittman authored House Bill 1976, also known as the "Ty Field School Bullying Prevention Act." Ty Field was an 11 year-old who committed suicide as a result of being bullied at school. The bill is designed to create a school environment free of unnecessary disruption, harassment, intimidation, bullying, and cyberbullying. According to the bill, "Harassment, intimidation, and bullying" means any gesture, written, visual or verbal expression,. . ." The bill is specific in making sure bullying does not occur on school grounds, vehicles, bus stops, school-sponsored activities, or events. Neither can it be practiced using mobile phones, pagers, or other electronic devices. Schools are required to report bullying behavior to the parents of the students involved in addition to having procedures of reporting to law enforcement agencies. The entire bill can be viewed on the House website.

THE ANASTASIA PITTMAN SHOW

Anastasia Pittman's talk show can be heard each Friday from 12 NOON until 12:30 PM on KTLV Radio AM 1220. "The Anastasia Pittman Show," is a tool used to keep the community informed about problems and issues that affect them. She also uses the forum as a means to let the community call in with issues and problems she may not be aware of that may need to be addressed.

ANASTASIA PITTMAN
Answer the true / false questions below.

1. _____ The Ty Field School Bullying Prevention Act is designed to create a school environment free from harassment, intimidation, and bullying.

2. _____ The Anastasia Pittman Show is aired on all of the Oklahoma television channels.

3. _____ A candidate for Oklahoma Representative must be at least 50 years old.

4. _____ The state of Oklahoma is divided into 300 house districts.

5. _____ Anastasia Pittman was elected to represent District 99 in Oklahoma.

6. _____ The Bill and Melinda Gates Foundation granted the SCCF $600,000 for the purpose of sickle cell research.

7. _____ The House of Representatives holds session from February through May.

8. _____ Anastasia uses her weekly radio talk show to keep the community informed and to hear about concern, problems and celebrations.

9. _____ The Governor is not able to call special sessions

10. _____ Bullying of any kind should be reported to parents and law enforcement.

BIOGRAPHICAL PROFILE

Michael "Mike" Shelton was born on February 28, 1973 in Tulsa, Oklahoma. He is the son of William and Sandra Shelton. Mike graduated from Millwood High School in Oklahoma City, Oklahoma. He furthered his education by going to Langston University, earning a bachelor of science degree in Economics with emphasis in Agricultural Business. Mike married his childhood sweetheart, Clarissa Franklin. They have one daughter.

POLITICAL IMPACT

District 97 in Oklahoma County voted in 2004 for Mike Shelton to represent them in the State House of Representatives. He is responsible for writing legislation to require insurance companies to provide coverage for supplies and medication to assist individuals to stop smoking when recommended by a health care provider. Shelton authored House Bill 1078 which authorizes a leave of absence for employees making a bone marrow or organ donation. The employee is able to use sick, vacation, or annual leave. Shelton said, "This has become a ministry of sorts for me, a passion to encourage people to get on the registry and follow through on their donation if they are called to donate." Shelton was called to donate marrow and was suprised to find, "Technology has changed so much that donating marrow is literally like donating blood." Statistics are grim for African Americans, Hispanics, Native Americans and Asian Americans. There are only 600,000 African American donors compared to more than 6 million white donors. According to Be The Match, a bone marrow donation organization, over 10,000 patients a year are diagnosed with life-threatening diseases but around 70 percent do not have a matching donor in the family. Shelton says that the state Capitol office is now equipped to register donors to the national Be The Match bone marrow registry.

MIKE'S COMMUNITY INVOLVEMENT

Mike is an active alumnus in the Millwood Alumni Association and Langston University's Alumni Association. He mentors at the Eagle Ridge Institute giving support and resources for mental challenges and substance abuse. Mike is involved in the Boy Scouts of America and has served as the District Executive. He also serves on the Ryan White Board. Ryan White contracted HIV/AIDS at the age of 13 through a blood transfusion. He faced many obstacles because of his condition. The Ryan White organization assists individuals and their families with resources and care.

PENALTY FOR UNAUTHORIZED MILITIA OR DOMESTIC TERROR GROUPS

In April 2010 Shelton proposed to amend Senate Bill 2018. The amendment would increase the penalty for people involved in unauthorized militias or domestic-terror groups. These groups would include gangs, Christian Knights of the Ku Klux Klan, and militia fanatics. Shelton says "In Oklahoma we have seen firsthand the dangers represented by those affiliated with militia fanaticism, and the Ku Klux Klan has a long history of domestic terrorism targeting both the African American community and all citizens who stand up for equality...Involvement in these organizations – which are often involved in drug trafficking and worse crimes – should be treated no differently than participation in a violent street gang." The bill has passed the House and is scheduled to go before the Senate. If passed, violators will face a penalty of five years' incarceration.

MICHAEL SHELTON

1. Discuss Mike Shelton's community involvement and some of the organizations he volunteers to assist

2. What is House Bill 1078? Write about it.

3. Mike Shelton is an Oklahoma representative. what is his job?

4. Discuss Representative Shelton's proposal to amend Senate Bill 2018.

5. Write about the schools Mike attended and name the degrees he earned.

BIOGRAPHICAL PROFILE

Ernest Lee Spivey, Jr. "Junior" was born in Oklahoma City, Oklahoma on January 28, 1975. His father is Ernest Lee Spivey Sr., he and Junior's mother had six children. Two boys; Curtis and Ernest Jr. and four girls. Junior's parents divorced when he was 13 years old. His father raised him in a single parent home. His dad worked very hard as a baker to take care of the family, but the Spiveys were poor. They lived in a housing project named Kerr Village located in Oklahoma City. Junior estimates a total of three fathers in the neighborhood households where he grew up. He greatly appreciates his father being a good role model and keeping him on the straight and narrow. Junior says, "I would've gone wrong without him. My dad wasn't rough on me, but he raised me to be a man. He told me at 16 that you make your own decisions." Although the family struggled, he sees the challenges as character builders. Junior's father always gave his family a lot of love. Ernest Sr. was his mentor and best friend. He taught him to never give up and to strive hard to be the best ballplayer and man possible. Junior played basketball at Douglass High School in Oklahoma City, Oklahoma, graduating in 1993. Junior and his wife, Tabitha, have one son, Ernest Lee Spivey III who was born in 2005.

MAJOR LEAGUE BASEBALL PLAYER

Junior's father exposed the family to a lot of positive things most inner-city black kids seldom experience. When he was 8, his father would drive him across town to play baseball in other neighborhoods. Junior would be the only black child on the team. Ernest Sr., did not push Junior to make it into the majors, but he believed the sport was his most likely ticket out of a tough neighborhood. After high school, Junior accepted a scholarship to play basketball at Northwestern Oklahoma State University. His coach red-shirted him so he transferred to Cowley County College in Kansas which allowed him to play baseball. Junior's Major League Baseball career began in 2001, with the Arizona Diamondbacks. He also played for the Milwaukee Brewers and the Washington Nationals. Being in the majors wasn't easy. Junior would work out every day, six days a week, and lift weights Monday through Saturday, in addition to strengthening and conditioning. Junior retired from major league baseball in 2005 due to multiple injuries. He returned to play baseball in 2007 at the Minor League level. Junior continued to be plagued by injuries for several years and in 2010, he retired again. He has started a new career in broadcasting and is currently working on a television show interviewing Major League baseball players about their big league journeys. Junior loves talking to the kids and never turns down autograph requests.

ERNEST L. SPIVEY JR.
Use the words below to fill in the blanks.

Curtis   **broadcasting**   **1993**   **dad**   **one**
injuries   **Saturday**   **eight**   **scholarship**   **love**
autograph   **basketball**   **baseball**   **Washington Nationals**
Northwest Oklahoma State University

1. Junior Spivey attended Douglass High School in Oklahoma City, he graduated in _____.

2. Junior made the decision to retire from baseball in 2005 and again in 2007 because of _____.

3. Ernest Spivey Sr., would take Junior across town to other neighhborhoods to play baseball with other kids, Junior was _____ years old.

4. The coach from this University red-shirted Junior his first year there. _____

5. Junior's only brother's name is _____.

6. Junior's father gave the family a lot of _____ as they grew up.

7. While attending Douglass High School, Junior played this sport. _____.

8. Junior and his wife Tabitha have _____ son.

9. Training in the Major leagues wasn't easy. Junior was required to lift weights Monday through _____.

10. Northwest Oklahoma State University offered Junior a _____ to attend there.

11. Since retiring in 2010, Junior has started a new career in _____ _____.

12. While visiting with fans, Junior never turns down a request for his _____ _____.

13. Junior feels he would have gone wrong without his _____.

14. Junior's dad did not push him to play _____.

15. During his professional career, Junior played for the Milwaukee Brewers, the Arizona Diamondbacks, and the _____.

BIOGRAPHICAL PROFILE

Jabar Shumate was born in Tulsa, Oklahoma on January 26, 1976. His parents are Joseph and Cleatta Johnson and Glenn E. Shumate. He is a graduate of Booker T. Washington High School in Tulsa. In addition, Jabar graduated with a bachelor of arts degree in Public Affairs/Administration from the University of Oklahoma (OU) in 1998. He also received his master of human relations degree from OU's Tulsa campus in 2007.

CREDIT FOR HIS SUCCESS

Jabar serves as an Oklahoma House Representative for District 73 in Tulsa, Oklahoma. He was elected to this position in 2004. Jabar says he knew he wanted to be a politician since the age of 6, even trying to run for Usher Board President. His first job was a waiter at a local restaurant. He credits OU President David Boren for bringing interest to his Political Science class. In addition to guiding and supporting him Jabar considers Boren his mentor. He applauds Senator Judy Eason McIntyre for teaching him how to run a campaign.

SERVING OKLAHOMANS

Jabar serves as Vice Chair of the Common Education Committee. He is also a member of the Insurance Committee, Redistricting North/Northwest Oklahoma Sub-Committee and the Appropriations and Budget Education Committees. He is responsible for authoring House Bill (HB) 1364, which concerns the safety of the children of Oklahoma. HB 1364 states "Children; modifying requirements and procedures to conduct certain criminal background searches on persons with access to children in child care facilities." Representative Shumate also authored a bill allowing the creation of a special license plate to honor the Greenwood District. It is hoped the tag will bring "hope, revitalization, remembrances and identity to a sector of north Tulsa's history." The plate pictures local jazz musician Christopher Clayton playing the saxophone on the corner of Greenwood Avenue and Archer Street. "Remembering Black Wall Street" appears at the bottom of the plate.

Tahrohon Wayne (T.W.) Shannon was born on February 24, 1978, he grew up in Lawton, Oklahoma. T.W. graduated from Lawton High School in 1996. He earned a bachelor's of arts degree in communications from Cameron University in 2000. Later receiving a Juris Doctor degree from Oklahoma City University. He is married to Devon and they have two children: Audrey Grace and Tahrohon Wayne II.

T.W. worked for United States Representatives J.C. Watts and Tom Cole as a Congressional Staffer. In 2006, T.W. was elected to serve District 62 in Lawton, Oklahoma as State Representative, making him the first African American to serve in this position. He is the first African American elected to serve the Legislature in southern Oklahoma since statehood. He currently serves as Chairperson of the Transportation Committee.

Governor Brad Henry consults with Representative Shumate at the State Capitol

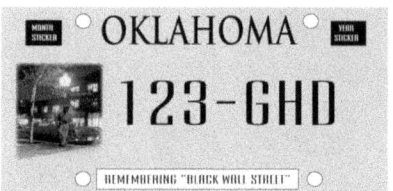

A replica of the proposed license plate honoring Tulsa's Greenwood District

JABAR SHUMATE & T.W. SHANNON
Answer the true – false statements below

1. _____ Jabar was born in 1998, in Tulsa, Oklahoma.

2. _____ Shumate wrote legislation creating an Oklahoma license plate to honor the Greenwood District in Tulsa.

3. _____ Jabar knew at the age of 45 that he wanted to become a politician.

4. _____ Jabar considers University of Oklahoma's president David Boren his mentor.

5. _____ Representative Shannon is the first African American to serve District 62 in Lawton, OK.

6. _____ The historical Greenwood District license plate displays a picture of Charlie Christian.

7. _____ Money from the Greenwood District license plates may bring live entertainment to the area.

8. _____ Representative Shannon earned his Juris Doctor degree from the University of Lawton.

9. _____ Representative Shumate represents District 73 in Tulsa, Oklahoma.

10. _____ Jabar appreciates Senator Judy Eason McIntyre for helping him with his campaign.

11. _____ T.W. Shannon considers OU President David Boren his mentor.

12. _____ T. W. Shannon formerly worked for U.S. Representative J.C. Watts.

13. _____ Representative Shannon has six children.

14. _____ Jabar Shumate's first job was working for U.S. Representative Tom Cole.

15. _____ T.W. Shannon graduated from Lawton High School in 2006.

The National Black Caucus of State Legislators (NBCSL) is an American political organization made up of African Americans and Latino Americans that have been elected to the state legislatures in the United States. The organization was founded over thirty years ago and has grown to over six hundred members. The NBCSL meets annually in a selected host state for its Annual Legislative Conference. Members are informed about growing policy trends and policy issues that may affect their constituents. Black caucus members focus on health, education, crime prevention, economic development and other important issues that affect all Oklahomans.

Oklahoma Legislative Black Caucus, left to right: T. W. Shannon, Anastasia Pittman, Judy Eason McIntyre, Constance Johnson, Mike Shelton, Jabar Shumate

BLACK CAUCUS FILES DISCRIMINATION COMPLAINT

In February of 2009, members of the Oklahoma Legislative Black Caucus (OLBC) filed a complaint of discrimination against the Oklahoma Department of Transportation (ODOT). The group contacted the U.S. Secretary of Transportation with allegations they had evidence of past and continuing discrimination against ethnic minority owned and economically disadvantaged businesses and contractors. Senator Constance Johnson stated that ODOT had not awarded any bids to black contractors in the Disadvantaged Business Enterprise Program since 2007. The black lawmakers are requesting that federal funding targeted for the public sector projects be held until a resolution is met.

SENATE APPROVES HIV/AIDS TASK FORCE

State Senators McIntyre and Johnson authored Senate Bill 1829 in 2008. The Bill will create a 13 member task force to look at the HIV/AIDS problem in Oklahoma's minority communities and recommend a course of action. The bill was approved through the senate and now needs to be considered by the House of Representatives. Senator Judy Eason McIntyre said, "HIV/AIDS is an epidemic nationwide and growing at an even faster rate within communities of color. I believe this task force is the first step in truly addressing this problem head-on. We have to raise awareness and increase the knowledge of this deadly disease in Oklahoma. Protecting Oklahoma minority citizens from HIV/AIDS is a critical priority. This task force will study the best ways to curb the rate of new cases and find the best options for testing and treatment." The task force will assess the problem of HIV/AIDS in the minority community, review the lack of success of having testing and treatment available, identify funding that is available on the state and federal level, and develop innovative and effective strategies to increase HIV testing. The task members included Gov. Brad Henry, and members from the following state agencies: Mental Health and Substance Abuse, Commissioner of Health, Department of Public Instruction, and Oklahoma Health Care Authority. HIV/AIDS testing information can be obtained by dialing 211.

OKLAHOMA LEGISLATIVE BLACK CAUCUS

Curly Words - Find the words below in the puzzle.

GOVERNOR	**ANASTASIA**	**PITTMAN**	**MIKE SHELTON**
CONTRACTORS	**JABAR**	**SHUMATE**	**CAUCUS**
JUDY MCINTYRE	**SENATE BILL**	**T.W. SHANNON**	**CONSTANCE**
JOHNSON	**THIRTY YEARS**	**SIX HUNDRED MEMBERS**	

```
S E C E O C S H N D M M H J V J L R O S
A A R Z O L Q H H T Y H X A Q P F X K K
B A I X I M Z R V V L E M B A E V M R F
V S L O I J S N R A U W E A U E Z N P A
Q E A Q S U E R M O L N L R O M E Q Y M
I N E A J D O D B B B C J L S D O B S E P
S A S A E Y F F U S P M Y N Q A O L L S
L T O L I M F T N T O E N A M T T I P C
I E M R E C I X I N N O N N A H S W T P
V B R S M I K E S H E L T O N I S N R N
S I X H U N D R E D M E M B E R S L A E
H L Q U B T E C E C L N N E O T Y N E R
E L S M O Y S U C U A C R T R Y F W Z R
X H S A O R P D N J P O C T O Y M L E O
S N S T S E J E A Y O A G L N E L L D S
N E W E S J A D T H R H U L R A A N I E
S O N R O W O C S T K E N N E R F E I N
N A I S A T S A N A Z X N S V S M U E N
O Y S S A S T O O S M I O F O N N T F N
F S A C A E C V C P O J D R G N T T L W
```

selected sources

Books

Altman, Susan. *The Encyclopedia of African-American Heritage.* New York, 1997

Ellison, Ralph. *Ralph Ellison: A Biography.* New York, 2007

Luper, Clara. *Behold the Walls.* Oklahoma City, 1979

Nevergold, Barbara Seals & Brooks-Bertram, Peggy. *Un-Crowned Queens: African American Women Community Builders of Oklahoma.* New York, 2007

Teall, Kaye (Moulton). *Black History of Oklahoma – a resource book.* Oklahoma, 1971

Newspapers

Cobblestone
Sunday Oklahoman
The Black Dispatch
The Daily Oklahoman
The Oklahoma Eagle
The Tulsa Tribune
Muskogee Phoenix
The Black Chronicle
The Capital Journal
The Oklahoma City Herald
The Oklahoman
The Tulsa World

Other Sources

Melvin B. Tolson Black Heritage Center located on the Langston University Campus in Langston, Oklahoma

Periodicals

Ebony Magazine
Journal of the National Medical Association
Journal Record
Oklahoma Magazine

Personal Interviews

Ballard, Currie - historian
Barclay, Mae Neece (wife of Dr. Carl A. Barclay)
Bass-LeSure, Tammy - judge
Bragg, Leon (husband of Judge Susan Woodard Bragg)
Brown, Glendale (Son of Leslie Brown, Sr.)
Colbert, Tom - judge
Cox, Kevin C. – former state legislator
DeLoney, Frances
Finley, Barbara (sister of Leona Mitchell)
Fisher, Bruce (son of Ada Sipuel Fisher)
Foley-Davis, Lelia - mayor
Goodwin, Ed and James
Johnson, Oren (Grand-son of Walter J and Frances Edwards)
Holmes, Carl and Marvella – Carl is one of original 12 black firefighters
Horner, Maxine – former state legislator
Johnson, Constance – state legislator
Johnson, Willa – Oklahoma county commissioner
Lewis, David B. - judge
McIntyre, Judy Eason – state legislator
Minner, Selby – (wife of D.C. Minner)
Mitchell, Leona P. – famed opera singer
Perry, Russell – newspaper and radio station owner
Pittman, Anastasia – state legislator
Ross, Don R. Sr – former state legislator
Shannon, Tahrohon W. – state legislator
Shumate, Jabar – state legislator
Stevenson, Horace – business owner
Watson, Kenneth - judge
Williams, Portwood, Sr. – driver for sit-in demonstrations

Websites

The African American Registry
http://www.aaregistry.com/

The African -Native American Genealogy Homepage
http://african-nativeamerican.com

Big Al Downing Home Page
http://www.bigaldowning.com/

BlackAmericans.com
http://blackamericans.com/

The Black Past: Remembered and Reclaimed
http://wwwblackpast.org

Booker T. Washington National Alumni Association
http://www.hornetalumni.org

Buffalo Soldiers Lawton- Ft. Sill Chapter
http://www.buffalosoldiers-lawtonftsill.org/index.htm

DC Minner's Dusk 'til Dawn Blues Festival in Rentiesville, OK
http://www.dcminnerblues.com/bluesfest.htm

The Encyclopedia of Arkansas History & Culture
http://www.encyclopediaofarkansas.net/encyclopedia
Encyclopedia of Oklahoma History & Culture
http://digital.library.okstate.edu/encyclopedia/

Explore Oklahoma
http://www.travelok.com

The History of Jim Crow
http://www.jimcrowhistory.org/

Juneteenth.Com
http://www.juneteenth.com/

Justia US Law
http://cases.justia.com/

Langston University
http://www.lunet.edu

Legends of America
http://www.legendsofamerica.com/

National Cowboy & Western Heritage Museum
http://www.nationalcowboymuseum.org

Oklahoma Bar Association
http://www.okbar.org

Oklahoma Higher Education Heritage Society
http://www.ohehs.org

Oklahoma Historical Society
http://okhistory.org

Oklahoma Senate
http://www.oksenate.gov

Oklahoma House of Representatives
http://www.okhouse.gov

Sand Town History
http://www.sandtownhistory.com/endn.html

Tulsa City-County Library African-American Resource Center
http://tulsalibrary.org/aarc/

The United States Department of Justice
http://www.usdoj.gov

The University of Oklahoma Graduate College
http://gradweb.ou.edu/History

Wikipedia
http://www.wikipedia.com

about the author

Rochelle Stephney-Roberson was born and raised in Oklahoma City. She grew up in a large family in northeast Oklahoma City. All of the Stephney children graduated from Douglass High School. Rochelle grew up in a close knit family where racial pride and importance of education were instilled from both parents. Rochelle received a bachelor of science degree in Education and a master's degree in Library Science with emphasis on Elementary School Administration from the University of Central Oklahoma in Edmond. She began working in the Oklahoma City Public Schools system in 1981 and again in 1986. She has worked with and educated youth for over 25 years.

Milton Keynes UK
Ingram Content Group UK Ltd.
UKHW052331141023
430632UK00018B/335